D1280628

Towards a Christian Literary Theory

Cross-Currents in Religion and Culture

General Editors:
Elisabeth Jay, Senior Research Fellow, Westminster College, Oxford
David Jasper, Professor in Literature and Theology, University of Glasgow

The study of theology and religion nowadays calls upon a wide range of interdisciplinary skills and cultural perspectives to illuminate the concerns at the heart of religious faith. Books in this new series will variously explore the contributions made by literature, philosophy and science in forming our historical and contemporary understanding of religious issues and theological perspectives.

Published titles:

Luke Ferretter
TOWARDS A CHRISTIAN LITERARY THEORY

Harold Fisch
NEW STORIES FOR OLD
Biblical Patterns in the Novel

Susan VanZanten Gallagher and M. D. Walhout (*editors*)
LITERATURE AND THE RENEWAL OF THE PUBLIC SPHERE

Michael Giffin
JANE AUSTEN AND RELIGION
Salvation and Society in Georgian England

Stephen Happel
METAPHORS FOR GOD'S TIME IN SCIENCE AND RELIGION

Philip Leonard (*editor*)
TRAJECTORIES OF MYSTICISM IN THEORY AND LITERATURE

Lynda Palazzo
CHRISTINA ROSSETTI'S FEMINIST THEOLOGY

Eric Ziolkowski
EVIL CHILDREN IN RELIGION, LITERATURE, AND ART

Lambert Zuidervaart and Henry Luttikhuizen (*editors*)
THE ARTS, COMMUNITY AND CULTURAL DEMOCRACY

Cross-Currents in Religion and Culture
Series Standing Order ISBN 0–333–79469–9
(*outside North America only*)

You can receive future titles in this series as they are published by placing a standing order. Please contact your bookseller or, in case of difficulty, write to us at the address below with your name and address, the title of the series and the ISBN quoted above.

Customer Services Department, Macmillan Distribution Ltd, Houndmills, Basingstoke, Hampshire RG21 6XS, England

---

Towards a Christian Literary Theory

Luke Ferretter

First published 2003 by
PALGRAVE MACMILLAN
Houndmills, Basingstoke, Hampshire RG21 6XS and
175 Fifth Avenue, New York, N.Y. 10010
Companies and representatives throughout the world

PALGRAVE MACMILLAN is the global academic imprint of the Palgrave
Macmillan division of St. Martin's Press, LLC and of Palgrave Macmillan Ltd.
Macmillan® is a registered trademark in the United States, United Kingdom
and other countries. Palgrave is a registered trademark in the European
Union and other countries.

ISBN 0–333–96421–7 hardback

This book is printed on paper suitable for recycling and made from fully
managed and sustained forest sources.

A catalogue record for this book is available from the British Library.

Library of Congress Cataloging-in-Publication Data
Ferretter, Luke, 1970–
   Towards a Christian literary theory / Luke Ferretter.
     p. cm. — (Cross currents in religion and culture)
   Includes bibliographical references and index.
   ISBN 0–333–96421–7 (cloth)
   1. Criticism. 2. Christianity and literature. 3. Literature—History
and criticism—Theory, etc. 4. Theology. I. Title. II. Cross-currents
in religion and culture (Palgrave (Firm))

   PN98.R44 F47 2002
   801′.95—dc21

                           2002026755

10 9 8 7 6 5 4 3 2 1
12 11 10 09 08 07 06 05 04 03

Printed and bound in Great Britain by
Antony Rowe Ltd, Chippenham and Eastbourne

For Jen

Contents

Preface

I would like to thank the many colleagues who gave of their time and expertise during the writing of this book. Ian Johnson and the late Stephen Boyd were instrumental in allowing me to begin the research out of which it developed, and provided me with shrewd criticism and constant support thereafter. Many of my former colleagues in the School of English at St Andrews went out of their way to assist me in the writing of this book, and I would like to thank especially Susan Sellers, Robert Crawford and Michael Alexander. I am grateful to Catherine Belsey for her generous support during my time at Cardiff University and after. Terry Wright provided me with the most productive criticism of the ideas presented here, and I continue to be indebted to his criticism. Perhaps my greatest debt, however, is to David Jasper, who has enthusiastically supported this project throughout its development, and without whom it may not have reached its final form. I also appreciate the patience of my editors at Palgrave Macmillan in allowing me to see it through to this form.

This book was completed during a British Academy Postdoctoral Fellowship, which I gratefully acknowledge. I would like to thank my parents for their help and support during the early years of my work on this project. Most of all, I would like thank my wife Jen, to whom this book is dedicated, for her love and constant belief in me.

Luke Ferretter

1
Introduction

Most contemporary literary theories are atheistic. In 'The Death of the Author' (1968), Roland Barthes describes the emphasis on textuality characteristic of post-structuralism as 'an anti-theological activity . . . since to refuse to fix meaning is, in the end, to refuse God and his hypostases – reason, science, law'.[1] The philosophers to whom modern literary theory is most indebted – Marx, Nietzsche and Freud – have argued that the truth-content of religious beliefs is negated by their social and psychological determinants. Post-structuralist theories emphasize that the language in which such beliefs are expressed cannot support the truth-claim that they imply. It seems that contemporary literary study is incompatible as such with Christian faith. This book argues that this is not the case.

In his book *Justifying Language* (1995), Kevin Mills writes that his goal is

> to affirm the viability of a critical belief which is cognisant of the array of philosophico-linguistic objections to its existence, and yet understands why faith, hope and love are able to remain in the face of this onslaught.[2]

One of the reasons why Mills can assert that it is possible consistently to hold a Christian faith after understanding the modern objections to it is that there is no system of thought that does not at some point involve an act of faith. In *Does God Exist? An Answer for Today* (1978), the Catholic theologian Hans Küng argues this point in his study of Nietzschean nihilism. He asserts that each of us makes a 'fundamental decision' about reality as a whole, a choice of what self, others and the world mean to us, which grounds all our subsequent actions and convictions.

1

Nietzsche has made clear that reality is not self-evident, Küng argues, and so this decision is ultimately a matter of trust. He writes:

> The fundamental alternative is a (considered or unconsidered) *Yes or No to reality* in principle: an unforceable and unprovable trust or mistrust in the reality of the world and of my own self.[3]

In the end, I either believe that reality has identity, meaning and value or I do not. Küng argues that the former choice, which he calls 'fundamental trust' in reality, is the basis both of science and of ethics. Citing philosophers of science from Karl Popper to Thomas Kuhn, Küng argues that 'all rational thinking rests on a choice, a resolution, a decision, an attitude; in a word, on a "faith in reason".'[4] A rationalism which attempts to base every proposition on arguments or experience cannot itself be based on arguments or experience, but must be *believed* to be a valid way of understanding reality. Küng adds that a similar act of faith is the precondition of ethics:

> Any acceptance of meaning, truth and rationality, of values and ideals, priorities and preferences, models and norms, presupposes a fundamental trust in uncertain reality.[5]

Every positive system of thought at some point involves an act of faith, a decision simply to commit oneself to something that cannot be proved. Even nihilism is based on such a decision. If this is true, then Christian theology and modern literary theory are not incommensurate discourses. It is not the case that whereas the latter is based on critical reason and ethics, the former derives from an irrational faith that results in unethical values. On the contrary, Christians share with modern literary theorists an understanding of reality whose most fundamental axioms are neither proved nor provable, but in the end simply believed.

Granted that literary theory and Christian faith are not in principle incompatible, it may be asked whether it is meaningful or valuable in practice to associate them. It may be objected that criticism should be practised according to strictly critical norms, and Christian faith should be reserved for theology and ethics, to which it properly pertains. This objection ignores the most fundamental insight of modern literary theory, however, that there is no critical discourse that does not derive from some theory or theories, however unconscious or ill-assorted. As Catherine Belsey writes, in *Critical Practice* (1980):

There is no practice without theory, however much that theory is suppressed, unformulated or perceived as 'obvious'. [Reading] pre-supposes a whole theoretical discourse...about the relationships between meaning and the world, meaning and people, and finally about people themselves and their place in the world.[6]

Whether I write about what John Donne's imagery tells me about his particular way of perceiving of the world, or about the political signifi-cance of his representations of women, I cannot but derive my interpret-ations and judgements from a more or less conscious system of opinions about the way the world is and about what should be done in it. Since Christian theology constitutes the basis of such a world-view, it is reasonable to imagine a critical discourse whose interpretations and judgements derive from it or from principles consistent with it. My aim in this book is to describe such a discourse.

I will begin with some working definitions. In *The Nature of Doctrine* (1984), George Lindbeck argues that Christian doctrines are

communally authoritative teachings regarding beliefs and practices that are considered essential to the identity or welfare of the group in question.[7]

This statement makes clear that any definition of Christian doctrine is determined by the community in which it is formulated. My definition is no exception, and is determined by the Roman Catholic community within which I write. I will mean by 'Christian' doctrines those Catholic doctrines from which the major Protestant confessions and the Eastern Orthodox communions do not dissent. There is no brief summary of Catholic doctrines, like the Church of England's Thirty-Nine Articles or the Presbyterian Westminster Confession. Even lengthy volumes such as Denzinger's *Enchiridion Symbolorum* and the *Catechism of the Catholic Church* do not represent the complete doctrinal content of the Catholic faith. This is partly because, as Vatican II asserts, the primary object of revelation is 'God...Himself', in Christ, whose meaning cannot be exhausted in dogmatic propositions.[8] Furthermore, as Catholic theologian Karl Rahner argues in 'The Development of Dogma' (1954), the devel-opment of these propositions is a necessity of the church's historical existence:

The real understanding of what is revealed and its existential appro-priation by men is wholly dependent on the transformations of the propositions of faith, as they were originally heard, into propositions which relate what is heard to the historical situation of the men who hear.[9]

In *Foundations of Christian Faith* (1976), Rahner argues that Scripture, as 'the objectification of the original church's consciousness of the faith', is the norm of Catholic doctrine. The church's teaching office, he writes, has the task of 'always interpreting it anew in historically changing horizons of understanding as the one truth which always remains the same'.[10] Vatican II's decree on ecumenism, *Unitatis Redintegratio* (1964), asserts that 'in Catholic teaching there exists an order or "hierarchy" of truths, since they vary in their relationship to the foundation of the Christian faith.'[11] The structure of this hierarchy has not been specified. For the purpose of this book, I will take those doctrines that are shared by the major Protestant and Orthodox confessions as its fundamental level, and will refer to them as 'Christian' doctrines.

I will mean by 'literary' texts, fictional texts which are found valuable. In *Literary Theory* (1983), Terry Eagleton argues that fictionality cannot be used as a criterion for defining literature, pointing out that much prose intended to accurately describe the author's understanding of reality is studied in literature courses.[12] The logic of his argument, that literature is constituted by readers' relations to texts, however, suggests that the same text can be read either as fiction or in a different way. If I read John Donne's sermons for advice on my spiritual life, or *The Cloud of Unknowing* to learn how to contemplate, then I am reading them as science. If on the other hand I read these texts without expecting them directly to describe some aspect of reality, then I am reading them as fiction, in the sense of that term that denotes a text or part of a text that is not understood as an accurate description of reality. In defining literature as texts read in this way and 'found valuable', I am accepting the modern axiom that, since values are determined by the social and historical context of the discourses in which they are formulated, literature is a historically variable category. I take 'literary theory' to denote discourse concerned with texts in general, and in particular with the nature and function of literary texts. By 'Christian literary theory', I will mean a theory of the nature and function of fictional texts found valuable, which is derived from those fundamental doctrines of the Catholic faith shared by the major Protestant and the Orthodox confessions, or from principles consistent with them.

I will construct such a theory in this book in two ways. Firstly, I will argue that, despite the rejection of the truth-claim and the value of

Christian theology by the most influential schools of contemporary literary and cultural theory, it remains legitimate to interpret literary and cultural works from the perspective of Christian faith and theology. In the first three chapters, I will examine the most influential critiques of Christian theology in contemporary literary theory, those of deconstruction, Marxism and psychoanalysis. In each chapter, I will analyse the significance of these theories for the concept of Christian literary theory, and argue that it remains legitimate, under certain conditions, to use Christian theology in literary theory and criticism, even after the critique of such theology which these theories articulate. I will also suggest that Christian literary theory should incorporate some of their characteristic insights. In Chapter 5, I will conclude my argument for the legitimacy of Christian literary theory and criticism on the basis of an analysis of hermeneutics. Here I will argue that literary theory and criticism practised from the perspective of Christian faith and theology are not exceptional forms of these discourses but rather examples of the way in which they are always practised. Having established the legitimacy of Christian literary theory in these ways, in Chapter 6 I will go on to examine the work of recent theologians and literary critics who have interpreted literary texts from the perspective of Christian theology. I will assess which of their principles and practices should be used in Christian literary theory, and how. On the basis of these analyses, I will conclude with the formulation of a contemporary Christian literary theory. By this, I mean a theory which derives Christian faith and theology on the one hand, and which takes account of the objections to such theology raised by contemporary literary theory on the other.

2
On Deconstruction

I will begin with an examination of deconstruction. Deconstructive analysis constitutes a serious challenge to Biblical exegesis and to Christian theology as such. It implies that neither the Biblical texts nor theological reflection upon them have a coherent or finally determinable meaning, and that they do not clearly or truly refer to objects beyond themselves. Derrida writes that his key-term *différance* 'blocks every relationship to theology'.[1] In this chapter, I will argue that, despite the challenge posed by deconstruction, it remains possible to use theological language in literary theory. I will examine the complex relations between deconstruction and the language of theology, and argue that deconstruction itself ultimately remains within the problematic of such language.

2.1 Derrida and the language of theology

In order to assess the consequences of deconstruction for the language of theology, we need first to understand Derrida's own concept of theology. He uses the term most commonly in the Heideggerian compound 'onto-theology', as a description of the language of metaphysics. In the *Critique of Pure Reason* (1781), Kant defined onto-theology as that kind of transcendental or rational theology which 'endeavours to know the existence of [a supreme being] through mere concepts, without the aid of experience'.[2] Transcendental theology in general, according to Kant, thinks of its object as *ens originarium, ens realissimum, ens entium,* that is, as the first being, the perfect being and as the Being of beings. In 'The Onto-Theological Constitution of Metaphysics' (1957), Heidegger argues that 'Western metaphysics . . . since its beginning with the Greeks has eminently been both ontology and theology', that is, has been concerned both with beings as such and with beings as a whole.[3] What these enquiries share, Heidegger asserts, is an understanding of Being as the ground (*grund*) of beings. He writes:

> When metaphysics thinks of being with respect to the ground that is common to all beings as such, then it is logic as onto-logic. When metaphysics thinks of beings as such as a whole, that is, with respect to the highest being which accounts for everything, then it is logic as theo-logic.[4]

By calling metaphysics 'onto-theology', Heidegger means that it thinks of the relation between Being and beings in terms of the relation between ground and grounded, and *vice versa*. Derrida follows him in this, further asserting that the distinction between each pair of terms is based on an understanding of the first term as presence. Theology, for Derrida, is therefore the name applicable to any discourse which posits or implies a point of presence as the ground of that which is grounded in the way that metaphysics thinks of Being as the ground of beings. Heidegger had described the self-grounding ground or *causa sui* as 'the metaphysical concept of God', suggesting that another concept may be available, but Derrida, at least until his most recent work, does not acknowledge that possibility.[5] He calls the semiotic opposition between signifier and signified a 'metaphysico-theological' distinction, that is, one which can be thought in terms of the distinction between God as ground and the world as grounded by which metaphysics thinks of the Being of beings as presence. He writes:

> The difference between the signifier and the signified belongs... to...the history of metaphysics, and in a more explicit and more systematically articulated way to the narrower epoch of Christian creationism and infinitism when these appropriate the resources of Greek conceptuality.[6]

Christian theology is integrally related to Western metaphysics, for Derrida. Its distinctions between God as creator and the world as created, and between God's infinity and the world's temporality, are paradigms of the attempt to determine the meaning of Being as presence. Any semiotics which distinguishes a non-worldly signified from a material signifier can therefore be called theological. This is what Derrida means when he writes, 'The age of the sign is essentially theological.'[7]

One of the earliest Anglo-American responses to Derrida's critique of theology so conceived was the enthusiastic reception of deconstruction into theological discourse by 'death-of-God' theologians such as Thomas J.J. Altizer and Mark C. Taylor. In the volume *Deconstruction and Theology* (1982), Carl A. Raschke describes deconstruction as 'the death of God put into writing', that is, as the latest Nietzschean lesson for theology that to distinguish between the sensible, temporal world and a supposedly transcendent intelligible, eternal world is an act of bad faith.[8] In Raschke's view, Derrida's work demonstrates the necessity of a theology that recognizes that 'neither language nor human self-awareness conceals any thread of reference to things as they are', a theology entirely resigned to the immanence of its own textual play, and therefore to the end of theology as such.[9] This view, echoed by other contributors to the volume, was most thoroughly expressed by Taylor, in his *Erring: A Postmodern A/theology* (1984). There Taylor describes deconstruction as 'the "hermeneutic" of the death of God', that is, as the mode of reading that most thoroughly responds to the postmodern resignation to the impossibility of any transcendental category of thought.[10] It is thus the way to do theology for those postmodern thinkers who, in Taylor's words, find themselves 'suspended between the loss of the old [metaphysical] certainties and the discovery of new beliefs'.[11] Of course, a deconstructive theology cannot be described as a 'theology' as such, since the binary oppositions which that term implies are precisely the objects of deconstruction. Hence Taylor calls his project 'a/theology', that is, a kind of open-ended textual analysis which is 'neither properly theological nor non-theological, theistic nor atheistic... believing nor non-believing'.[12] He situates his discourse on the / of a/theology, between theology and atheology, and writes of it:

Along this boundless boundary the traditional polarities between which Western theology has been suspended are inverted and subverted.[13]

'Erring', that is, both deviating from the right and wandering, will be the characteristic action of this discourse, according to Taylor.

The value of this kind of analysis, he argues, is that by liberating Western theology from the network of hierarchical oppositions upon which it is based, deconstruction 'creates a new opening for the religious imagination'.[14] Having offered a Derridean reading of the theological axioms of God, self, history and the book, Taylor suggests that a deconstructive a/theology will correspond to a 'radical Christology', in which the divine is understood as the 'incarnate word' of 'script(ure)'.[15] This coinage reflects the double meaning of Derrida's French term *écriture*: both 'writing' and 'Scripture'. The differance or 'writing' which, for Derrida, characterizes all experience, is that *milieu* in which alone we can now find God. Taylor writes:

> God is what 'word' means and word is what 'God' means. To interpret God as word is to understand the divine as scripture or writing.[16]

There is nothing outside the text, Derrida wrote. It is therefore in this postmodern text of experience, Taylor concludes, that God is to be found. The text, he asserts, *is* God. 'This complex web of interrelations is the divine milieu.'[17]

John D. Caputo criticizes Taylor for failing to remain within the genuinely Derridean problematic of undecidability that his term a/theology is supposed to describe. By understanding deconstruction as the last phase in the history of the death of God, in which God has simply become *écriture*, Caputo argues, Taylor has made 'a reductionist decision against God, to reduce the ambiguity of a genuine a/theology and to turn *différance* against God'.[18] It is not entirely fair to say that Taylor turns deconstruction 'against God', however. This is true only of the concept of God as a transcendent entity. Granted, it is difficult to imagine that the term can be meaningfully used in an absolutely immanent sense, but this is Taylor's argument. He does not assert that there is no God, but that Being, in the sense of ground, is not a divine attribute. A more serious critique comes from John Milbank, who writes:

> The theological content in ... endeavours [such as *Erring*] turns out to be small: the transcendental rule of anarchic difference can be renamed God or the death of God, Dionysiac celebration can be declared to include a contemplative mystical moment – and very little has really been added, nothing is essentially altered.[19]

This is true: the theological content of Taylor's work on deconstruction is small. Taylor is at his best in his deconstructive readings of the axioms of Western theology. The a/theology he claims to reconstruct from its ruins amounts to little more than a renaming of Derridean motifs with fragments of traditional theology. His 'radical Christology' is ultimately a matter of ascribing theological names to the law of differance. The same can be said of his association of the deconstruction of the autonomous subject with the Pauline 'crucifixion of the self'.[20] Nothing is added to the latter doctrine, which is simply described as another name for *différance.* Whilst Taylor might object that theological content is precisely that which he is attempting to displace, the fact remains that he tells us almost nothing about the 'implications of the insights' of deconstruction for Christian theology.[21] Ultimately, 'deconstructive a/theology' differs in no significant respect from deconstruction.

A second, relatively recent, theological response to deconstruction is the argument that Derrida, like Heidegger before him, is wrong to characterize the entire history of Western philosophy as onto-theology, and wrong in particular to assimilate Christian theology as such into this history. This response is characteristic of John Milbank's work on Derrida. In *The Word Made Strange* (1997), Milbank writes:

> Whereas Heidegger read the entire philosophical tradition and the Christian appropriation of philosophy as the history of metaphysics or onto-theology ..., it now seems at the least unclear as to whether this describes Platonism, Neoplatonism and Christian theology before Henry of Ghent and Duns Scotus.[22]

Milbank traces a tradition of Christian thought that, he argues, cannot be assimilated into a history of metaphysics as onto-theology, that is, a tradition in which God is not conceived as a transcendent ground. He argues that there is a history of Christian speculation on language that, far from subordinating utterance to an absolute and transcendental *logos* as Derrida asserts, in fact anticipates elements of his critique of logocentrism, and does so precisely insofar as it is determined by the distinctive categories of Christian theology. He writes, 'The post-modern embracing of a radical linguisticality, far from being a "problem" for traditional Christianity, has always been secretly promoted by it.'[23] Milbank traces the 'linguistic turn' characteristic of twentieth-century philosophy in particular to orthodox Christian thinkers of the eighteenth century. He finds in Robert Lowth's accounts of the pleonasm or 'repetition with variety' that characterizes Hebrew poetry, and of the future clarification of its prophetic figures, an anticipation of the Derridean principle of supplementarity or 'non-identical repetition'.[24] The significance of this anticipation, for Milbank, is that it is 'peculiar to a Biblical construal of reality', that is, determined by a distinctively Christian discourse which turns out not to be reducible to onto-theology, as Derrida would imply.[25] In the same way, he argues that J.G. Hamann's theory of meaning as a play between remembered past meanings and anticipated future ones, as well as between elements of the present language system, shows that he 'understands as well as Derrida that *logos* is a "supplement at the origin"'.[26] Again, this view derives from Hamann's Christian view of creation as a divine language and of human language as its elevation to expression. Milbank finds it particularly significant with respect to deconstruction that these differential theories of language are theories primarily of oral language. This means that Derrida would be wrong to incorporate them into a history of metaphysics which depends on the fading breath of speech for the illusion of self-presence. For Hamann in particular, Milbank argues, it is precisely writing that allows metaphysics the illusion of presence. Eighteenth-century Christian thinkers such as Lowth and Hamann, Milbank argues, based their differential theories of language on a 'temporally fading present', which leads to a theory of language whose meaning is neither absolutely present nor absolutely indeterminate but a continual process of 'tradition'.[27] Milbank describes this view as:

> a trust that all the words we now use with a particular range of relative determination will be able to carry an endless succession of significations as yet undreamt of, and yet remained recognisably 'circumscribed' by precious usage.[28]

Milbank's thesis that Christian theology cannot always and everywhere be assimilated into the history of metaphysics as onto-theology is also that of Graham Ward, in *Barth, Derrida and the Language of Theology* (1995). There Ward argues that Barth's doctrine of the analogy of faith is a structural equivalent to Derrida's law of *différance*, and can be understood as a 'theological [reading]' of the latter.[29] He writes:

> Barth's theological discourse is ... a rhetorical strategy presenting both the need to do and the impossibility of doing theology. This is exactly the form, method and content of Derrida's philosophical discourse.[30]

Ward is perhaps too concerned to emphasize the similarities between Derrida's discourse on *différance* and Barth's theology of the Word fully to acknowledge some of the differences that remain between them. Barth's emphasis on the absolute interiority of God, for example, rests on the kind of axiological distinction that Derrida deconstructs in Husserl. Barth writes, 'In and for himself, [God] is I, the eternal, original and incomparable I ... He is known – from outside ... as Thou and He.'[31] The value consistently ascribed throughout Barth's theology of the Word of God to the interiority of God, to 'God's side' as opposed to 'our side', makes it difficult simply to describe this theology as a 'reading of *différance'*, which is opposed to all such oppositions. Furthermore, the presupposition of faith in Barth's theology, that God 'is actually known' through his Word in the Church, so that 'we cannot ask whether God is known', but only how far this is the case, has no equivalent in Derrida's ultimately rationalist thought.[32] It is true, however, that Barth's theology of language cannot be reduced to a metaphysics of language in the sense Derrida ascribes to Western thought as such. Barth is continually at pains to distinguish his theology of revelation from the scope of metaphysics. He writes that the Word of God as the object of church proclamation is 'in contrast to all the objects of metaphysics or psychology', insofar as it is 'not...primarily the object of human perception'.[33] He continues that the Word of God is 'not a reality in the same way as the totality of what we otherwise call reality is real', precisely because it is 'not universally, i.e. always and everywhere present'.[34] The Word of God, for Barth, is not that kind of present-being which, for Derrida, is the object of metaphysics. It is not even a supreme being.[35] Barth writes, 'The question: What is God's Word? is utterly hopeless.' Like Derrida's trace, it 'exceeds the question, *What is?*'.[36] The Word of God is precisely that about which we cannot form definitions or proofs, because to do so would be to slip into the metaphysical enquiry as to what it is, which Barth calls the 'illegitimate yearning' of theology.[37] He writes:

> We must not...base the hiddenness of God on the inapprehensibility of the infinite, the absolute, that which exists in and of itself, etc. For all this in itself and as such...is the product of human reason in spite of and in its supposed inapprehensibility.[38]

This statement could scarcely make it more clear that Barth aims to write something other than metaphysical theology in the sense in which Derrida understands metaphysics as onto-theology. Milbank is right, therefore, to assert that Western theology cannot be univocally reduced to onto-theology, as Derrida claims. It is precisely insofar as Barth analyses the distinctive categories of Christian theology that he ceases to write theology in Derrida's sense of the term.

In fact, Derrida's concept of theology is untenably reductive. He takes the use of the term 'God' as the ground of metaphysical systems such as those of Descartes, Leibniz and Hegel, to indicate discourse on God as such. He takes a species of theology to indicate the genus. Hence the most common theological response to deconstruction has been the assertion that it is only the metaphysical species of theology which is the proper object of deconstruction, and not theological discourse in general. In *Theology and Contemporary Critical Theory* (1996), Graham Ward argues that it is only theology which 'does not recognize the limitations of its own language' which is open to deconstruction, and not theology as such. He writes, 'Derrida is attacking a certain form of theology: the use of God within classical rationalism and Enlightenment Deism.'[39] In *The Trespass of the Sign* (1989), Kevin Hart takes a similar view. He argues that whilst theologies have often been, at least in part, metaphysical, that is, discourses based on a point of presence, 'there does not seem to be a compelling reason why theology *should* be a discourse on presence.'[40] He argues that deconstruction pertains only to 'that which is metaphysical in theology', leaving open the possibility of a non-metaphysical theology which would not be susceptible to deconstruction. Derrida is concerned with 'how God has been made to *function* in philosophical and theological systems', Hart argues, and not with the God in whom Christians profess to believe nor with belief in God itself.[41] As Terry Wright writes:

> The real target of deconstruction is not the religious imagination... but the belief that... religious discourse can be the last word..., transparent upon a fixed and absolute truth.[42]

For Derrida, theology denotes a discourse that uses the term 'God' as the ground of an ontological system, or that which uses an equivalent term in a similar way. It is quite legitimate, therefore, to conceive of theological discourse that is not 'theological' in this sense. Here and there, Derrida acknowledges that this is the case. He writes that the concept of God is the ground of presence 'from Descartes to Hegel', and again that this is true of 'the name of God, at least as it is pronounced within classical rationalism'.[43] In fact, this sort of qualification ought to be repeated each time Derrida uses the concept of God or the term 'theology'. In Brian D. Ingraffia's words, Derrida's 'God', particularly in the early texts, is 'only the god who acts as a metaphysical ground for the operations of the independent and autonomous ego' in rationalist metaphysics, and his 'theology' is only the discourse upon this god.[44]

Most critics agree that the deconstruction of metaphysical theology, once the latter is distinguished from theology in general, is a valuable exercise for Christian theology. As James J. Dicenso writes, 'While there is a degree of cogency to the deconstructionist "critique of metaphysics", there exist, within the very procedures of that critique, valuable insights for religious thought.'[45] In *Postmodern Theory and Biblical Theology* (1995), Ingraffia argues that 'in breaking the Enlightenment faith in reason, of our concept of truth as residing in self-presence, as our own' Derrida's deconstruction of metaphysical theology makes clear what should never have become confused, that 'Biblical theology' is not at all metaphysical.[46] He argues that the God of Biblical revelation 'does not make possible but rather makes impossible, an absolutely pure and absolutely present self-knowledge', insofar as Paul's thought is opposed to the effort to claim one's life as one's own, calling this sin.[47] Insofar as metaphysical theology is deconstructed, for Ingraffia, the non-metaphysical nature of the Biblical revelation becomes clearer. I will examine the truth of this and other similar claims in more detail in Chapter 6, but for now will simply point out that, as with other recent attempts to distinguish a 'Biblical' or Hebraic stratum of Christian theology from its distortion by Greek metaphysics, Ingraffia does not satisfactorily explain how the difference between the Biblical content and its interpretations is to be maintained. He writes:

> Ontotheology makes the same reversal as the Colossian philosophy condemned by Paul by beginning with Greek (or existential or post-structuralist, etc.) philosophy and then using this philosophy to interpret the Bible.[48]

The question he does not answer is how else it is possible to interpret the Bible than with one set or another of philosophical first principles. As Paul Ricoeur writes, with respect to Biblical interpretation in the postmodern era:

> It is now with an anti-ontological conceptuality that theology has to come to grips. But the fundamental situation has not radically changed. It is still as a function of an external problematic that theology has to interpret its own meanings.[49]

We cannot accept Ingraffia's rigorous distinction of 'Biblical' thought from its 'philosophical' interpretations. There must be an interpretation of some kind even to articulate a system of Biblical theology. Terry Wright is more judicious as to the value of the deconstruction of metaphysical theology, as he writes that 'Christianity can benefit from some of [Derrida's] critique, coming to a clearer understanding of its complex

"Jewgreek" construction.'[50] The value of deconstruction is less that it highlights a purely Hebraic conceptuality to which Christian theology should adhere than that it insistently reminds such theology, if it had ever forgotten, that it is, in Karl Barth's words, 'a conglomerate of philosophies', none of which are in themselves adequate to the task of full or certain representation of its objects.[51]

This is the essence of the value of deconstruction for theology, that it insists on the proper limits of the function of theological language. In an essay entitled 'Why is Derrida Important for Theology?' (1992), Graham Ward argues this case. He writes that deconstruction implies that 'as a discourse, [theology] has no more privileged access to truth than any other form of writing'.[52] He asserts:

> *Différance* draws attention to the fact that theology cannot make dogmatic claims about God, not without accepting that it speaks with and through metaphors. This ineradicable metaphorical character of language does not negate the meaning of theological statements but it puts them into question.[53]

This is, on the whole, true. Ward perhaps over-emphasizes the 'metaphorical' character of theological language here, by which he means that a word's meaning is as determined by its relation to the language-system as by its relation to an object. It is not so much that the differential language-system, on the structuralist account, prevents our words from simply or purely denoting God, but that God is not an object within the scope of or appropriate to our words on any account. It is this point that the deconstruction of metaphysical theology insists that theology as such must acknowledge. It is engaged in a task which is fundamentally impossible, namely to apply the worldly phenomenon of language to that which is wholly other than all worldly phenomena as such. Deconstruction will not allow it to forget that this is so.

Let us be clear. I am not arguing, in the manner of Mark Taylor, that deconstruction teaches Christian theology something new, to which it must thereafter conform. On the contrary, deconstruction repeats for theology a fundamental caveat of which, in its depths, it has always been aware, namely that it exists in a double bind. On the one hand, it does and must use our language to speak of God. On the other hand, our language is as such inadequate to the task. As Ward says, this does not negate the meaning of theological statements. Derrida himself supports this view. In his reading of philosophical texts, a deconstructed text is not simply assigned to meaninglessness. The conclusion is not that the text is metaphysical and therefore not true. This approach Derrida describes as 'turning the page of philosophy (which usually amounts to philosophising badly)', by which he means that there is no question of a non-metaphysical language in which one could dismiss or falsify metaphysics.[54] Rather, what is necessary, for Derrida, is:

> to surround the critical concepts with a...discourse...to mark the conditions, the medium and the limits of their effectiveness...and, in the same process, designate the crevice through which the yet unnameable glimmer beyond the closure can be glimpsed.[55]

This double task is, in a certain sense, that of theology. On the one hand it must use the worldly material of language to speak of God, since this is all that is available. On the other hand, and with precisely this language, it must also point out its incapacity to name God, who is wholly other than the world to which it applies. It is a question, as Derrida puts it elsewhere, of 'conserving all [the] old concepts...while here and there denouncing their limits'.[56] This kind of qualification does not amount to a negation of theological statements, since the same kind of qualification would have to be applied to the negation as to the position, but to an acknowledgement that they are not and never can be the final words with respect to their object. As Karl Barth writes, 'The issue is not an ultimate "assuring" but always a penultimate "de-assuring" of theology, or, as one might put it, a theological warning against theology.'[57]

It is not only negative theologians but also systematic theologians such as Aquinas and Barth who were already aware of the double bind of theological language. As he formulates the doctrine of analogy in the *Summa Theologiae*, Thomas Aquinas makes this double bind clear. He argues that we know God from the way in which creatures represent (*repraesentant*) him, which they do insofar as they possess any *perfectio*, or completeness in any respect.[58] In his simplicity, God is perfect in every respect, and the limited perfections of creatures are limited participations in his perfect perfection. A 'good' man or a 'good' dog, that is, participate to the limited degree determined by their respective natures in the unlimited and complete goodness of God. When we say that God is 'good', Aquinas writes, such words 'do say what God is [*significant substantiam divinam*]; they are predicated of him in the category of substance, but they fail to represent adequately what he is [*deficiunt a repraesentatione ipsius*]'.[59] We know that they say something about God, or are properly predicated of him, because the perfections they signify (*perfectiones significata*) belong pre-eminently to God.[60] If I say that God is good because of what I have learnt about goodness from good men and good dogs, I am speaking ultimately about a divine quality in which these creatures participate insofar as their limited nature allows. On the other hand, in the sense that the signifying apparatus (*modus significandi*) pertains entirely to such creaturely participations, such words are not properly predicated of God. Ultimately, Aquinas writes, our words for God, such as 'living' in the statement 'God is living', are used to indicate that that which they signify 'does pre-exist in the source of all things, although in a higher way than we can understand or signify [*eminentiori modo quam intelligatur vel significatur*]'.[61] This is a crucial sentence, naming the relationship at the heart of the doctrine of analogy. It means that, for Aquinas, we can speak truly of God, but that we cannot know in what sense we are doing so. This is not to say that Aquinas in any way anticipates deconstruction. The metaphysical system in which creatures variously participate in the simple and universal perfection of God which is the context of the theory of analogy would itself be open to deconstruction. Nevertheless, Aquinas is aware of the consequence of the deconstruction of metaphysical theology, namely that while theology must proceed in worldly language suited to worldly phenomena, since there is no other kind, this language is not capable of signifying God, at least in the way in which it signifies everything else. In order to signify God in any way at all, theological language must be submitted to the critique which insists that, if it does so, it is in such a way that we do not know with certainty what it is that it signifies. What Aquinas already knew about deconstruction is that theology proceeds and must proceed by the dual movement of position and critique of position.

Barth approaches the double bind of theological language from the other side, as it were, of Aquinas' natural theology, by means of his theology of the Word of God. Graham Ward has shown that there are similarities in Barth's and Derrida's attempts to name the wholly other than that to which our language applies. I will simply add one or two points here to support my contention that Barth was already aware of the consequences of the deconstruction of metaphysical theology. He emphasizes that our concepts and language are inapplicable as such to God, who, apart from his revelation, is altogether hidden to us. 'In contrast to that of all other objects', he writes, '[God's] nature is not one which... lies in the sphere of our power' to view, conceive and express.[62] He writes:

> The lines which we can draw to describe formally and conceptually what we mean when we say 'God' cannot be extended so that what

is meant is really described and defined; but they continually break apart so that it is not actually described and therefore not defined.[63]

Barth is equally emphatic that, if God's revelation is true, then, in church proclamation and theology, we must conceive and speak truly of God in response. He writes:

> It is disclosed to us that we do not view and think of God, that we cannot speak of Him; and because this is disclosed to us, it is brought home to us that the very thing which has to happen ... is that we must not fail to do it.[64]

God's Word tells us that he is not an object within our capacity to name, and that we must use the language he has given us to speak of him nevertheless. Hence, Barth writes:

> The success of our undertaking stands or falls with the fact that we are on the way; that therefore any goal that is attained becomes the point of departure for a new journey on this way.[65]

Again, it is not the case that Barth has simply anticipated deconstruction. The double bind in which he describes theology derives from an event of revelation of the other that has no equivalent in Derrida's thought. Nevertheless, within the problematic of revelation, Barth is aware of the consequences of the deconstruction of metaphysical theology, namely that theology must comprise 'the saving unrest ... of a continual enquiry', which responds to revelation with positive language at the same as it points out in that language the limits of its function as such.[66]

I am now in a position to draw my first conclusions with respect to the consequences of deconstruction for theological language. I have argued that Derrida is wrong to assert or imply that theology in general can be assimilated into the history of metaphysics as onto-theology. Not all theology is onto-theology, and deconstruction applies only to the latter. This is not to say that any given theology consistently avoids thinking of God in terms of what Derrida calls presence, but that not every theology uses such a concept of God, even by implication, to determine the meaning of Being. The deconstruction of theology which is metaphysical in this sense, however, shows that theology in general must proceed by means of a critique of its own language, whose grammar and lexicon have been essentially determined by the history of metaphysics as onto-theology. I have argued that deconstruction's own task is, in its own way, that of theology, which both must and cannot use language to speak of the wholly other than that to which it applies, namely beings. Deconstruction, therefore, teaches theology nothing radically new, but insists with a new rigour on what it already knew, that its positive statements must be qualified with an acknowledgement of the incapacity of position as such finally and certainly to represent God.

2.2   Derrida and negative theology

It has been argued almost since deconstruction began that it is closely related to negative theology. Derrida himself opened the debate in '*Différance*' (1968), asserting that whilst deconstruction might employ similar locutions to those of negative theology, the objects of the two discourses are distinct. He writes:

> The detours, locutions and syntax in which I will often have to take recourse will resemble those of negative theology, occasionally even to the point of being indistinguishable from negative theology.[67]

Both deconstruction and negative theology deny the predicate of Being to the object of their inquiry, which is precisely that which precedes Being, and hence both begin by delineating all that it is not. In the discussion following the original presentation of Derrida's paper, an interlocutor argued that the two discourses could be identified, saying that *différance* 'is the source of everything and one cannot know it: it is the God of negative theology'.[68] Derrida was therefore led to defend and to qualify his claim with the proposition that *différance* cannot be identified with God 'if, that is, this name is given to a being, even to a supreme being'.[69] The debate as to the relationship between deconstruction and negative theology has continued unabated ever since, and in this section I will examine the precise nature of this relationship.

I will begin with an analysis of Derrida's own arguments concerning the relations between the two discourses. As I will discuss below, his views on this question are complex. Nevertheless, there is a fundamental level of Derrida's response, in which he asserts, 'No. What I write is not "negative theology".'[70] *Différance*, for Derrida, is not another name for God. He says, '*Différance* is not, it is not a being and it is not God.'[71] His reason for this is that, although negative theology denies God the predicate of Being, it does so ultimately in order to attribute to him a higher, more eminent mode of Being than those we understand by the term. In *'Différance'*, he writes that negative theologies are

> always concerned with disengaging a superessentiality beyond the finite categories of essence and existence ... and always hastening to recall that God is refused the predicate of existence only in order to acknowledge his superior, inconceivable and ineffable mode of being.[72]

In 'How to Avoid Speaking' (1986), Derrida repeats that negative theology, at least to some extent, 'seems to reserve beyond all positive predication, beyond all negation, even beyond Being, some hyperessentiality, a being beyond Being'.[73] However, it may deny the attribute of Being to God, in Derrida's view, negative theology remains an ontological discourse, since it continues to posit God as Being in an inconceivable and transcendent mode. It is therefore altogether distinct from deconstruction, whose object is not any manner of being. Derrida describes this distinguishing quality of negative theology as the 'ontological wager of hyperessentiality'.[74]

He argues that this wager is 'at work both in Dionysius and in Meister Eckhart', and it is at this point that his argument breaks down.[75] On two occasions, Derrida cites a passage in support of his claim from Eckhart's sermon *Quasi stella matutina*, on the nature of God, which reads:

> In saying that God is not a being and that God is above Being, I have not denied Being to God; rather, I have elevated it in him.[76]

Derrida comments, 'The negative moment of the discourse on God is only a phase of positive ontotheology.'[77] Clearly, this comment is a fair exposition of the passage Derrida cites. It is not, however, a fair description of negative theology in general, as Derrida takes it to be. In particular, it cannot be applied to the work of Pseudo-Dionysius, which is an important point with respect to Derrida's account of negative theology, firstly because he argues that Dionysius exemplifies this account, and, secondly because the latter is often taken to represent the most radical expression of negative theology in the Greek and Christian traditions.[78]

Pseudo-Dionysius (c. 500) writes a complex and interdependent series of accounts of the meaning of theological language, according to what Rosemary Lees calls the 'logic of the theology of transcendence'.[79] On the one hand, God is known for Dionysius through Scriptural revelation, which confirms the natural theological deduction that he is the universal cause. On the other hand, both Scripture and natural theology tell us that God is beyond our capacity to know. As Deirdre Carabine writes:

> The tension between transcendence and causality (as the foundation for divine immanence) is the axis upon which the Dionysian system revolves, and, as such, can be said to reflect the central dialectic at the heart of theism.[80]

As the cause of all that is, God can be predicated with every name applicable to beings, but since he transcends existence, these predicates must also be negated. Dionysius writes, 'As cause of all and as transcending all, [God] is rightly nameless and yet has the names of everything that is.'[81] It is for this reason that Dionysius follows Ex. 3:14 in attributing Being to God. As Derrida points out, in the course of Dionysius' account of the meaning of this divine name, God is said to be a transcendent being. Dionysius writes that God is 'being for whatsoever is [*to einai tois hopôsoun ousi*]', and 'the being of beings [*tôn ontôn ousia*]'.[82] These formulations are onto-theological, both positing the relation between Being and beings as that between ground and grounded, and identifying God with that ground.[83] Furthermore, Dionysius offers an analogical account of the meaning of this divine name, according to which God is Being, but in a higher and fuller mode than we can understand from what we know about Being from creatures. He writes that God is 'a "being" [*ôn*] in a way beyond being [*huperousiôs*]', which is open to interpretation in an analogical sense, and he describes such hyperbolic terms for God as examples of 'a denial in the sense of a superabundance [*huperokhikês aphaireseôs*]', which would corroborate such an interpretation. In a similar vein, he writes that in the divine Good beyond being, 'non-being is really an excess of being [*to anousion ousias huperbolê*]'.[84] These texts all seem to support Derrida's claim that Dionysius reserves a higher mode of Being for the divinity of whom he ostensibly denies Being.

If this were Dionysius' complete account of the meaning of theological language, then Derrida would be right to describe his thought as an ontological wager. This is not the case, however. Dionysius qualifies his analogical explanation of Scriptural names with several other accounts of their meaning. Firstly, he writes that 'what the Scripture writers have to say regarding the divine names refers... to the beneficent processions [*agathourgous proodous*] of God.'[85] Dionysius' account of the divine names is set in the context of a Neoplatonic metaphysics, in which divine causality is understood as a series of processions from the divine unity. It is only in these processions, for Dionysius, that God can be known in any way, since his unity is absolutely transcendent, and it is to them alone that Scripture intelligibly refers when it ascribes the names of conceptual qualities to God. He writes:

> The truth is that everything divine and even everything revealed to us is known only by whatever share of them is granted [*tais metokhais*]. Their actual nature [*auta de*], what they are ultimately in their own source and ground [*kata tên oikeian arkhên kai hidrusin*], is beyond all intellect and all being and all knowledge.[86]

The first divine name, for Dionysius, because it accounts for the divine processions through which alone we have any knowledge of God, is 'Good'. He writes, 'The Godhead is granted as a gift to all things. It flows over in shares of goodness to all.'[87] In his goodness, that is, God causes all existence as a series of processions from his unity. His goodness carries him outside of himself, as it were, into the creation and preservation of all creatures, and into their return to himself as their end.[88] Dionysius writes, 'The divine name "Good" tells of all the processions [*tas holas proodous*] of the universal Cause.'[89] Dionysius identifies these good processions with the Christian category of Providence. He writes:

> The first [divine] name tells of the universal Providence of the one God, while the other names reveal general or specific ways in which he acts providentially.[90]

This text is important because it introduces Dionysius' explanation of the second divine name, 'Being'. Dionysius' account of this name is based entirely upon the premise that it refers only to a providential procession of God and not to God's unity or 'essence' in itself. Dionysius writes:

> The purpose of what I have to say is not to reveal that being in its transcendence [*tên huperousion ousian, hêi huperousios*], for this is something beyond words, something unknown and wholly unrevealed [*pantelôs anekphanton*] ... What I wish to do is to sing a hymn of praise for the being-making procession [*ousiopoion proodon*] of the absolute divine Source of Being [*ousiarkhias*].[91]

This qualification of Dionysius' account of the meaning of the attribution of Being to God contradicts Derrida's assertion that his negative theology is a species of onto-theology. Firstly, it makes clear that Dionysius does not think of God as the Being of beings or as Being itself, according to Heidegger's definition of onto-theology. On the contrary, for Dionysius, Being is logically consequent upon its cause, the divine Goodness. He writes, 'The first gift . . . of the absolutely transcendent Goodness is the gift of being [*to auto einai dôrean*].'[92] Secondly, this aspect of Dionysius' account of theological language makes clear that, although the term 'Being' is to be attributed to God in an analogical sense, its referent is a procession of the divinity, and not the divinity in itself, about which nothing can be known or said, including the proposition that it is the fullness of Being.

The other element of Dionysius' account of theological language that contradicts Derrida's claim that his thought is ultimately onto-theological is the double sense of negation which he prescribes for such language. He writes:

> Theological tradition has a dual aspect, the ineffable and mysterious on the one hand, the open and more evident on the other. The one resorts to symbolism and involves initiation. The other is philosophic and employs the method of demonstration.[93]

The second of these theological modes, for Dionysius, is that of affirmative theology, which is metaphysical. Its object is the knowledge of God derived from beings, namely the ways in which God is like beings and those in which he is unlike them. It is crucial in understanding Dionysius' thought to recognize that the first stage of negative theology functions within the framework of affirmative theology. It is in this sense that he writes:

> Since [the divinity] is the cause of all beings, we should posit [*tithenai*] and ascribe to it all the affirmations [*kataphaskein theseis*] we make in regard to beings, and, more appropriately we should negate [*apophaskein*] these affirmations, since it surpasses all being.[94]

As the cause of Being, God can be likened to all that is with positive predications, but since he transcends Being, he must be distinguished from all that is with negative predications. It is at this level of negative theology that the analogical explanations of the divine name Being which support Derrida's claim function. As the cause of Being, God must be, but since he transcends Being, he is not. We must therefore say that he is, but in a higher sense than we understand by the term. As John D. Jones writes:

> Negative theology functions within affirmative theology or, more specifically, metaphysics, to express the pre-eminence of the divine cause. Here, if you will, the negations are 'super-affirmations'.[95]

Derrida's claim is contradicted by the existence of a second level of negative theology, which Dionysius describes first in the text at the head of this paragraph. In this theological mode, affirmative theology as such, and hence all reference to Being, is denied. Whereas affirmative theology was concerned with the similarity and difference of the divinity to beings, the second level of negative theology denies that the divinity can be intelligibly predicated with any relationship whatsoever to beings. It is in this sense that Dionysius writes:

> We should not conclude that the negations are simply the opposites of the affirmations, but rather that the cause of all is considerably prior to this, beyond privations [*sterêseis*], beyond every denial [*aphairesin*], beyond every assertion [*thesin*].[96]

Denys Turner describes this as a move from 'negating propositions' to a strategy of 'negating the propositional'.[97] Dionysius employs the latter strategy when he writes, 'We make assertions and denials of what is next to it [*met'autên*], but never of it [*autên*], for it is both beyond every assertion ... and beyond every denial.'[98] It is in this sense that he writes that the divinity is 'more than ineffable [*huperarrêtou*]' and 'more than unknowable [*huperagnôstou*]'.[99] It cannot be intelligibly related to anything that can be said or known. As John Jones puts it, this level of negative theology is not 'one logos among many' but 'the denial of all logos'.[100] Whilst there is a sense of Dionysian negative theology of which Derrida's claim that it is onto-theological is true, there is a further sense in which the first mode is negated, and which falsifies Derrida's claim. Dionysius predicates Being analogically of God, but goes on to deny that predication as such is applicable to him.

Many commentators have followed Derrida in arguing that deconstruction differs from negative theology insofar as the latter is a species of onto-theology. In most cases, Derrida's thesis is merely expounded and accepted as such. This is the case in Mark Taylor's essay, 'nO nOt nO' (1992), in which he writes:

The via negativa turns out to be implicitly affirmative ... In Christian theology, God, who is beyond Being, is not discontinuous with it. The apophatic God, like the Platonic Good, is surreal, hyperreal, hyperessential, or 'supereminent Being'.[101]

In the same way Shira Wolosky writes, in 'An "Other" Negative Theology' (1998), 'Apophatics, far from transcending ontology, is itself fundamentally structured by ontology.'[102] Both essays simply repeat Derrida's point, as if its truth were either clear or already established. The case is argued most thoroughly by John Caputo, in *The Prayers and Tears of Jacques Derrida* (1997), and it is to his argument there that I will now turn. The thesis of Caputo's book is that 'Derrida's religion is more prophetic than apophatic, more in touch with Jewish prophets than with Christian Neoplatonists, more messianic ... than mystical.'[103] As a comparison of the relative prominence of religious traditions in Derrida's work, this thesis is true. Caputo's supporting claim, however, that deconstruction can be altogether dissociated from the problematic of negative theology, is false. The essence of his argument is that the object of deconstruction is something 'less than real', empty of Being, whereas the object of negative theology is something 'hyper-real', or the fullness of Being.[104] In fact, this distinction cannot be maintained. Caputo writes:

Différance is but a quasi-transcendental anteriority, not a supereminent ulteriority.[105]

There are two problems with this comparison. Firstly, it is not one that is tenable within the terms of deconstruction, which is important here because Caputo is explaining why Derrida is right with respect to negative theology. If he is right, he can be so only within the terms of his own argument, and deconstruction does not permit a distinction between one object which is less than or before Being on the one hand and one which is more than or beyond Being on the other. There is no distinguishing between this side and that side of presence on the one hand *and* asserting that Derrida is right to make such a distinction on the other. Secondly, the object of negative theology is not restricted to the terms of just one side of this distinction. Pseudo-Dionysius' God could be described both as 'quasi-transcendental', in the sense that it is neither a transcendental nor a non-transcendental, and as 'anteriority', since it precedes Being. When Caputo reformulates the difference, the same applicability of negative theology to both its sides obtains. He writes:

> The namelessness of *différance* does not consist in being an unnameable being but in pointing to the differential matrix that generates names and concepts.[106]

In the first place, we have seen that Pseudo-Dionysius' God is not an unnameable being. In the second place, the God of negative theology cannot rigorously be distinguished from the matrix that generates names and concepts. Derrida himself says as much of negative theology:

> This is what God's name always names, before or beyond other names: the trace of the singular event that will have rendered speech possible even before it turns itself back toward...this first or last reference.[107]

We can speak of God in negative theology because God makes such speech possible, just as we can speak of *différance* in deconstruction because *différance* makes it possible. Even Caputo's most apparently solid distinction, of which the previous one is an expansion, that deconstruction is not mystical but grammatological, does not hold absolutely. The 'mystical' element of negative theology is that in it which is concerned with relation to the wholly other, and it has become increasingly clear in Derrida's later work that deconstruction shares this concern. Deconstruction cannot be distinguished from negative theology in the manner that Caputo claims, because his distinctions are based upon the premise that the object of negative theology is a supreme being, and, as I have argued, it is one the intentions of that discourse to negate precisely this proposition.

Derrida's own assessment of the question of the relationship of deconstruction to negative theology has always been complex, however. From the beginning, there has been an undercurrent of uncertainty in his work with respect to his fundamental assertion that negative theology is a species of onto-theology. He recognizes that negative theology is a plural discourse, referring to the 'most negative of negative theologies' and to the 'dissimilar corpuses, scenes, proceedings and languages' to which the term refers.[108] In 'How to Avoid Speaking', he cites this heterogeneity as a reason to be cautious in defining negative theology as such.[109] He expresses this caution himself most clearly in a letter to John P. Leavey, Jr. (1981), in which he writes:

I believe that what is called 'negative theology' (a rich and very diverse corpus) does not let itself easily be assembled under the general category of 'onto-theology-to-be-deconstructed'.[110]

Clearly, this remark is in striking contrast to the fundamental theme of Derrida's response to negative theology. Whereas he almost always describes the latter as a kind of onto-theology, he here expresses a doubt that this is the case. He displays a similar doubt in 'From Restricted to General Economy' (1967), in which, having written that negative theology is 'perhaps' ontological, he continues, 'Perhaps: for here we are touching upon the limits and the greatest audacities of discourse in Western thought.'[111] The closest Derrida comes to resolving the question as to whether he believes that negative theology is onto-theological or not is in 'How to Avoid Speaking', where he writes that negative theology is as open to being described as onto-theological as deconstruction is open to being described as metaphysical. He writes:

If the movement of this [onto-theological] reappropriation [of hyperessentiality] appears in fact irrepressible, its ultimate failure is no less necessary.[112]

Like deconstruction, that is, negative theology can always be described as onto-theological, since its language is directed as such towards beings. Nevertheless, Derrida suggests, like deconstruction it can also be considered to draw attention to the limits of this language from within, as the only medium available in which to do so.

In his most recent work on negative theology, 'Sauf le nom' (1993), Derrida acknowledges this similarity between deconstruction and negative theology more explicitly than in previous essays. During the 1990s, Derrida has increasingly been characterising deconstruction as the attempt to experience that which is presently impossible. In *Circumfession* (1991), he writes that he has 'never loved anything but the impossible', and in *Specters of Marx* (1993), he writes:

Wherever deconstruction is at stake, it would be a matter of linking an affirmation ... *if there is any*, to the experience of the impossible, which can only be a radical experience of the *perhaps*.[113]

It is this response to the unthinkable and the unrepresentable that Derrida recognizes that deconstruction shares with negative theology. In his analysis of the apophatic poetry of Angelus Silesius, Derrida writes that, like deconstruction, Silesius' discourse on communion with God 'introduces an absolute heterogeneity in the order and in the modality of the possible..., an absolute interruption in the regime of the possible'.[114] Derrida writes, 'This thought seems strangely familiar to the experience of what is called deconstruction.'[115] He goes on to characterize negative theology as the 'essence' of language, insofar as it 'exceeds language', aiming at precisely that which lies beyond the limits of language's capacity to refer.[116] He writes:

> Negative theology would be... above all the most thinking, the most exacting, the most intractable experience of the 'essence' of language: a discourse on language... in which language and tongue speak for themselves.[117]

Derrida comes to characterize negative theology, that is, as the most revealing kind of discourse on discourse, insofar as it reveals the limits of propositional discourse. In this it shares precisely the same goal as deconstruction. Derrida goes further, and argues that negative theology finds itself in the same *double bind* as deconstruction. However much its essence is to question the essence of language, he writes, 'by testifying it *remains*'.[118] On the one hand, that is, negative theology is 'a movement of internal rebellion, [which] radically contests the tradition from which it seems to come'.[119] On the other hand, even in the act of denying predicates to a subject, negative theology continues to use the language founded on the very categories of subject and predicate whose validity it is attempting to transcend. It says the unsayable, but it is still forced to *say* it, and hence betray it. As Derrida writes, this is precisely the situation in which deconstruction finds itself.

Derrida continues to deny, however, that deconstruction and negative theology have comparable objects. He regards negative theology as relatively more constrained in its questioning of the limits of language than deconstruction, which aims at something absolutely unconstrained. This distinction cannot be maintained, however. There are two characteristics of negative theology that lead Derrida to make it. Firstly, negative theology is always circumscribed by prayer or celebration. Derrida writes:

> An experience must guide the apophasis towards excellence, not allow it to say just anything, and prevent it from manipulating its negations like empty and purely mechanical phrases.[120]

This is the experience of the 'you', of the relatively determinate other to whom the discourse is either directly addressed or indirectly concerned with relation to. Now it is true that negative theology can be characterized in this way. It is not true, however, that deconstruction is not determined in a similar way by the context of the other which precedes the discourse. In *The Gift of Death* (1992), Derrida reads Kierkegaard's exposition of the Biblical account of Abraham's sacrifice of Isaac to indicate that 'duty or responsibility binds me to the other, to the other as other, and ties me in my absolute singularity to the other as other'.[121] The name of this absolute other in the story of Abraham is God. In *Specters of Marx*, Derrida makes clear that deconstruction as an ethical discourse consists precisely in fulfilling this responsibility to the other. Its ethics consist in a faithful response to 'the singularity of the other, to his or her absolute precedence or to his or her absolute previousness, to the heterogeneity of a *pre-*'.[122] Deconstruction, that is, is in part a response to the wholly other which precedes it. Derrida grants that this wholly other has been named 'God'. It is therefore wrong to distinguish deconstruction from negative theology by attributing to the latter a relative determination by the other which precedes the discourse, since deconstruction is also characterized by this relative determination.

The second characteristic of negative theology by which Derrida distinguishes it from deconstruction is its dependence on revelation history. The difference between Plato's idea of the Good beyond Being and Dionysius' God beyond Being, Derrida writes, is 'the event of the event, the story, the thinking of an essential "having-taken-place", of a revelation'.[123] Negative theology, that is, is dependent on a view of history in which there has been a revelation of the meaning of history, and it takes this revelation as the point of departure for all its negations and de-negations. Deconstruction, on the other hand, neither has nor could have such a point of departure. Again, whilst this is true of negative theology, it is also true in a certain way of deconstruction. As John Caputo writes, the latter has its being *in alio* rather than *in se*. It is a 'parasitic' practice which requires a prior discourse on which to operate. It has nothing to say, but '[inhabits] the discourse of those who have something to say', and shows them how difficult it is to do so.[124] In this it can be compared to negative theology. Now deconstruction can inhabit any kind of discourse that makes a positive claim to refer to reality, whereas negative theology works in the context of a theological tradition. Nevertheless, both share this fundamental characteristic, that their concern is the limits of the capacity of language to refer to reality in given positive discourses. Deconstruction, in this sense, is to the Western metaphysical tradition what negative theology is to any given theological tradition. Derrida is right to say that deconstruction knows no concept of revelation as such, but wrong to imply that it is thereby less relatively determined than negative theology. Both discourses question the limits of the referential function of the texts of previous systems of thought with respect to fundamental realities, and do so entirely within the context of these texts.

I am now in a position to sum up my conclusions with respect to the relationship between deconstruction and negative theology. I have argued that Derrida is wrong to claim that deconstruction can be distinguished from negative theology insofar as the latter is a species of onto-theology. Pseudo-Dionysius in particular, one of the most radical exponents of negative theology in the Christian tradition, and of whom Derrida makes this claim, gives an analogical account of the Scriptural attribution of Being to God on the one hand, but goes on to qualify this account in several important ways on the other. Firstly, he denies that it applies to God in himself, arguing that its referent is a providential procession of the divine unity, and, secondly, he denies that any kind of language whatever can be intelligibly predicated of God. This dual sense of negative theology, in which propositions are negated on the one hand and propositional language as such is negated on the other, leads to the breakdown of the distinctions Derrida and his commentators draw between deconstruction and negative theology. Ultimately, Derrida, who has always betrayed a current of uncertainty concerning his fundamental assertion that negative theology is a species of onto-theology, begins to recognize that it shares with deconstruction the double bind of using language to denote the wholly other than that to which language applies, namely beings. This is not to say that deconstruction can be reduced to negative theology, since the two discourses relatively determine the other in different ways. Rather, I would claim that, as a discourse of the wholly other, which denotes this object by means of a negation both of the positions of a given tradition and of positional language as such, deconstruction remains within the problematic of negative theology.

2.3   The messianic

I will conclude this section with an examination of Derrida's most recent point of contact with Christian theology, namely his exposition of the ethics of deconstruction in terms of messianic eschatology. He describes himself as 'the last of the eschatologists', that is, as thoroughly eschatological in his thinking even as he deconstructs the concept of eschatology.[125] In *Specters of Marx* (1993), Derrida writes that what remains valuable in Marx's thought today is what he calls 'the messianic', that is, an openness to 'the coming of the other, the absolute and unpredictable singularity of the *arrivant as justice*'.[126] Derrida had written of the word 'Come!', addressed to the risen Christ at the end of the book of Revelation, that as a prayer for the wholly other, which 'does not address itself to an identity determinable in advance', it exceeds the scope of ontology, which is concerned with present beings.[127] He finds this apocalyptic thought to obtain also in Marx, whose ontology '*must carry with it, necessarily* ... a messianic eschatology'.[128] Marx's thought shares this eschatology with the religion whose critique he argues is the essence of ideology-critique. What Marx shares with Jewish and Christian religious thought is not the content of their eschatologies, not a particular account of the last things, but a 'formal structure of promise [which] exceeds ... or precedes' any such account.[129] This formal structure, which Derrida describes as the '*epokhê* of the content' of messianism, is what deconstruction inherits from Marxism. Derrida writes that what remains irreducible to any deconstruction, itself undeconstructible, is 'a certain experience of the emancipatory promise', which he expounds as:

> the formality of a structural messianism, a messianism without religion, even a messianic without messianism, an idea of justice – which we distinguish from law or right ... – and an idea of democracy – which we distinguish from its current concept and from its determined predicates today.[130]

Deconstruction is all about a justice to come, Derrida asserts, a justice beyond all present moral and political discourses and that cannot be thought within their terms. This is what he means when he calls it a messianism without religion, or a messianic without messianism.

Derrida insists on the distinction between the strictly formal 'messianic', whose structure informs deconstruction, and the determinate historical 'messianisms', including Judaism, Christianity and Marxism. These last, insofar as they determine to some degree the future event for which they wait, betray the absolute otherness of that of which deconstruction is an expectation. Derrida writes:

> Ascesis strips the messianic hope of all its biblical forms, and even all determinable figures of the wait or expectation; it thus denudes itself

in view of responding to...the 'come' to the future that cannot be anticipated.[131]

Derrida calls deconstruction a 'desert' messianic, therefore, since it constitutes a 'waiting without horizon of expectation', which he sees as the condition of possibility of the historical messianisms that wait within such a horizon.[132] In 'Faith and Knowledge' (1996), Derrida links the historical religions with violence, with the 'wars of religion' which return today like the repressed of the technology which itself perpetuates new political and economic wars whose interests are ultimately reducible to determinate religions.[133] If the Enlightenment project of a universal religion 'within the limits of reason alone' is to be thought today, Derrida argues, it must be by means of the kind of 'desert-like' abstraction of the content of the historical religions that he proposes in *Specters*.[134] This abstraction, he writes, 'liberates a universal rationality and the political democracy that cannot be dissociated from it'.[135] A universal and rational religion, that is, would consist precisely in that messianic structure of openness to the wholly other as justice by which Derrida characterizes the ethics of deconstruction. This can be taken as a gloss on Derrida's comment in 'Circumfession' (1991) concerning his 'religion about which nobody understands anything', that 'the constancy of God in my life is called by other names so that I quite rightly pass for an atheist'.[136] The constant and atheistic religion of Derrida's is, insofar as he expresses it in his work, this desert messianism which he associates with a universal rational religion. He calls it a 'desert within a desert', that is, not merely a kind of negative-theological eschatology, but an abstraction even of the content of negative theology.[137]

Derrida calls this universal 'religion without religion' a 'faith without dogma', and argues that it is legitimate to describe such a position as rational because the faith on which it rests cannot ultimately be distinguished from that which also underwrites rational discourse.[138] He writes that 'critical and technoscientific reason, far from opposing religion, bears, supports and supposes it'.[139] Both religion and reason, he argues, share a 'performative of promising', which calls for 'an elementary act of faith' without which there could be no address of the other in general.[140] Both religious and scientific discourse, that is, are addressed to their hearers or readers under the sign of the *promise*: they have the hermeneutic structure of the statement, 'I promise you that what I am saying to you is true.' Derrida calls this 'the testimonial signature', and it can be responded to only by faith, which, he writes, 'is, in its essence or calling, religious'.[141] One can negate any given article of faith, Derrida argues, but what cannot be denied is the fiduciary structure of address, which opens the 'possibility' of given religions although not their determinate necessity, and which underwrites all scientific discourse whatever. Derrida writes that this fiduciary structure is 'the place where...reason, critique, science, tele-technoscience, philosophy, *thought* in general, retain the *same* resource as religion in general'.[142]

It is difficult for Derrida to associate deconstruction with a universal form as opposed to its particular historical contents in this way, since it is precisely this kind of distinction whose structure the non-concept of the messianic is intended to challenge. Derrida has so far professed to be unable to explain this anomaly. In *The Gift of Death* (1992), he explicitly defers the 'immense and thorny' question, and at the Villanova roundtable (1994), he says:

> The problem remains – and this is really a problem for me, an enigma – whether the religions, say, for instance, the religions of the Book, are but specific examples of this general structure, of messianicity...[or whether they] have been absolute events, irreducible events which have unveiled this messianicity.[143]

Whether Derrida were eventually to conclude in favour of either one of these options, the problem would still remain that the ethics of deconstruction is described by means of precisely the kind of binary opposition – between form and content, or universal and particular – of which this ethics is intended to be a critique. Even if, as Derrida continues, 'some other scheme has to be constructed to understand the two at the same time', the opposition remains.[144] He has so far been helped out of this difficulty by John Caputo, who suggests that the early Heidegger's concept of 'formal indication', that is, 'an anticipatory sketch [as compared] to the idiomatic fullness of concrete life', glosses the kind of universal category with which Derrida is concerned.[145] The formal indication is a sign of an ontic region in which it does not itself participate, as opposed to the traditional universal which is held to contain its particulars. One can only *be involved* in that of which is a sign, since it is of another order than that which can be grasped conceptually. According to this structure, thought is related to existence in a merely 'quasi-transcendental' manner, which, Caputo argues, is the relation in which it could be said that Derrida's messianic stands to the historical messianisms.[146] Whilst Derrida uses the term 'quasi-transcendental', however, this analogy between Heidegger's formal indication and

Derrida's universal structure limps, as Caputo recognizes. He writes that Derrida's messianic denotes engagement itself, whereas Heidegger's formal indication contrasts conceptuality precisely with such engagement.[147] But further than this, it is based on the kind of distinction between existence as presence and conceptuality as distance that deconstruction contests, which perhaps explains why Derrida himself has not used the analogy. In fact, it is impossible for Derrida to maintain, within his own terms, the strict distinction between the formal messianic and the historical messianisms. No amount of talk about 'quasi-transcendentality' will alter the fact that it remains within what Derrida calls 'the problematic opposition between form and content', which is a potential object of deconstruction.[148] Ultimately, Caputo is right to say that deconstruction is in fact '*one more* messianism', and not a rigorously formal structure that has been abstracted from such discourses.[149] This is true not just at the level of deduction, in the sense that it follows from deconstruction's own terms, but also at the level of induction, in the sense that it follows from what Derrida in fact writes about the messianic. In 'Faith and Knowledge', Derrida speaks of the 'phenomenal form' of the messianic, as peace and justice, and asserts that it 'always' takes this form.[150] At the Villanova roundtable he says, 'The expectation of the coming has to do with justice.'[151] The wholly other which deconstruction awaits can be *relatively determined* as peace and justice. In precisely the same way, that which is awaited in Christian eschatology is predicated with absolute otherness at the same time as it is relatively determined by precisely such predication. In this sense there is no doubt that deconstruction constitutes the expectation of a relatively determinate other, or is one more messianism.

My claim that Derrida does not escape the problematic of negative theology is supported by this conclusion. Like negative theology, he begins to delineate the object of his discourse by negating the positions of a given tradition. In *Specters*, he asks himself, 'Why keep the name, or at least the adjective [i.e. messianic]...there where no figure of the *arrivant*, even as he or she is heralded, should be pre-determined, prefigured or pre-named?'[152] It is an important question, since it names an apparent inconsistency in the ethics of deconstruction. In 'Faith and Knowledge', Derrida suggests that he is 'obliged...to continue' to use the language of the Abrahamic religions because the language of Western philosophy has been irreducibly formed by its development in the history of the West as Christendom.[153] In precisely the same way as negative theology, that is, Derrida describes the other by means of a series of abstractions from the positive terms of a determinate tradition, without which tradition this other could not be thought or described at all. He writes that the formal messianic '*resembles to a fault*, but without reducing itself to, that *via negativa* which makes its way from a Graeco-Judaeo-Christian tradition'.[154] This is true. As an ethics, deconstruction resembles to a fault, that is, has precisely the same structure as, negative theology. The object of both discourses is the wholly other, and their method of indicating this object is to negate the positive terms of a given tradition, and then to go on to negate position as such. When Derrida writes that the thought of the messianic 'makes its way through the risks of absolute night', the night of non-knowledge to which he refers is no more absolute than in negative theology. It remains dimly illuminated by a series of determinations, the negation of which is the pre-condition of the thought of the other.

I will conclude this analysis of Derrida's concept of the messianic with the assertion that the ethics of deconstruction remains within a theological problematic. The distinction between the messianic and messianism cannot be rigorously maintained, as Derrida is ultimately aware. As a discourse of the wholly other, deconstruction remains within the theological double bind of the relative determination of the other by the discourse itself. To be precise, it remains within the double bind of negative theology, thinking the wholly other by negating the positive terms of the discourse in which it is named. This is not to contain or domesticate the critique which deconstruction constitutes, but to assert that, as Derrida is well aware, it remains a profoundly traditional Western discourse. Furthermore, as Derrida has begun to indicate in his most recent work, deconstruction shares with theology the response of faith to its double bind. The compromised attempt to indicate the other in deconstruction 'belongs from the very beginning to the experience of faith...that is irreducible to knowledge'.[155] Deconstruction shares with theology, that is, not only the incapacity consistently to speak of the wholly other, but also the continuing attempt to do so based on a *belief* in the other and in the heterogeneous event of its arrival.

I am now in a position to conclude my argument with respect to the significance of deconstruction for the use of theological language in literary theory which I am proposing in this book. Ultimately, Derrida is wrong to assert that deconstruction 'blocks every relationship to theology', at least insofar as this statement is taken to mean that, after deconstruction, discourse on God in general collapses into self-contradiction. On the contrary, deconstruction remains within the theological problematic of using language to denote the wholly other than that to which language applies. As a critique of position in a language that is necessarily positive, deconstruction remains in particular within the problematic of negative theology, negating both the positions of previous discourse on the other and its own negations. It cannot, therefore, be said to prohibit or render meaningless theological language, since, as Derrida is ultimately aware, it remains within the circle of precisely such language itself. The consequence of deconstruction for the use of theological language in literary theory is in the end simply a rigorous insistence on a point of which theology was always aware, namely that its statements cannot be taken as finally and certainly true. Rather, they represent the current provisional articulation of what Barth calls the saving unrest of the church's continual enquiry, which are ultimately believed to be true, although this truth cannot be demonstrated. Derrida has become increasingly clear that the faith in which theological meaning is grounded is shared not only by deconstruction but also by all other rational discourse, which includes all other modes of literary theory.

3
On Marxism

I will now move on to an analysis of Marxist literary theory. In the historical materialist world-view, religious ideas are a contingent mental reflection of the reality of human life, the production relations of a given social formation. This means not only that Marxism in its classical forms is atheistic, negating the truth-claim of religious beliefs, but also that it is based upon a critique of such beliefs, exposing their imaginary quality in order to emphasize the reality of material human life. In Marx's well-known phrase, 'The criticism of religion is the presupposition of all criticism.'[1] On the other hand, there are long-established similarities between certain fundamental Marxist and Christian ideas. Alisdair MacIntyre, for example, claims that 'Marxism shares in good measure both the content and the functions of Christianity as an interpretation of human existence.'[2] In this section, I will assess the consequences of Marxist literary theory for the use of Christian theology in literary theory for which I am arguing in this book. I will examine some of the major bodies of work which deal with the relations between Marxism and Christianity, and assess their significance for the concept of Christian literary theory. I will begin, however, with an analysis of the Marxist critique of religion, since this seems to rule out the possibility of using theological language in literary theory in the way in which I propose.

3.1 The Marxist critique of religion

Marx was born a Jew, both of his parents coming from rabbinical families, but his father converted to Protestantism shortly before Marx's birth, in order to advance professionally. His children followed when Karl was six years old. Marx's father's religion was the moralistic deism of the Enlightenment, of which he writes to his son, 'What Newton, Locke and Leibniz believed, everyone can submit to.'[3] Marx himself showed early signs of outward acceptance of this religion, writing an essay for his final examination at school in 1835 on 'The Union of Believers with Christ according to John 15:1–14'. He closed this essay with a view of Christian faith as a kind of passive endurance of adverse circumstances that would remain with him throughout his life:

> Once man has attained this virtue, this union with Christ, he will await the blows of fate with composure, courageously oppose the storms of passion, and endure undaunted the wrath of the iniquitous, for who can oppress him, who could rob him of his Redeemer?[4]

It was during his studies in Berlin that Marx became an atheist, becoming a member of the circle of left-wing Young Hegelians, which included Bruno Bauer, Max Stirner and Ludwig Feuerbach. In the foreword to his doctoral thesis on ancient materialism (1841), Marx expresses the view that he formed in this circle, that philosophy must be able to pursue the question of man freely, without the hindrance of religious dogma or authority:

> Philosophy makes no secret of it. Prometheus' admission – 'in sooth, all gods I hate' – is its own admission, its own motto against all gods, heavenly and earthly, who do not acknowledge the consciousness of man as the supreme divinity.[5]

The Young Hegelians placed great emphasis on the criticism of religion. Bauer argued that the gospels were the artistic creations of their individual authors, and wrote a book, on which Marx collaborated, invoking Hegel as a 'atheist and anti-Christian'.[6] Most influential of all the works of the Young Hegelian school was Feuerbach's *The Essence of Christianity* (1841). Engels writes that 'Enthusiasm for [this book] was general; we all at once became Feuerbachians.' He describes 'how enthusiastically Marx greeted the new conception, and how much – in spite of all critical reservation – he was influenced by it'.[7]

Feuerbach argues that, in religion, men project qualities of human nature into an object opposed to themselves, namely God. He writes, 'Consciousness of God is self-consciousness, knowledge of God is self-knowledge.'[8] His presupposition is that the object of knowledge in general is the objective nature of the subject.[9] If religion, therefore, can be defined as consciousness of the infinite, it is ultimately 'nothing else than the consciousness of the infinity of the consciousness', in which man contemplates the infinity of his own nature in the form of an object.[10] Indeed, it is in religion above all that the law of the coincidence of self-consciousness and consciousness of the object holds most true, for Feuerbach. He writes:

> The divine being is nothing else than the human being, or rather the human nature purified, freed from the limits of the individual man, made objective – i.e., contemplated and revered as another, a distinct being.[11]

Man's own most self-evident qualities, such as existence and subjectivity, are those which he attributes first and with the greatest conviction to God in religion. Furthermore, all the highest perfections of his own nature, such as goodness, justice and love, he also attributes to God, who therefore becomes 'the highest subjectivity of man abstracted from himself'.[12] As a result of this process, Feuerbach writes, 'To enrich God, man must become poor; that God may be all, man must be nothing.'[13] In order to constitute God as another subject, in whom all the perfections of human nature appear, that is, man must deny these perfections of himself. In order that God may be thought of as infinitely good, goodness must be denied as a quality of human nature, and so Christianity tells us that man is corrupt and incapable of good. Feuerbach's goal is to invert the false relationship of subject and predicate in religion, and restore to man those qualities of human nature which he has hitherto attributed to God. Having demonstrated that 'the true sense of theology is anthropology', Feuerbach wants to 'exalt anthropology into theology'.[14] He writes:

> That in religion which holds the first place – namely, God – is, as we have shown, in itself and according to truth, the second, for it is only the nature of man regarded objectively; and that which to religion is the second – namely, man – must therefore be constituted and declared the first.[15]

In 1843, after the closing of the journal of which he was editor-in-chief, Marx moved to Paris, where he came into close contact with revolutionary socialist ideas, and, as a result of his friendship with Engels, began to study and write on economics. The following year, Marx produced his two most extended meditations on religion, both under the influence of Feuerbach, in the 'Introduction to the Critique of Hegel's Philosophy of

Right', and the *Economic and Philosophical Manuscripts*. The 'Introduction' begins with the presupposition that, as far as Germany is concerned, 'the criticism of religion is essentially complete'.[16] As a subsequent remark in *The Holy Family* (1845) confirms, this is a reference to Feuerbach, whom Marx describes as 'the first to complete the criticism of religion'.[17] He rehearses Feuerbach's view of religion as a projection of human nature, writing:

> The foundation of irreligious criticism is this: man makes religion, religion does not make man. Religion is indeed the self-consciousness and self-awareness of man who has either not yet attained to himself or who has already lost himself again.[18]

What Marx adds is an account of the social conditions which generate the illusory phenomena of religion. He writes, 'Man is no abstract being squatting outside the world. Man is the world of man, the state, society.'[19] Society as it is presently organized produces religion as an inverted consciousness of the world, for Marx, because it is itself an inverted world, that is, an unjust and irrational one. As a result, 'the struggle against religion is indirectly the struggle against the world whose spiritual aroma is religion'.[20] It is no longer religion that alienates man from his nature, as in Feuerbach, but rather the social conditions in which he lives; religion reflects these alienating conditions. The truth of the religious reflection of the inverted world is its positive value for Marx, since it constitutes a primitive form of protest against such a world. It is in this sense that he writes:

> Religious suffering is at the same time an expression of real suffering and a protest against real suffering. Religion is the sigh of the oppressed creature, the feeling of a heartless world, and the soul of soulless circumstances. It is the opium of the people.[21]

The proper response to religion, then, for Marx, is not the rationalistic criticism of Feuerbach and the Young Hegelians – such a response is the paradigm of what he will call 'ideology' – but rather an active engagement in the transformation of the social conditions which render religion necessary as an opiate. He writes, 'The abolition of religion as the illusory happiness of the people is the demand for their real happiness.'[22] Feuerbach's criticism of religion has led to the doctrine that 'man is the highest being for man'. For Marx, it must be taken a step further, and become 'the categorical imperative to overthrow all circumstances in which man is humiliated, enslaved, abandoned, and despised'.[23] In the fourth of the *Theses on Feuerbach* (1845), he writes:

> His work consists in resolving the religious world into its secular basis. But that the secular basis detaches itself from itself and establishes itself as an independent realm in the clouds can only be explained by the cleavages and self-contradictions within this secular basis. The latter must therefore, in itself be both understood in its contradiction and revolutionized in practice.[24]

After 1845, Marx turned his attention from the question of alienation primarily to questions of the economic base of society from which alienating forms of consciousness such as religion arise, and his subsequent remarks on religion are made largely in passing. In *The German Ideology* (1845), written with Engels, Marx first assigns religion its specific place within the scheme of historical materialism. A fundamental premise of the latter is that, 'The phantoms formed in the brains of men are ... necessarily sublimates of their material life-process.'[25] Religion is one of these forms of consciousness, and Marx and Engels write of it, along with other ideological forms, such as morality and metaphysics:

> They have no history, no development; but men, developing their material production and their material intercourse, alter, along with this their actual world, also their thinking and the products of their thinking.[26]

Religion is therefore no more than a reflection of the sum total of the production relations of the society in which it inheres. In the first volume of *Capital* (1867), Marx describes the latter as the 'earthly kernel of the misty creations of religion'.[27] Hence, the feudal mode of production of the Middle Ages gives rise to the hierarchical structure of medieval Catholicism: 'It is the manner in which they gained their livelihood that explains ... why Catholicism played the chief part.'[28] In the same way, Marx asserts that the post-Enlightenment forms of Christianity are particularly suited to capitalist society, since they posit man in general, abstracted from his individual conditions, just as capitalism thinks of labour in general, abstracted from individual conditions:

> For a society of commodity producers ... Christianity, with its religious cult of man in the abstract, i.e. in Protestantism, Deism, etc., is the most fitting form of religion.[29]

In such later formulations, therefore, Marx ceases to think of religion as an inverted reflection of the conditions of the proletariat, and argues that it is, rather, an accurate reflection of the mode of production. He continues, however, throughout his work, to regard religion as the paradigm of alienated consciousness, illustrating the 'fetishism of commodities', for example, that is, the way in which relations between people appear in the commodity form as relations between things, with 'the misty realm of religion', in which:

> The products of the human brain appear as autonomous figures endowed with a life of their own, which enter into relations both with each other and with the human race.[30]

Once the bourgeois society based on the production of commodities is revolutionized, for Marx, so its religious reflection will vanish. He writes, 'The religious reflections of the real world can ... vanish only when the practical relations of everyday life between man and man, and man and nature, generally present themselves to him in a transparent and rational form.'[31]

In contrast to Marx, Engels wrote many essays and meditations on religion. Whereas the religion of Marx's household had been of a liberal bent, Engels grew up in Barmen, a centre of Pietism, where his father held office in the local church. Engels himself was a sincere believer as a youth, but, by 1839, as an apprentice businessman in Bremen, he had begun to have serious doubts about the rationality of his faith.[32] After a crisis of faith lasting some months, Engels found Strauss' *Life of Jesus* (1835), which argued on Hegelian grounds that the gospels should be understood as mythical expressions of a philosophical truth, above all that the unity of the divine and human natures cannot be found in the historical individual Jesus, but rather in the human race itself. Engels soon described himself as an 'enthusiastic Straussian', and by the time he became a member of the Young Hegelian circle in Berlin in 1841, had become an atheist, convinced that communism was the necessary result of Young Hegelian philosophy.[33] His continued interest in religion, however, led him to produce the first sketches of a Marxist history of religion. In this history, Christianity is seen in some respects as a prototype of communism, and in other respects as the kind of ideology which communism will supersede.

Engels accepts Marx's critique of religion as the reflection at the level of ideas of contradictions within the economic base of society. Having read E.B. Tylor on primitive culture, however, he adds a historical dimension, namely that deities were originally projections of natural forces beyond the control of primitive peoples. In *Anti-Dühring* (1878), he writes:

> All religion is nothing but the fantastic reflection in men's minds of those external forces which control their daily life, a reflection in which the terrestrial forces assume the form of supernatural forces.[34]

Engels then asserts, 'In the beginnings of history, it was the forces of nature which were so reflected', and argues that such reflections can be traced throughout the religions of the ancient world.[35] As social and production relations begin to develop, however, Engels argues that people also project these relations as alien forces standing over against them:

> It is not long before social forces begin to be active – forces which confront man as equally alien and at first equally inexplicable, dominating him with the same apparent necessity as the forces of nature themselves.[36]

As this second group of forces becomes deified, Engels argues, so later gods bear their characteristics. He then gives a rather hurried explanation of the eventual development of monotheism, in which all the natural and social attributes of previous deities are transferred to 'one almighty god, who is but a reflection of the abstract man'.[37] The first such god was the Jewish Jehovah, who has remained as the God of Christianity. Engels writes:

> In this convenient, handy, universally adaptable form, religion can continue to exist as the immediate, that is, the sentimental form of men's relation to the alien natural and social forces which dominate them.[38]

Indeed, Engels goes so far as to identify God in contemporary society with 'the alien domination of the capitalist mode of production'.[39] As a result, he follows Marx in believing that, once this mode of production has been superseded by the communist revolution, then the religion which comprises its reflection will also be superseded. When men have taken conscious control of the means of production, he writes:

> Only then will the last alien force which is still reflected in religion vanish; and with it will vanish the religious reflection itself, for the simple reason that there will then be nothing left to reflect.[40]

Despite his conviction of the falsity of its content, Engels nevertheless has a certain amount of respect for early Christianity. In *Bruno Bauer and Early Christianity* (1882), he describes the dogmatic content of the religion as 'nonsense', but argues that 'a religion that brought the Roman world empire into subjection and dominated by far the larger part of civilized humanity for 1800 years' cannot be dismissed as merely fraudulent, but rather must be accounted for in terms of the socio-historical conditions in which it arose.[41] Engels follows the early, and now outdated, Biblical criticism of Bauer and Ferdinand Benary, whose lectures he attended in Berlin in 1841, in order to provide such an account. From the latter, he takes the argument that Revelation is the oldest book in the New Testament, dating from 67–69 AD. From this book, therefore, 'one can get an idea of what Christianity looked like in its early form'.[42] For Engels, this is characterized by the absence of later Christian dogmas and morals, and the presence of the single doctrine of the salvation of the faithful by Christ, and of the single moral principle of the mortification of the flesh. Engels follows Bauer in asserting that the later theology of the gospels and the epistles were derived from Philo and from Seneca.[43] The early Christianity of the Book of Revelation is not conscious of itself as a new religion at all, but as a visionary Jewish sect, awaiting the imminent overthrow of the Roman Empire. Engels follows Benary's identification of the number of the name of the beast of Rev. 13:18 with the Emperor Nero. The popularity of the Christian sect, he argues, derived from 'the general right-lessness and despair of the possibility of a better condition' experienced by all the three classes he identifies in Roman imperial society of the period, and above all by the largest of those classes, the slaves.[44] Engels writes:

> In all classes there was necessarily a number of people who, despairing of material salvation, sought in its stead a spiritual salvation.[45]

He adds, 'We need hardly to note that the majority of those who were pining for such consolation of their consciousness ... were necessarily among the slaves.'[46] It was among the slaves, then, that Christianity found the greatest number of adherents. In *On the History of Early Christianity* (1895), Engels writes:

> What kind of people were the first Christians recruited from? Mainly from the 'labouring and burdened', the members of the lowest strata of the people, as becomes a revolutionary element.[47]

Engels draws a series of comparisons between early Christianity and the socialist movement. We have already seen that, for Engels, early Christianity drew most of its members from the lower classes of society, and that one of its most essential constituents was its belief in the overthrow of the Emperor Nero. Engels describes the Christianity of the book of Revelation, like socialism, as 'opposed to the ruling system, to the "powers that be"'.[48] He argues that both early Christianity and socialism came into being as 'the struggle against a world that at the beginning was superior in force, and at the same time against the innovators themselves', that is, against the ruling class of their society.[49] Engels twice cites a remark of Renan's that, to get an idea of the nature of the early Christian communities, one should now look not at church parishes, but at local sections of the International Working Men's Association, and agrees with it. Indeed, he argues that early Christianity constituted the closest form of organization to socialism possible in its time.[50] Both were movements of the oppressed; both 'preach forthcoming salvation from bondage and misery'; both were persecuted and legislated against as enemies of society; and both either have developed or will develop from small sects into the dominant ideology of their time.[51] There are even institutional parallels.[52] The only difference, Engels writes, necessitated by the historical conditions of their relative epochs, is that Christianity 'did not want to accomplish the social transformation in this world, but beyond it, in heaven, in eternal life after death, in the impending "millennium"'.[53]

Despite this late assertion of the value of pre-Nicene Christianity, Engels remains convinced of the ideological character of religion, and in several places sketches out a history of doctrinal conflicts within the church as ideological expressions of socio-economic conflicts. In *Ludwig Feuerbach and the End of Classical German Philosophy* (1886), Engels argues that, having arisen as a result of the projection of natural and social forces, as an ideology religion develops in the terms of the content thus established.[54] Having developed into a world religion in the conditions of Roman empire, Engels writes, in the Middle Ages, with the advent of feudal society, Christianity 'grew into the religious counterpart' to that society, with a corresponding feudal hierarchy and doctrine of authority.[55] The various heresies of the early modern period are to be explained in terms of the class oppositions to feudalism which they embody. As he puts it in *The Peasant War in Germany* (1850), as a result of the universal significance attributed to theology, 'All social and political, revolutionary doctrines were necessarily at the same time and mainly theological heresies.'[56] The dominant

Catholic ideology upheld contemporary feudal conditions, whereas the 'burgher-moderate heresy' of Luther represented the interests of the rising burgher class, 'directed primarily against the clergy, whose wealth and political importance it attacked'.[57] The peasant opposition to the conditions of feudalism, by contrast, took the form of the 'plebeian-revolutionary' heresy of Thomas Münzer, whose doctrine Engels describes as follows:

> By the kingdom of God Münzer understood a society in which there would be no class differences or private property and no state authority independent of or foreign to the members of society.[58]

Hence he identifies Münzer's doctrine as 'less a compilation of the demands of the plebeians of that day than a visionary anticipation of the proletarian element' beginning to develop among the plebeians.[59] Engels goes on to identify the bourgeois interests represented by the development of Calvinism, and concludes that with the access of freethinkers to political power at the beginning of the eighteenth century, Christianity enters its final stage of ideological significance, becoming 'incapable for the future of serving any progressive class as the ideological garb of its aspirations'.[60]

Although Lenin portrays himself as an expositor of the views of Marx and Engels on religion, in fact he develops their views in a number of ways, above all evolving a militant hostility towards religion and its representatives not found in his predecessors. As Lenin himself makes clear, his views are formed in the specific context of the Russian situation of his time, in which the Russian Orthodox church had become integrated into the political apparatus of the state and identified with the interests of the autocracy. Lenin describes the Orthodox clergy represented in the Duma as 'feudalists in cassocks', whose political objectives are essentially 'defence of the Church's feudal privileges' and 'outspoken support of medievalism'.[61] Furthermore, as David McLellan writes, the Church had traditionally been set against the intellectual and political progress represented by the Enlightenment, and Lenin takes up an anticlerical stance typically associated with the Russian intelligentsia in his writings on religion.[62]

Lenin wrote comparatively little on religion, but his concrete deliberations on the attitude of the Communist Party towards the subject proved to be of great influence on the practice of later Soviet governments.

In 'Socialism and Religion' (1905), he broadly follows the account of Marx and Engels in arguing that religion is the ideological reflection of the wretched conditions imposed upon the proletariat by the incomprehensible forces of capitalist economy. He writes, 'Impotence of the exploited classes in their struggle against the exploiters... inevitably gives rise to the belief in a better life after death.'[63] He places much greater emphasis than Marx or Engels, however, on the conscious use of religion by the ruling classes to keep the proletariat in their situation of exploitation. He describes religion as 'one of the forms of spiritual oppression' of the masses, and writes:

> Those who toil and live all their lives in want are taught by religion to be submissive and patient while here on earth, and to take comfort in the hope of a heavenly reward.[64]

Hence, as many commentators point out, Lenin, in this essay, silently alters Marx's dictum that religion is the opium of the people to the formulation that it is 'opium *for* the people', 'a sort of spiritual booze, in which the slaves of capital drown their human image'.[65] Whereas for Marx, religion was experienced as a real consolation by the proletariat, although in fact illusory, for Lenin it is a stultifying narcotic, peddled by the ruling classes to keep them unaware of the socialist solution to the conditions of exploitation under which they suffer. Hence he describes all modern religions and religious institutions as 'instruments of bourgeois reaction that serve to defend exploitation and to befuddle the working class'.[66]

On this account, it is clear that the party which represents the interests of the proletariat must eschew all connections with religion. This is true, for Lenin, both on philosophical and on political grounds. In the first place, as a Marxist organization, the Communist Party's actions are based on its conviction of the scientific truth of dialectical materialism, which logically precludes religious belief. In 'The Attitude of the Workers' Party to Religion' (1909), Lenin writes:

> Social-Democracy bases its whole world-outlook on scientific socialism, i.e. Marxism. The philosophical basis of Marxism, as Marx and Engels repeatedly declared, is dialectical materialism ... – a materialism which is absolutely atheistic and positively hostile to all religion.[67]

As a result of this hostility, Lenin disapproves of the tendency within German Social Democracy in particular to assert, as it did in the Gotha programme of 1875 and the Erfurt programme of 1891, that 'religion is a private matter'. Whilst religion should be treated as a private concern by the state, Lenin argues, in the sense that the state must sever all ties with religious organizations, it cannot be treated so by the workers' party. He writes:

> Our Party is an association of class-conscious, advanced fighters for the emancipation of the working class. Such an association cannot and must not be indifferent to lack of class-consciousness, ignorance or obscurantism in the shape of religious beliefs.[68]

The Party is committed primarily to the emancipation of the proletariat. Whilst it will necessarily disseminate atheist propaganda in its pursuit of this goal, it must also subordinate its atheism to it. Nor should the Party raise the question of the existence of God in an abstract or 'idealist' manner, in which it is artificially divorced from the class-struggle from which context it truly derives.[69] In his earlier essays, Lenin allows that proletarians who continue to hold religious beliefs must not be prohibited from joining the party which represents their interests, and even envisages working with religious groups insofar as they act in these interests.[70] In many cases, he argues, it would prove impossible to remove religious beliefs from the masses by ideological means alone until the social conditions which cause such beliefs are themselves removed.[71] The ultimate goal of the Party, therefore, for Lenin, must be to fight religion by fighting 'the *root* of religion, ... the *rule of capital* in all its forms'.[72] With the development of the movement of 'God-builders' within the Bolshevik party, however, Lenin began to take a sterner view of religious ideology. This movement, of which Lunacharsky and Gorky were among the most prominent members, saw the Marxist philosophy of history in religious terms, and equated the progress of socialism with the human 'building' of God. Lenin viewed these and similar ideas as 'clearly wrong and clearly reactionary', describing their equation of socialism and religion as 'a form of transition *from* socialism to religion'.[73] Lenin writes to Maxim Gorky:

> Any, even the most refined and best-intentioned, defence or justification of the idea of God is a justification of reaction ... The idea of God *always* put to sleep and blunted the 'social feelings', replacing the living by the dead, being *always* the idea of slavery.[74]

Hence, in the programme of the Russian Communist Party, drawn up in 1919, Lenin sets out the Party's intention to maintain a broad anti-religious campaign:

> The Party's object is to completely destroy the connection between the exploiting classes and organized religious propaganda and really liberate the working people from religious prejudices. For this purpose it must organize the most widespread scientific education and anti-religious propaganda.[75]

3.2 An assessment of the Marxist critique

The first point to be made with respect to the Marxist critique of religion is that, insofar as it constitutes an argument for the non-existence of God, this argument is fallacious. It violates the relevance criterion of a good argument, according to which the premises of such an argument must be relevant to its conclusion.[76] Insofar as the Marxist authorities argue that God does not exist, they draw this conclusion from premises concerning the determination of religious beliefs by the socio-economic conditions in which they are held. The question of this kind of determination is a different one than that of the truth or falsity of religious beliefs, however. As J.L. Mackie writes, 'The origin of a belief is in general irrelevant to the question of its truth.'[77] In *Does God Exist?*, Hans Küng traces this kind of argument back to Feuerbach, of whom he writes, 'From [his] time onward, there has been no form of atheism that did not draw on Feuerbach's arguments.'[78] Feuerbach claimed that religion is the consciousness of the infinite, and therefore of the infinity of the consciousness. But the phenomenological orientation of consciousness to the infinite does not entail either the existence or the non-existence of an infinite independent of consciousness, despite Feuerbach's repeated assertions that the latter is the case. The same holds with respect to the psychological justification of his projection theory, namely that God is 'the realized wish of the heart, the wish exalted to the certainty of fulfilment'.[79] Whilst psychological factors play a part in both the genesis and content of religious beliefs, it does not follow, as Feuerbach asserts, that there is no reality which corresponds to such beliefs. Küng writes:

> I can deduce psychologically my experience of God, but this still implies nothing against the existence of a God independent of

me, as the reference point of all my needs and wishes. In a word, something real can certainly correspond in reality to my psychological experience; a real God can certainly correspond to the wish for God.[80]

This is true. Insofar as Feuerbach raises the question of the existence of God, therefore, it remains open. The only conclusion that follows from his argument that the concept of God fulfils certain human needs and wishes is that it constitutes no evidence either for the existence or non-existence of a reality corresponding to this concept.

As we have seen, Marx thought of the work of Feuerbach as the completion of the criticism of religion, and he accepts the latter's view that religion is a projection of human realities in objective form as a case that has been definitively established. He takes it as given that, by the time he is writing, 'theology itself has failed'.[81] In the same way, Engels writes that Feuerbach 'proves' that God is no more than a reflection of man.[82] Whilst Marx argues against Feuerbach that it is not the human essence but the social conditions in which human beings actually live that are projected as the illusory objects of religion, he does not question the projection theory as such. His critique is therefore open to the same objection as that of Feuerbach. Whilst the socio-economic conditions in which religious beliefs are held may be shown to influence the content of those beliefs, that is, it does not follow that these beliefs correspond to no reality other than the conditions in which they are held. As Küng writes:

From the undeniable influence of economic and sociological factors on religion and the idea of God, we can . . . draw no conclusion about the existence or non-existence of God.[83]

In fact, the premises of the Marxist argument against the existence of God would be relevant to its conclusion only if it could be shown that the social determinants of religious beliefs are their *only* determinants. As we have seen, however, no such demonstration is attempted. Indeed, it is a striking feature of Engels' essays in the history of religion that he offers very little account of the correlation between the class-interests of the various groups he discusses and their characteristic religious beliefs. The Marxist perception that religious beliefs cannot be fully be understood without reference to the material conditions in which they are held does not necessitate the conclusion that these conditions exhaust their claim to be true. As Nicholas Lash writes, in *A Matter of Hope* (1981):

> It may well be the case that, in social situations marked by class conflict, the forms of religion do indeed 'reflect' the interests of conflicting parties ... It does not follow, however, that the truth-content of religious forms is exhausted by the circumstances they 'reflect' and the social functions which they serve.[84]

As with Feuerbach, insofar as Marx raises the question of the existence of God, it remains open. It is true that religion can function as the opium of the people, inasmuch as it offers the exploited classes the hope of the kind of justice and happiness in the next world that they see no hope of achieving in this one. It is true that it can function as opium for the people, inasmuch as it can be used by the ruling classes to justify a social organization from which they benefit at the expense of others. It does not follow that the God in whom either group believes either exists or does not exist, however. The only conclusion which can be drawn with respect to the determination of religious beliefs by the social conditions in which they are held is that it does not constitute evidence either of the truth or falsity of the content of those beliefs. As Lash also points out, none of the Marxist authorities recognizes the possibility of a *theological* critique of religious beliefs that can be shown to be so determined.[85]

Despite this logical fallacy in its argument against the existence of God, the Marxist critique nevertheless has a certain degree of historical justification, insofar as it represents the social attitudes of the churches with which the Marxist authorities were confronted. The Protestant church in Germany had been closely integrated into the administrative structure of the state since the Reformation, and by the eighteenth century, state bodies were responsible for the government of the church, whose clergymen had increasingly become agents of the political authorities. In *The Politics of German Protestantism* (1972), Robert Bigler writes, 'A Protestant clergyman's main duty was to carry out the orders of the ruler faithfully and unquestioningly and thus assist him in the task of strengthening and consolidating the Prussian state.'[86] After the French Revolution and the war with Napoleon, the church became even more closely integrated into the state. Whilst individual efforts were made on behalf of the rural and urban poor, the Lutheran tendency to assign responsibility to the state for the worldly affairs of its citizens and to the church for their salvation was predominant during the first half of the nineteenth century. The church proposed no solution to the increasingly wretched condition of the proletariat beyond individual acts of charity, which in practice were infrequent. Even the charitable societies, such as Wichern's Inner Mission, supported the existing order and opposed the social and political principles represented by the French revolution. During the 1848 revolution, the church allied itself with the conservative reaction of the monarchy, and engaged in a widespread campaign to convince the people that the revolution was against the God-given order. Afterwards, it continued to support the discredited regime, with its authoritarian institutions and hostility to democratic movements, thereby finally alienating itself from the proletariat. In *German Protestants Face the Social Question* (1954), William Shanahan writes:

> Protestant opinion remained aloof, punctuated only here and there by individual outcries, from all that concerned the worldly life of the people, their economic insecurity as well as their longing for political and social recognition. By this attitude, Protestantism virtually renounced the allegiance of the urban and industrial masses in Germany.[87]

The Catholic Church in Europe was similarly reactionary with respect to social change in the nineteenth century. Both liberals and revolutionaries cited the French revolution as a model of social and political change, and the Catholic hierarchy associated such change primarily with the extreme hostility towards the Church which quickly developed after 1789. Arthur McGovern writes, 'This memory influenced all the Church's responses...The very words, "liberty", "equality", and "democracy", because of their association with the French Revolution, often carried threatening connotations.'[88] Parish priests and bishops were stripped of their tithes and salaries, church property was nationalized, and monasteries and convents were dissolved. The Civil Constitution of the Clergy required bishops and priests to be elected by the laity and demanded that clergy swear an oath of fidelity to the Constitution, on penalty of deportation. Over 200 priests and bishops were killed in the September Massacres of 1792, and nearly 1000 more were condemned in the Terror. Twenty-five thousand, nearly one-sixth of the entire clergy, were deported or had fled. Religious dress and services were prohibited, and the cathedral of Notre Dame was re-named the 'Temple of Reason'.[89] Pope Pius VI quickly condemned the Declaration of the Rights of Man, and had severed all links between the Catholic Church and revolutionary France by 1791. During the Restoration period, the Church allied itself strongly with the monarchy and the aristocracy, and its members were often involved in counter-revolutionary reaction. As in Prussia, the Church's identification with the interests of the monarchy alienated the working class, who, as H. Daniel-Rops writes, experienced its function within the state as 'a political undertaking intended to repress them'.[90] Furthermore, the popes were monarchs themselves, of the Papal States in central Italy. In an encyclical of 1860, Pius IX threatened excommunication to anyone who challenged the legitimacy of the pope's temporal power over these states, and four years later, in the *Syllabus of Errors*, anathematized the belief that 'abrogation of the civil sovereignty enjoyed by the Holy See would greatly advance the freedom and happiness of the Church'.[91] The *Syllabus* condemned socialism and communism as 'pests' to be 'reprobated in the severest terms'.[92] The latter, in the pope's view, incited revolution 'in order to pillage, ruin and invade first the property of the Church and then that of all other individuals'.[93]

It is clear, therefore, that, during the period of the Industrial Revolution, the churches were on the whole characterized by alliance with the existing order and by resistance to social and political change, particularly in revolutionary form. Whilst movements of social concern among both Protestants and Catholics attempted to involve the churches in the problems faced by the industrial proletariat, they met with only limited success. The Catholic Church was concerned primarily to maintain its threatened authority, and the German Protestant Church to defend a traditional ideal of Christian monarchy which did not recognize the needs of the urban working classes. With respect to the historical expressions of Christianity with which they were confronted, therefore, the Marxist authorities were on the whole accurate in criticizing religion as an instrument of the ruling classes, serving to justify existing political structures and to discourage the exploited classes from any effort to change them. Marx's contemptuous diagnosis of the social ethics of Christianity was true enough of the churches of his time:

> The social principles of Christianity preach the necessity of a ruling and an oppressed class, and all they have for the latter is the pious wish the former will be charitable.[94]

Having pointed out that the Marxist critique of religion is justified with respect to certain historical expressions of Christianity, however, it must be added that this critique cannot be justified insofar as it generalizes from these historical expressions to the essence of Christianity. In *Christians and Marxists* (1976), José Miguez Bonino makes this point. Having endorsed the historical and Biblical justification of the Marxist critique, he writes:

> We should not see it primarily as a general denunciation of religion as such – this is indeed a secondary, unoriginal and quite questionable generalisation – but as a very specific exposure of the ideological function of Christianity . . . in relation to the individualistic, egoistic and profit-crazy bourgeois world.[95]

Bonino's commitment to Marxist praxis perhaps obscures the degree to which Marx certainly intended to denounce religion as such, but he is right to point out that the Marxist critique, whilst on the whole true of Christianity during the rise of the industrial bourgeoisie, is not generally true either of every historical manifestation of Christianity or of Christianity itself. This is what Roger Garaudy means when he writes that 'Marx criticizes religion, not metaphysically but historically.'[96] In the first place, as Engels himself points out, whilst Christianity has served to discourage social change in the interests of the ruling classes, it has also served as a stimulus to precisely such change. In *The Alternative Future* (1972), Garaudy describes this as the dialectic of 'the Constantinian and the apocalyptic' in Christian history, or 'the opposition between those who were contented to prepare souls for the coming of the Kingdom of God through repentance and those who wished to prepare for this coming by changing the world'.[97] He cites the Exodus, the denunciations of the Old Testament prophets and the Revelation of St John as Biblical examples of the element of protest against social injustice in Christianity, and Joachim of Fiore and Thomas Münzer as historical examples. Such a faith, as he rightly argues, is 'not an opiate but a leaven for changing the world'.[98]

In the second place, whilst Christianity has in certain cases preached a commitment to God that impoverishes human life, demanding a submission to authority that prevents the full expression of human potential, it has also preached a commitment to God that enriches human life. Whilst, for some Christians, religion has been an experience that engenders fear and guilt, demands submission to rules and promotes an individualistic concept of salvation, for others it is an experience that enriches and fulfils them as human beings. As Arthur McGovern writes, in *Marxism: An American Christian Perspective* (1980):

> Countless Christians . . . experience faith in Jesus and in God's power as sources which enable them to love more deeply, to act more justly and courageously, and to live more freely and hopefully.[99]

Contemporary theology has stressed that the Gospel is a call to become fully human. This has been the repeated message of the Catholic Church since the Second Vatican Council. The council's Pastoral Constitution on the Church in the Modern World, *Gaudium et Spes* (1965), asserts, 'Whoever follows Christ the perfect man becomes himself more a man', and sums up the relationship between Christian faith and human culture as follows:

> In their pilgrimage to the heavenly city Christians are to seek and relish the things that are above: this involves not a lesser but a greater commitment to working with all men towards the establishment of a world that is more fully human.[100]

The council derives this commitment to a fully human society from its renewed emphasis on 'the sublime dignity of the human person, who stands above all things and whose rights and duties are universal and inviolable'.[101] Its first principle in calling to Christians to work for such a society is that, 'All things on earth should be ordained to man as to their centre and summit.'[102] It can no longer be justly said, therefore, that Christianity involves a choice of submission to God over the exercise of human freedom. In his *Marxism and Christianity* (1966), Giulio Girardi makes this point. As a religion, Christianity undoubtedly affirms the primacy of God in the relationship between God and man. Nevertheless, Girardi writes:

> Christianity cannot be resolved into an affirmation of the primacy of God, but sees itself as an answer to the problem of man and of terrestrial existence in the light of God.[103]

Following the council's definition of the 'common good', Girardi argues that, as the history of salvation, Christianity is 'totally ordered towards enabling man – every man – to fulfil himself as an end'.[104] For Marxism, the relationship of man to God in religion is exhausted in that of master to slave, in which man's power to determine his own life is surrendered to God. In Christianity, however, whilst man indeed affirms the greatness of God, he does not do so at the expense of his own greatness, but rather finds the latter precisely in the former. Since this consists in God's love for man, the affirmation of God is at the same time the affirmation of man. As Girardi writes:

> If, in the Christian universe, not only God, but man too, is endowed with absolute value, then ethics will not be oriented to the glory of God alone, but also to the liberation of man.[105]

Despite the justification of Marx's critique of the practice of the churches of his time, therefore, it remains an incomplete account of Christianity. As several theological commentators point out, Marx never devoted serious attention to Biblical or Christian theology.[106] As a result, although his observations on the 'social principles of Christianity' constitute a significant critique not only of certain historical expressions of the Christian faith but also of a historical tendency of Christian practice, they remain one-sided. As Küng writes, in the end Marx 'was not at all familiar with the social principles of Christianity', because he was not fully familiar with the theological grounds of such principles.[107] He rightly criticizes historical abuses of Christianity, but he wrongly identifies those abuses with the essence of the Christian faith, and hence with any historical practice whatever of its principles. McGovern rightly argues that 'ideological use or abuse of religion should not be equated with the very nature of religion'.[108] Christianity cannot be identified either with the institutions to which it has given rise nor with the practices of those who have held power in such institutions. Marx's critique of religion, therefore, is a partially justified but incomplete account. He does not acknowledge either that there have been forms of Christianity which have striven for rather than hindered the development of a more fully human society, or that the Bible and much theological reflection upon its message call for precisely such a society.

I am now in a position to draw my first conclusions with respect to the consequences of Marxism for the use of theological language in literary theory for which I am arguing in this book. I have claimed that the Marxist critique of religion is fallacious, arguing from the socio-economic determinants of religious beliefs to their truth-content, whereas in fact the latter is logically independent of the former. The atheism of the Marxist world-view remains a hypothesis that cannot be proved either true or false. Despite the influence of the Marxist critique of religion, therefore, it remains possible meaningfully to use such language in literary theory after Marxism. Furthermore, whilst Marxism is on the whole justified in criticizing the churches of the Industrial Revolution for their resistance to the kind of social change that would improve the material conditions of the working classes, it is wrong to generalize from this situation to the essence of Christianity. Whilst Christianity has served in this and other historical situations to defend the interests of ruling classes, as Marxism claims, it has also inspired efforts to bring about greater justice in social relations. The gospel is a call to full humanity, to a faith that enriches human life, both individually and socially, and contemporary theology emphasizes this aspect of the Biblical message. It remains ethically possible to use the language of Christian theology in literary theory after Marxism, therefore. The latter claims that such theology is an ideological defence of social conditions that degrade the lives of men and women, but in fact it can and should constitute reflection upon a faith that calls men and women to a fully human individual and social life. The Marxist critique functions as a reminder to Christian theology that it has both justified and protested against situations of social injustice, and that it can still function in either way. Küng calls it a 'warning dark shadow continually accompanying belief in God', and it is a warning that an ethically justifiable practice of theology must constantly heed.[109]

3.3 Liberation theology

The value of the Marxist critique of religion for Christian theology, therefore, is that it constitutes a continual reminder to the latter of its historical tendency to subordinate the radical challenge of the Gospel of the Kingdom of Heaven and of the commandment of love, with their inescapably social relevance, to an identification with political structures which guarantee material prosperity to churches and to Christians who benefit from these structures, but which deny such prosperity to large numbers of their fellow men and women. Garaudy puts it well when he speaks of the dialectical structure of Christian history, in which Christianity has functioned socially both as opium and as leaven, both as an ideology which supports unjust social relations and as a challenge to bring about greater justice in those relations.[110] Marx reminds Christians that their faith can still function in either way, and that it is of the essence of the Biblical revelation upon which it is based that they choose the latter. This has been one of the insights of liberation theology, the movement which began in the 1960s in Latin America as theologians responded to the situation of poverty and exploitation suffered by most of their countries' inhabitants and to the social unrest that it provoked. An important stage in the development of this theology was the Second General Conference of the Latin American Bishops at Medellín, Colombia, in 1968, which met to relate the teaching of Vatican II to the specific situations faced by the church in Latin America. The bishops spoke of the misery of the majority of the population of the continent as 'an injustice which cries to the heavens'.[111] They affirmed that God intended the goods of the earth for everyone in common, and that he sent his Son to 'liberate all men from the slavery to which sin has subjected them', namely from 'hunger, misery, oppression and ignorance, in a word, that injustice and hatred which have their origin in human selfishness'.[112] They criticized the political authorities for decisions which tended to favour privileged groups and to militate against the common good, and asserted:

> The Church – the People of God – will lend its support to the downtrodden of every social class so that they might come to know their rights and how to make use of them.[113]

Liberation theology follows the Latin American bishops in moving from an analysis of the situation of oppression by which it sees the continent to be characterized to reflection upon the meaning of the word of God for the liberation of the poor for which such a situation calls.

The closest comparison of Marxist concerns to those of the Bible has been made in the works of the Mexican exegete José Porfirio Miranda. In *Marx and the Bible* (1971), he takes a position derived from Emmanuel Lévinas, according to which the primacy accorded to the concept of being in Greek metaphysics must be submitted to an ethical critique. The Western tradition of philosophy and theology has on the whole assumed the validity of the Greek concept of being-in-itself, for Miranda, but it is precisely this validity which both Marx and the Bible deny. He writes:

> Our century is definitively challenging the very concept of being, the 'in itself' which was the absolute criterion of the Greek mind. This criterion was adopted without question by Western culture...as the indisputable norm of truth.[114]

Lévinas argues that 'ontology, as a fundamental philosophy that does not call into question the self, is a philosophy of injustice'.[115] Miranda agrees, and adds that the concept of being-in-itself produces a 'philosophy of injustice' when used with respect to the object of knowledge. He writes, 'Greek philosophy was born to neutralize reality and prevent it from disturbing us, to reduce it to a cosmos in which everything is all right.'[116] The concept of being-in-itself, that is, has come to justify a culture in which the subject is considered as an autonomous individual on the one hand, and in which others are considered as objects in themselves, available for use as means to an end, on the other. In Miranda's view, the Bible systematically anticipates Marx in criticising the injustice of such a culture. He writes:

> What Marx criticizes in Western science is the same thing that today prevents it from being challenged by the fact, which is recognized by that science itself, that to a great degree Marx coincides with the Bible.[117]

The God of the Bible, Miranda argues, is not understood as a being of any kind, but is known only insofar as he commands Israel. The content of this command is clearly specified: it is 'to achieve justice for the poor'.[118] Miranda cites numerous texts from the prophets in support of this position, the most clearly stated of which is Jer. 22:13–16:

> Woe to him who builds his house by unrighteousness,
>   and his upper rooms by injustice;
> who makes his neighbours work for nothing,
>   and does not give them their wages...
> Did not your father eat and drink
>   and do justice and righteousness?
>   Then it was well with him.
> He judged the cause of the poor and needy;
>   then it was well.
> Is this not what it means to know me?
>   says the LORD.

No causal relationship is intended in the last four lines of this citation, Miranda argues, according to which the just man first knows Yahweh and therefore acts for justice on behalf of the poor. When the Bible intends to denote such a relationship, it does so. What Jeremiah means is that to act justly *is* to know Yahweh. Miranda comments, 'Here we have the explicit definition of what it is to know Yahweh. To know Yahweh is to achieve justice for the poor.'[119] He goes on to argue that this is what all the prophets understand by the knowledge of God, namely the practice of 'interhuman justice'.[120] He cites Hosea 4:1–2:

> There is no faithfulness or loyalty,
>   and no knowledge of God in the land.
> Swearing, lying, and murder,
>   and stealing and adultery break out;
>   bloodshed follows bloodshed.

Miranda comments that, since knowledge of God is here opposed to the 'interhuman crimes' of v. 2, the former is 'naturally understood to mean "justice among men"', and that this is reinforced by the synonymous relationship between knowledge of God and 'faithfulness and loyalty'.[121] The word here translated as 'loyalty', *ḥesed*, means goodness or kindness, especially to those in need, and appears again in Hos. 6:6.

> I desire steadfast love and not sacrifice,
>   the knowledge of God rather than burnt offerings.

Again, Miranda argues, knowledge of God is placed in synonymic parallelism with steadfast love, or, as he proposes to translate *ḥesed*, 'compassion'. It is opposed to the crimes of murder and robbery in the following verses, and contrasted in v. 6 with sacrificial rituals, a contrast repeated throughout the prophets. These factors, he argues, demonstrate that the meaning of knowledge of Yahweh in the prophets is 'almost like a technical term: to have compassion for the needy and to do justice for them'.[122] Nor does this meaning depend upon the use of the verb 'to know', he continues; the same meaning can be attributed to 'turning to' God (Hos. 12:6) or to 'seeking' him (Hos. 10:12). Miranda concludes:

> The God who does not allow himself to be objectified, because only in the immediate command of conscience is he God, clearly specifies that he is knowable exclusively in the cry of the poor and the weak who seek justice.[123]

The reason for the prophets' denunciation of the ritual observance of the Law, Miranda argues, is clear. The prophets are not asking for justice in addition to ritual worship, nor that such worship be reformed. Their message is that Yahweh does not want Israel to observe rituals but rather to act justly. Miranda cites Amos 5:21–25:

> I hate, I despise your festivals,
>   and I take no delight in your solemn assemblies.
> Even though you offer me your burnt offerings and grain offerings,
>   I will not accept them...
> But let justice roll down like waters,
>   And righteousness like an ever-flowing stream.

The message of this and many other similar prophetic texts, Miranda argues, 'can be summarized in this way: I do not want cultus but rather interhuman justice'.[124] At Isa. 1:15–17, Yahweh even denies that he will listen to Israel's prayers, until they 'learn to do good, seek justice, rescue the oppressed, defend the orphan, plead for the widow'. This stark opposition of ritual worship to justice, Miranda argues, means that, if there is injustice in a society, then its worship and prayer do not in fact have Yahweh as their object, however much that may be its intention. The prophets do not condemn worship as such, that is, but only worship offered by a society characterized by injustice. It will be acceptable to them only 'at the time when justice has been achieved'.[125] It must be clearly recognized, therefore, Miranda argues, that 'the prophets were convinced that justice would be achieved on earth', and he cites Isa. 2:2–4, Mic. 4:1–8 and Zeph. 3:9–13 in support of this position. Only in this context does their message, 'First justice and then cultus', make sense. Here Marx is of assistance in properly interpreting the Bible, Miranda adds, since, like Marx, the prophets look forward to a society characterized by just social relations. He writes, 'Everything they wrote, did and said stems precisely from the fact that they did not resign themselves to injustice.'[126]

Miranda finds a close anticipation of Marx's critique of the injustice of Western society in the New Testament as well. He argues that the 'sin' (*hamartia*) of which St Paul speaks in Rom. 4–11 should be understood to acquire its meaning from the first time it appears in the letter, Rom. 3:9, where, according to Miranda, it functions as a 'summary of the *adikia* [unrighteousness, injustice] of the Jews and Gentiles' to which Paul refers in Rom. 1:29 and 3:10. Miranda argues that the *adikia* which Paul places at the head of the catalogue of evils in Rom. 1:29–31 should be understood as the 'predominant concept' or 'comprehensive title' of that catalogue, in which 'great emphasis is put on interhuman injustices'.[127] The term 'sin', introduced in 3:9, he claims, should be defined by all the injustices of which Paul speaks in Rom. 1:18–3:20: 'The only thing he understands as "sin", with respect to content, is injustice.'[128] Miranda concludes:

> Paul defines sin with regard to its specific content by this interhuman injustice . . . *Adikia* constitutes the qualitative characterisation of what Paul understands by *hamartia* ('sin') in the whole rest of the letter.[129]

It is in this sense that Miranda understands Paul's repeated assertions that the law serves an instrument of sin (Rom. 5:20; 7:7–11; 1 Cor. 15:56).

Although it entered the world through one man (Rom. 5:12), he writes, sin 'has become structured into human civilisation itself, whose characteristic and most quintessential expression is the law'.[130] Citing Rom. 7:1 and 13:8–10, Miranda argues that concept of law in Paul must be understood formally, so that even when he alludes specifically to the Mosaic Law, his meaning can also be applied to law as such, 'law insofar as it is law'. Hence, when in Gal. 3:21 Paul writes, 'If a law had been given that could make alive, then righteousness [or 'justice', *dikaiosunê*] would indeed come through the law', Miranda comments:

> He denies not only to Mosaic law the power to achieve justice on earth; *a fortiori* he denies this ability to all law.[131]

Miranda goes on to compare Gal. 1:4, where Paul speaks of Christ's redemption from 'the present evil age [*aiôn*]', with Gal. 4:5, where he speaks of his redemption of 'those under the law'. He argues that Paul equates law with 'the entire cultural and social structure which we call human civilisation', and which Paul calls *aiôn*, 'this age' and *kosmos*, 'the world'.[132] Like Marx, that is to say, Paul 'wants a world without law', because he believes that justice cannot be achieved in the world as long as law and the culture of which it is the essence exists.[133] Miranda spells out the parallels he discerns clearly:

> Marx and Paul coincide in their intuition of the totality of evil. Sin and injustice form an all-comprehensive and all-pervasive organic structure. Paul calls this totality *kosmos*. Marx calls it capitalism.[134]

It is often argued that Miranda's work is one-sided, reducing the Biblical message to just one of its aspects, namely that God desires social justice. In 'Latin American Liberation Theology' (1976), Philip Berryman describes it as an 'extreme form' of liberation theology.[135] It is true that Miranda's exegeses tend to be reductive in this way. His account of Paul's understanding of sin as injustice, especially towards the poor, is an example. The Greek text does not support Miranda's contention that the *adikia* of Rom. 1:29 should be understood as the title or summary of the vices which follow. Rather, these nouns are listed in three grammatically distinct groups – the first in the dative singular, qualified by the adjective *pasêi*, 'all', and dependent upon the participle *peplêrômenous*, 'filled'; the second in the genitive singular and dependent upon the adjective *mestous*, 'full'; and the third in the accusative plural in apposition to *autous*, 'them', in 1:28. *Adikia* is the first term in the first of these groups. Cranfield comments that the list is 'arranged in three distinct groups', and Fitzmyer describes all four nouns in the first group as 'generic terms'.[136] The text does not support Miranda's exegesis, therefore, that *adikia* or injustice is the essence of the subsequent vices. It is difficult, as a result, fully to identify the 'sin' of which Paul speaks in Rom. 3:9 with injustice, as Miranda does, and to specify the latter as social injustice. Nor can the citations from the psalms and prophets in Rom. 3:10–18 which follow this first mention of sin, be entirely equated with such injustice and oppression, as Miranda goes on to do. Whilst these citations mention bloodshed and actions which result in 'ruin and misery' as characteristics of sinful humanity, other qualities such as unkindness and deceit do not refer only to political relations, and the 'seeking God' of 3:11 clearly refers to man's relation to God. Cranfield writes of this passage, 'It is expressed in fairly general terms – for the most part, but not exclusively, with reference to men's relation to God.'[137] In fact, Paul clearly and repeatedly condemns injustice and oppression as sinful, but he does not identify them with sin as such. Miranda argues that the term 'sin', introduced in Rom. 3:9, encapsulates Paul's indictment of humanity in 1:18–3:20. Most commentators agree. This passage does not refer only to injustice, however. First among the effects of sin is false religion, of which Miranda gives no account. Not only is this the first sin which Paul discusses (1:19–23), but he also describes it as logically prior to the others. After his account of the way in which the Gentiles 'exchanged the glory of the immortal God for images', he writes: '*Therefore* [*dio*] God gave them up in the lusts of their hearts to impurity' (1:24). In the next two verses, he repeats that the Gentiles 'worshipped and served the creature rather than the Creator' (1:25), and '*for this reason* [*dia touto*], God gave them up to degrading passions' (1:26). The causal link is explicit at 1:28, where Paul writes:

Since [*kathôs*] they did not see fit to acknowledge God, God gave them up to a debased mind . . .

Failing to acknowledge God as God is first and foremost among the effects of sin in Paul's thought. Furthermore, as these citations suggest, sexual sins, which James Dunn describes under the generic term 'self-indulgence', also feature strongly in his indictment of humanity in Rom. 1:18–3:20.[138] Whilst such sins can indeed constitute interhuman injustice, they do not do so in the social sense Miranda intends by this term, nor does Paul emphasize the oppressive aspect of such sins. It is clear, therefore, that when Miranda writes that 'the only thing [Paul] understands as sin' is injustice, his argument represents only a part of the truth. Whilst Paul does indeed condemn social injustice and oppression as sinful, these evils do not exhaust his understanding of the term 'sin'.

As Miranda goes on to argue that, for Paul, sin, understood as injustice, is a phenomenon which inheres in social structures and the ideological expressions of these structures, he continues to represent only a part of Paul's thought. It is true that Paul, especially in Romans, thinks of sin as a phenomenon that transcends the individual and that cannot be reduced to the sum of individual sins. In *The Theology of Paul the Apostle* (1998), James Dunn writes:

> 'Sin' is the term Paul uses for a compulsion or constraint which humans generally experience within themselves or in their social context, a compulsion towards attitudes and actions not always of their own willing or approving.[139]

As Dunn makes clear, for Paul, individuals experience sin both as an inner compulsion against the demands of conscience, and as a social compulsion, which derives from their insertion into a society whose structure is determined by godless values. Miranda is wrong to suggest that only the latter is the case. He interprets Rom. 7:14–25 as an account of the conflict between the human conscience and the unjust structure of the societies in which men and women have so far found themselves, but the text neither mentions nor implies any such social force. As Fitzmyer writes, it concerns the 'conflict in the inmost depths of a human being, the cleavage between reason-dominated desire and actual performance'.[140] Paul speaks of the conflict between the 'inner man' or 'mind' on the one hand and the 'members' or 'flesh' on the other, which makes of him a 'wretched man', with a 'body of death'. All these references are to individual experience, to an inner conflict between contradictory impulses within the human being. Whilst Paul does indeed think of society as governed by systems which do not recognize God or his will for just relations between its members, it is not in such structures alone that he finds sin to inhere.

Miranda's case is more cogent with respect to the Old Testament texts he cites. Social justice is, as his citations show, strongly emphasized as the will of Yahweh throughout the Old Testament. When Miranda interprets Jer. 22:16 to mean that achieving such justice is the *only* way in which Yahweh is known in the Old Testament, however, he states the case too strongly. The text clearly states that to know Yahweh is to defend the rights of the poor and needy. One who does not do the latter, like Jehoiakim son of Josiah, against whom the passage is directed, cannot claim to do the former. McKane comments on the reference to knowing Yahweh in Jer. 9:24:

> [Yahweh's] aim is to create a community in which there is mutual trust and solidarity and where justice is effectively expressed. This is what he wills for the world and those who 'know' him are committed with him to this great enterprise.[141]

Miranda is right, therefore, with respect to the texts he cites, that knowledge of Yahweh consists in defending the rights of the poor. The Old Testament also speaks of knowledge of Yahweh in other ways, however. Even in Jeremiah, the term is not restricted to working for social justice. At Jer. 5:4, it is precisely 'the poor', as contrasted with 'the rich', who 'do not know the way of the LORD', and at Jer. 31:34, knowledge of Yahweh stands in parallel to the experience of his forgiveness:

> They shall all know me, from the least to the greatest, says the LORD, for I will forgive their iniquity, and remember their sins no more.

In Hosea, whom Miranda also cites, lack of knowledge of God is placed in synonymic parallel with 'the spirit of whoredom' at Hos. 5:4, which 4:12 explains as 'forsaking their God'. Not to know God is to worship another or a false god, for Hosea, as the emphasis on idolatry throughout the book indicates. At Ps. 9:10, knowing Yahweh is further described as trusting in him: 'Those who know your name put their trust in you.' Whilst Miranda is right to argue that relationship to Yahweh is illusory without an active commitment to his will for social justice, he is wrong to go on to argue that the one consists only in the other. Knowledge of God in the Old Testament is a complex phenomenon, of which defence of the poor is an integral part but not the whole. Mays comments:

> To know God/Yahweh is Hosea's formula for normative faith, the apprehension of Yahweh's history with Israel in the classical era before her life in Canaan, the revealing acts and words of those days, an apprehension so single and whole that it would define and condition the life of the whole people.[142]

Miranda fails in his stated aim not 'to attempt to find parallels between the Bible and Marx, but rather simply to understand the Bible', and in fact interprets the Bible in the light of Marx, reducing those aspects of the Biblical message which anticipate Marx to the whole of that message.[143] Whilst the Bible cannot be reduced to Marxist concerns for social justice, however, Miranda's work makes clear that it nevertheless systematically describes such concerns as the will of God and as the duty of Christians.

This case is argued cogently by most of the major liberation theologians. Although critics of liberation theology have charged the movement with an uncritical acceptance of Marxist concepts, in fact Marxism plays a relatively small part in liberation theology.[144] In *Introducing Liberation Theology* (1988), Leonardo and Clodovis Boff write that 'liberation theology uses Marxism as an instrument' rather than treating it as an authority, a status which it reserves for the gospel.[145] They argue that such theology borrows 'methodological pointers' from Marxism in order to analyse the situation of oppression with which, as Latin American theologians, they are confronted. They mention among such pointers the importance of economic factors in determining this situation, attention to the fact of class struggle, by which it is constituted, and to the mystifying power of ideologies, including religious ideologies, which contribute to its remaining in place. Liberation theology uses these Marxist concepts insofar as they assist it in analysing the situation of the Latin American poor, and rejects them and others insofar as they fail to do so. The Boffs conclude:

> Liberation theology, therefore, maintains a decidedly critical stance in relation to Marxism. Marx (like any other Marxist) can be a companion on the way, but he can never be the guide, because 'You have only one teacher, the Christ' (Matt. 23:10).[146]

This critical stance towards Marxism allows the major liberation theologians to analyse more objectively than Miranda the ways in which aspects of Biblical revelation and of theological reflection upon that revelation do in fact coincide with Marxism.

In *A Theology of Liberation* (1971), Gustavo Gutiérrez asks the question of the theological meaning of liberation, a process that, like all liberation theologians, he sees as the immediate need of the majority of Latin Americans. He argues that the Christian concept of salvation must be understood to include liberation as an integral part:

> There are not two histories, one profane and one sacred, 'juxtaposed' or 'closely linked'. Rather, there is only one human destiny, irreversibly

assumed by Christ, the Lord of history. His redemptive work embraces all the dimensions of existence and brings them to their fullness.[147]

This is established early in the Biblical revelation, Gutiérrez argues, by the story of the Exodus, in which God delivers Israel from slavery and leads them to establish a society he intends to be just and humane. He rightly points out that this event is fundamental to the Old Testament's concept of God, and that Yahweh is constantly recalled as the God who delivered his people from slavery in Egypt. Gutiérrez writes of the Exodus:

> The liberation of Israel is a political action. It is the breaking away from a situation of despoliation and misery and the beginning of the construction of a just and comradely society.[148]

The early chapters of Exodus, as Gutiérrez points out, describe the oppressive situation of the Jewish people in Egypt. They are forced into slave labour, which contributes to the King's increased power, which keeps them in slavery (Ex. 1:11). Their work is cruel and inhuman (1:13–14): the Egyptians 'made their lives bitter with hard service in mortar and brick'. Their right to life is denied (1:15–22), and when Moses and Aaron begin to preach that they should be freed, their labour is increased to intolerable proportions (5:9). Gutiérrez describes this as 'alienated work', and adds that such work is even described as producing an alienated consciousness – initially the Israelites 'would not listen to Moses, because of their broken spirit and their cruel slavery' (6:9; cf. 14:11–12; 16:3). In this situation of oppression, Gutiérrez continues, 'Yahweh awakens the vocation of a liberator: Moses.'[149] In the account of the burning bush, in which the divine name is revealed, Yahweh tells Moses:

> I have observed the misery of my people who are in Egypt; I have heard their cry on account of their taskmasters. Indeed, I know their sufferings, and I have come down to deliver them from the Egyptians, and to bring them up out of that land to a good and broad land, a land flowing with milk and honey. (Ex. 3:7–8)

Gutiérrez comments, 'The Exodus is a long march towards the promised land in which Israel can establish a society free from misery and alienation.'[150] The religious event, God's covenant with Israel, and the political event, his deliverance of Israel from slavery, he argues, are inseparable: 'The Covenant and the liberation from Egypt were different aspects of the same movement, a movement which led to encounter with God.'[151] It is an essential part of the Biblical concept of salvation, that is, that it begins in the material, historical sphere. Gutiérrez writes:

> Building the temporal city is not simply a stage of 'humanisation' or 'pre-evangelisation'... Rather it is to become part of the saving process which embraces the whole of humanity and all human history.[152]

Biblical eschatology also suggests the unity of the history of salvation for which Gutiérrez argues. The coming kingdom of peace announced by the prophets, he writes, 'presupposes the defence of the rights of the poor, punishment of oppressors, a life free from the fear of being enslaved by others, the liberation of the oppressed'.[153] Isa. 65:21–22 lists the following characteristics of the 'new heavens and a new earth' (65:17) that Yahweh will create:

> They shall build houses and inhabit them;
>   they shall plant vineyards and eat their fruit.
> They shall not build and another inhabit;
>   they shall not plant and another eat;
>   for... my chosen shall long enjoy the work of their hands.

A society without oppression or exploitation is envisaged. It should not be understood that the New Testament 'spiritualizes' such promises, Gutiérrez argues, so that what the Old Testament thinks of in historical terms, the New explains in spiritual terms. He cites Lk. 4:21, arguing rather that the eschatological promises of the Old Testament are 'a matter of partial fulfilments through liberating historical events, which are in turn new promises marking the road towards total fulfilment'.[154] Whilst these promises, as the New Testament makes clear, are completely fulfilled only with the Second Coming of Christ, they are nevertheless partially fulfilled by the struggle to establish the kind of just society in this world of which they speak. Citing Isa. 29:19–21, in which it is said that 'the neediest people shall exult in the Holy One of Israel', and that 'the tyrant shall be no more', Gutiérrez writes:

> The struggle for a just world in which there is no oppression, servitude, or alienated work will signify the coming of the Kingdom. The Kingdom and social injustice are incompatible.[155]

The liberation brought about by Christ, therefore, is what Gutiérrez calls an 'integral liberation', which 'embraces all persons and the whole person', body and soul.[156] Paul says, 'For freedom Christ has set us free' (Gal. 5:1), and describes the new life in Christ as a state of liberation from sin (Rom. 6:18; 8:2). Jesus describes himself as one who brings true freedom (Jn. 8:36), and Rev. 1:5 says that he has 'freed us from our sins'. Gutiérrez defines the sin from which Christ frees as 'a selfish turning in upon oneself' that constitutes 'a breach of friendship with God and with others'.[157] This is not only a private or individual reality, he argues, but also a 'social, historical fact', since the situations of oppression with which he is directly confronted ultimately derive from sin.[158] Gutiérrez writes:

> Sin is evident in oppressive structures, in the exploitation of humans by humans, in the domination and slavery of peoples, races and social classes. Sin appears, therefore, as the fundamental alienation, the root of a situation of injustice and exploitation.[159]

If Christ liberates us from sin, and oppressive social relations have their ultimate foundation in sin, then the 'radical liberation' which Christ offers includes a liberation from such relations. The freedom for which the Christian is set free, Gutiérrez argues, is the freedom to love, which consists in 'the going out of oneself, the breaking down of our selfishness and of all the structures that support our selfishness'.[160] Christ frees us from sin insofar as it is a breach both in relationship to God and in relationship to others, and calls those who accept such a liberation to 'communion with God and with other human beings'.[161]

In *Jesus Christ Liberator* (1972), Leonardo Boff argues that this integral concept of liberation is the meaning of the kingdom of God which is the object of Jesus' teaching. To Jesus' listeners, he argues, the term indicated an eschatological fulfilment of human desire, an intervention of God at the end of the world in which 'all human alienation and all evil, be it physical or moral, would be overcome, when the consequences of sin – hate, division, pain and death – would be destroyed'.[162] In Jesus' teaching, however, this utopia 'will no longer be utopia but a reality introduced by God'.[163] The kingdom of God, in other words, will not only come into being at the end of the world, but begins with the ministry of Jesus himself, and with the signs that accompany it – healing the sick, raising the dead, driving out demons and forgiving sins. Boff writes, 'Christ understands himself as liberator because he preaches, presides over and is already inaugurating the kingdom of God.'[164] This kingdom, Boff argues, which is both present and future, indicates the transformation of the entire world: 'It embraces all: the world, the human person, and society. The totality of reality is to be transformed by God.'[165] It is a reality that includes every dimension of human life, material and spiritual, individual and social. Boff writes:

> The kingdom of God means a total, global, structural revolution of the old order, brought about by God and only by God.[166]

As well as an interior revolution, therefore, the kingdom implies a 'revolution of the human world'.[167] Jesus makes this clear as he systematically breaks with the social conventions of his time, associating with the poor and the marginalized members of society, the prostitutes, tax collectors, lepers and other 'sinners'. It is to these people to whom he is especially called: 'Those who are well have no need of a doctor, but those who are sick . . . I have come to call not the righteous but sinners' (Mt. 9:12–13). In the kingdom of God, the social order is negated and transcended – 'Many who are first will be last, and the last first' (Mk. 10:31). 'The tax collectors and the prostitutes are going into the kingdom of God ahead of you' (Mt. 21:31). The kingdom of God, therefore, is an entirely new world brought about by God, a transformation of the human person in relationship to God and in relationship to others. It is to be completely fulfilled in the future, but, since the ministry of the Incarnate Word, it begins in the present. In *Christology at the Crossroads* (1978), Jon Sobrino puts this case well when he argues that Jesus' twofold commandment of love of God and of neighbour is 'grounded in the logic of the kingdom'.[168] Sin, that which the kingdom overcomes, he writes, has two dimensions for Jesus:

> The personal dimension was a refusal to accept the future of the God who was approaching in grace. The social dimension was a refusal to anticipate that future reality in our here-and-now life.[169]

Whilst it is not the intention of the major liberation theologians, therefore, to incorporate Marxist ideas into Christian theology nor even to reflect theologically upon those ideas, nevertheless in the theological works they write in response to social structures of political and economic exploitation similar to those analysed by Marx a century earlier, they make clear that the ethics of the Bible coincide in many ways with those of the Marxist critique of capitalism. Exploitation of all kinds, social, political and economic, of some human beings by others, particularly of weaker by more powerful social groups, is systematically revealed in the Bible as contrary to the will of God, who calls men and women to work for a society from whose structures and relations such exploitation is eliminated. Without a response to this call, it is impossible to be in a saving relationship to him. The Biblical concept of salvation is a holistic one in which God frees men and women from egotism and its consequences in order to live in a relationship of love with him and with one another. Whilst this relationship is completed only in eternity, we are called to begin it in this world. This is the meaning of the gospel of the kingdom of God and of the twofold commandment in which it is summed up. Whilst the areas of agreement between the social ethics of the Bible and the Marxist critique of capitalism do not exhaust either Marxism or Christianity, liberation theology makes clear that, despite their wide divergences, there is a certain amount of ethical agreement between the two systems.

This agreement is significant for the Christian literary theory for which I am arguing. Since there is a certain amount of common ground between Biblical and Marxist ethics, there will be a similar common ground between the ethics of Christian literary theory and those of Marxist theory. To the extent that they are supported by the ethics of the Biblical revelation, therefore, Christian literary theory can incorporate some of the characteristic principles of Marxist theory. I would suggest that, in concrete terms, it should do so in the following respects. Firstly, Christian literary theory can agree with Marxism that literary texts are determined by the economic relations which govern the social and political conditions of the situation in which they are produced. The Bible does not support the Marxist view that such texts are *entirely* so determined, but, insofar as economic relations can be shown to be of relevance to any aspect of a literary text, it makes clear that they are of ethical significance. A Christian critical practice, therefore, would, where appropriate, judge the economic determinants of a text in the terms of Biblical social ethics. Secondly, Christian literary theory should recognize the Marxist category of ideology, that is, discourse which serves to promote the economic interests of powerful social groups over those of the less powerful. There is little agreement among Marxists as to how precisely literary texts are related to ideology, but I would suggest that, insofar as it can be shown to play any role in the determination of a literary text, Christian critical practice should again judge it in the terms of Biblical social ethics. Finally, I would suggest that Christian literary theory should incorporate the Marxist category of utopia, but that it should extend the range of this category to include all that is meant by the kingdom of God. As Marxist theory recognizes, literary texts can express desires for the kind of fully human society that does not exist at present. Boff acknowledges as much when he describes the Epic of Gilgamesh as a utopian vision generated by the principle of hope.[170] In Christian theology, the referent of such utopian desire is the kingdom of God, which, as liberation theology makes clear, is a life of love with God and others which will be completely fulfilled in the future but which we are called to begin in the present. Literary texts can in various ways express the desire for such a completely fulfilled human life. If, as Boff writes, Jesus is God's answer to the question of the human condition, then the utopian desires expressed in certain texts can, in Christian terms, be understood as statements of that question.

3.4 Catholic social teaching

Despite certain points of agreement in the social ethics of Marxism and Christianity, the two systems nevertheless derive their ethics from widely divergent views of man. The difference between these views has been repeatedly emphasized in the 'social teaching' of the Catholic magisterium, a tradition of encyclicals and other documents from the magisterium that dates back to Pope Leo XIII's encyclical *Rerum Novarum* of 1891, 'On the Condition of the Working Classes'. For several decades, prominent Catholics had become increasingly involved in efforts to improve the living conditions of the industrial working class, and church leaders were aware of the socialist efforts to organize and lead them in a revolutionary class struggle.[171] Pope Leo therefore set out to define the Church's teaching with respect to two of the major ethical questions raised by the capitalism of the Industrial Revolution, the plight of the working class and the socialist response to it. Since then, the magisterium has continued to develop this teaching, and, especially in its more recent documents, has built up a body of theological reflection upon the ethical issues raised by the Marxist critique of capitalism and upon the theory and practice of Marxism itself. In the latter respect in particular, this has come to represent a significant theological critique of Marxism.

Rerum Novarum acknowledges the inhuman living conditions of the majority of the industrial proletariat, and condemns the system which allows the desire for profit and competition amongst employers to subject their workers to such conditions. Leo writes, 'The present age handed over the workers, each alone and defenceless, to the inhumanity of employers and the unbridled greed of competitors.'[172] He adds that 'a devouring usury' has increased the dispossession of the majority of the working class, preventing them from owning a decent human minimum of essential goods. He characterizes the economic situation thus:

> A very few rich and exceedingly rich men have laid a yoke almost of slavery on the unnumbered masses of non-owning workers.[173]

He condemns this situation, arguing that 'it is shameful and inhuman to use men as things for gain and to put no more value on them than what they are worth in muscle and energy'.[174] He argues that state laws should protect workers from the numerous abuses and dangers that they suffer under the factory system, and even goes so far as to assert that 'the oppressed workers ought to be liberated from the savagery of greedy men' who use them as things rather than as human beings.[175] Nevertheless Leo condemns revolutionary 'socialism' along with the excesses of unchecked capitalism. He argues that private property is the worker's legitimate hope and not in itself unjust. He follows Thomas Aquinas in arguing that a person should be allowed to own goods but that this right is qualified by the duty to use them for the benefit of all. The socialist program to abolish private property, therefore, is for Leo a further injury rather than a hope for the worker. In fact, if the socialist state were to intervene at all levels of private and family choice, Leo argues, this would itself constitute a kind of moral slavery to the state. He writes:

> The equality conjured up by the socialist imagination would in reality, be nothing but uniform wretchedness and meanness for one and all, without distinction.[176]

He calls for a return to Christian ethics and institutions on the part both of employers and employees, and advocates ethical social legislation and the formation of Catholic trades unions. Such a 'return' to a truly Christian society, for Leo, would result in a just relationship between the employing and the employed classes, a goal to be preferred to the abolition of class distinction through revolutionary struggle proposed by socialism.

Pope Leo formulated these analyses in terms of Thomistic natural law theory and with respect to a normative model of Christian society. Whilst neither of these methods remain in the more recent documents of the magisterium, Leo's teaching that neither liberal capitalism nor the Marxist response to it result in a society which respects the God-given dignity and rights of the human being has been a continued emphasis. In his apostolic letter *Octagesimo Adveniens* (1971), Paul VI expresses this as follows:

> [The Christian] cannot adhere to the Marxist ideology, to its atheistic materialism, to its dialectic of violence and to the way it tends to absorb individual freedom in the collectivity, at the same time denying all transcendence to man and his personal and collective history; nor can he adhere to the liberal ideology which believes it exalts individual freedom by withdrawing it from every limitation, by stimulating through exclusive seeking of interest and power, and by considering social solidarities as more or less automatic consequences of individual initiatives.[177]

This is also the view of Pope John Paul II, who writes in his encyclical *Sollicitudo Rei Socialis* (1987), 'The Church's social doctrine adopts a critical attitude towards both liberal capitalism and Marxist collectivism.'[178] As the first non-Italian pope for nearly 400 years, John Paul brought to the magisterium a personal experience of life and Christian ministry under a Marxist-Leninist regime. It is perhaps as a result of this that his teaching emphasizes the practice of Marxism as much as the theory of Marx. Both, for John Paul, along with the liberal capitalism to which they are opposed, fail to respect the dignity and the rights which belong to the human person insofar as he or she is created in God's image and destined for communion with God. In his first encyclical, *Redemptor Hominis* (1979), John Paul asserted that man, considered 'in the full truth of his existence, of his personal being and also of his community and social being', is 'the primary and fundamental way for the Church', since, in the Incarnation and Redemption, God became fully a man in order to lead mankind back to him.[179] In his first social encyclical, *Laborem Exercens* (1981), 'On Human Work', he writes that his aim in the letter is to 'call attention to the dignity and rights of those who work'.[180] It is from this perspective that he judges the theory and practice of both liberal capitalism and Marxist collectivism.

Like Leo XIII, John Paul acknowledges that human rights were not respected by the industrial capitalism of the nineteenth century, under which system human work was considered as a commodity possessed by the worker and sold to the employer. The purpose of human work, John Paul argues, is ultimately that it serve to 'realize the humanity' of the worker. Gen. 1:28 speaks of mankind's mandate to 'subdue' the earth by means of his labour, and this divine command is fulfilled when men and women are truly 'the subject of work', that is, realizing themselves through it in a planned and rational way.[181] The early capitalist mode of production did not allow the worker to achieve the subjectivity proper to him and which is God's will for his work, John Paul argues. Under this system, he writes:

> Man is treated as an instrument of production, whereas he – he alone, independently of the work he does – ought to be treated as the effective subject of work and its true maker and creator.[182]

In modern capitalist economies, at least in Western countries, the unbridled injustices of early industrial capitalism are to some degree checked by social legislation, trades unions, and so on, but John Paul argues that capitalism as such can be defined by this 'reversal of order' in Biblical values, in which man is treated as an instrument in the production system rather than as its effective subject. This can occur just as much in economies that are called socialist as in those which are called capitalist. As a result of the dehumanizing conditions of work under capitalism, John Paul writes that the movements of protest against such conditions among industrial workers in the nineteenth century were a 'just social reaction'. In the face of the social situation analysed by Marx, in which man was degraded as the subject of labour, and exploited in inhuman ways as an instrument of production, John Paul writes:

> The reaction against the system of injustice and harm that cried to heaven for vengeance and that weighed heavily upon workers in that period of rapid industrialisation was justified from the point of view of social morality.[183]

Furthermore, John Paul argues that, whilst Western societies in particular have developed beyond early industrial capitalism, 'the human inadequacies of capitalism and the resulting domination of things over people are far from disappearing'.[184] This is particularly true of the Third World, where the majority of people lack not only adequate material goods but also the kind of knowledge and training that would enable them to participate in the current global economy. In these conditions of systematic inequality, John Paul writes, 'It is right to speak of a struggle against an economic system, if the latter is understood as a method of upholding the absolute predominance of capital.'[185]

Despite his condemnation of the injustices of unregulated capitalism, however, John Paul does not accept either the Marxist analysis of these injustices or its proposals for their solution. He argues that Marxist analysis shares with capitalism the error of 'economism', that is, of 'considering human labour solely according to its economic purpose', or, more generally, of reducing man to the economic sphere alone.[186] This in turn derives from what he calls a 'practical materialism', which judges that man's needs can be satisfied in the material sphere alone. Whilst he acknowledges the injustice of the social inequalities generated by capitalism, he nevertheless regards the Marxist response to them in terms of class-conflict as a 'non-humanistic way of stating the issue'.[187] He explains this further in *Centesimus Annus* (1991), where he discusses the collapse of Soviet socialism in Eastern Europe. There he argues that 'the fundamental error of socialism is anthropological in nature', insofar as it considers the individual only as an element of the social totality and therefore subordinates his or her good entirely to that of the totality. In practice, for John Paul, this means a society governed on the principle that the good of the individual can be determined from above by the governing elite, without reference to his or her responsible choice. In such a society, he writes, 'The concept of the person as the autonomous subject of moral decision disappears, the very subject whose decisions build the social order.'[188] He particularly condemns the Leninist concept of the dictatorship of the proletariat, therefore, according to which a professional executive governs in the name of working class interests, which it determines through a knowledge of the laws of history, as an abuse of human freedom.[189]

The first cause of the anthropological error in Marxism, John Paul argues, is its atheism. The person is not completely fulfilled in the state or society, as Marxism presupposes, but rather in God. Response to the call of God contained in nature and in revelation leads man to become aware of the dignity that derives from precisely his relationship to God. This response, for John Paul, is 'the apex of [the individual's] humanity, and no social mechanism or collective subject can substitute for it'.[190] He writes:

> The denial of God deprives the person of his foundation and conse-quently leads to a reorganisation of the social order without reference to the person's dignity and responsibility.[191]

Indeed, John Paul goes so far as to attribute the collapse of the Marxist regimes of Eastern Europe, in which he himself played a part, ultimately to the atheism which those regimes imposed. He writes that beneath the violation of workers' rights, the economic inefficiency and the denial of national and cultural traditions in the socialist states of Eastern Europe was 'the spiritual void brought about by atheism'.[192] Christ is the fulfilment of the human desire for goodness, truth and life, for John Paul, and the official negation of religion did not eliminate this desire in the peoples of Eastern Europe or prevent their return to their countries' Christian tradition in seeking to fulfil it. He writes:

> Marxism had promised to uproot the need for God from the human heart, but the results have shown that it is not possible to succeed in this without throwing the heart into turmoil.[193]

When John Paul considers the Marxist concept of alienation, therefore, he argues that the term does not merely refer to the material relationship between the worker and the product of his labour under capitalism. He recognizes that, in Western capitalist economies, alienated labour can remain a reality, when work is 'organized so as to ensure maximum returns and profits with no concern whether the worker, through his own labour, grows or diminishes as a person'. He adds that, since Marx's time, alienation can also be discerned in the promotion of consumerism, in which 'people are ensnared in a web of false and superficial gratifications' rather than authentically fulfilling themselves as human beings. But these systems alienate, for John Paul, not at the material level of production relations, as in Marxism, but rather at the moral level of the humanity of the person. According to Christian revelation, John Paul writes, the individual person finds his fulfilment in 'that relationship of solidarity and communion with others for which God created him', and, ultimately, with God himself.[194] He calls this the 'person's essential capacity for transcendence', that is, for giving himself to another human being and ultimately to God, who, as the creator of the person, 'alone can fully accept our gift'.[195] One cannot give oneself authentically to an idea, 'to an abstract ideal or to a false utopia', as the citizen of a socialist state is required to do, but only to another person. The essence of alienation, for John Paul, which persists in both capitalist and socialist societies, is failure or inability to fulfil one's humanity in this way. He writes:

> A person is alienated if he refuses to transcend himself and to live the experience of self-giving and of the formation of an authentic human community oriented towards his final destiny, which is God.[196]

A society is alienated if its organization of systems of production and consumption prevents its members from exercising this capacity to transcend themselves and their own interests in what John Paul calls 'solidarity' with God and with one another.

John Paul's critique of Marxism, as I have expounded it so far, is based upon the latter's exclusively socio-economic account of the human being, an account which fails to do justice either in theory or practice to the dignity and rights of the individual as he or she is conceived in Christian anthropology. This emphasis on the theological value of the human person is characteristic of his magisterium and of the positive attitude that the Catholic Church has adopted towards the secular world since Vatican II. John Paul adds that the historical materialist view of man also fails adequately to account for the complex moral conflict within the human person which Christian theology explains with the doctrine of original sin. According to this doctrine, men and women have both the capacity to transcend their own immediate interest but also the tendency to remain bound to that interest. As Vatican II puts it:

> Man ... is divided in himself. As a result, the whole life of men, both individual and social, shows itself to be a struggle, and a dramatic one, between good and evil.[197]

John Paul writes that the doctrine of original sin is of 'great hermeneutic value' in understanding human reality, and argues that a social order will be the more stable insofar as it takes the internal division of man to which it refers into account.[198] The goal of Marxism, therefore, namely a social organization from which injustice and exploitation have been eliminated, is ultimately an 'illusion', since the egoism at the root of these evils will remain a tendency of the human will, however production relations are organized. In the perspective of Marxist hope, John Paul writes:

> Politics ... becomes a 'secular religion' which operates under the illusion of creating paradise in this world.[199]

Protestant commentators have also emphasized the one-sided view of human nature implied in Marxist teleology, in which society is to be so rationally organized that the desire to further one's own interests at the expense of those of others will be eliminated from all. In *Moral Man and Immoral Society* (1932), Reinhold Niebuhr writes:

The expectation of changing human nature by the destruction of economic privilege to such a degree that no-one will desire to make selfish use of power, must probably be placed in the category of romantic illusions.[200]

He points out that, if the revolutionary Russian oligarchy were to strip itself of its own power once the entire community accepted the ideals of communism, rendering unnecessary the dictatorship of the proletariat, it would be the first oligarchy in history ever to have done so. In fact, Niebuhr argues, man will always be imaginative enough to enlarge his needs beyond an essential minimum, and selfish enough to feel the pressure of these needs as greater than those of others. The goal of communist society, therefore, in which each will take freely from the social process 'according to his need', 'completely disregards the limits of human nature', from which it is unrealistic to imagine the complete elimination of the tendency to self-interest.[201] Whilst it is conceivable and indeed desirable to approximate such an ideal through social legislation and ethical education, Niebuhr writes:

It is sentimental and romantic to assume that any education or any example will ever completely destroy the inclination of human nature to seek special advantages at the expense of, or in indifference to, the needs and interests of others.[202]

In 'Religious Socialism' (1930), Paul Tillich makes the same criticism. He describes Marxist anthropology as 'idealist', insofar as it implies 'the expectation that human nature will be transformed and completely subjected to the idea of justice' under the communist mode of production.[203] Whereas Christian doctrine makes the fall of man from essential integrity into internal conflict a universal phenomenon, from which all stand in need of redemption, the Marxist 'fall' is historically specific and its effects are reversed historically by one particular social class, who themselves do not stand under judgement.[204] Even in his earlier work, in which his commitment to socialism is strongest, Tillich rejects this anthropology. He writes, 'In the light of the brokenness of man's being, religious socialism rejects every utopian ethic.'[205] This brokenness, the internal conflict which derives from original sin, does not disappear, he argues, even in the most perfect institution or social organization.

As the views of Niebuhr and Tillich on original sin suggest, the critique of Marxism from the perspective of Christian anthropology by the Catholic magisterium, particularly under John Paul II, would be acceptable to many theologians from the other major denominations. Protestant commentators also share John Paul's view of the theological dignity of the human person. In 'Christianity and Marxism' (1961), Tillich speaks of the 'value and dignity of personhood' affirmed by Christianity, and in his *Systematic Theology* (1988–1993), Wolfhart Pannenberg writes:

> The destiny of fellowship with God confers inviolability on human life in the person of each individual. It is the basis of the inalienable dignity of each human person.[206]

The critique of the Catholic magisterium can be summarized in the proposition that Marxist anthropology does not give a full account of the human person. In the exclusively socio-economic terms of historical materialism, man is reduced to his role in the production relations by which a society is organized and ultimately to the material needs which such production is intended to satisfy. He is not recognized as an autonomous subject of moral decision, nor is his spiritual dimension acknowledged. Biblical revelation, however, tells us that men and women are created in the image of God and destined for communion with God and with one another. The human person cannot and does not find the fulfilment he or she seeks at the material level alone, but only in a relationship of faith and love to God, which grounds all other finite and contingent relationships. In Augustine's well-known formulation, 'You have made us for yourself and our heart is restless until it rests in you.'[207] Not only does Marxism not recognize the transcendent dignity of the human being that derives from his or her creation by and for God, but it also does not recognize the internal moral conflict in man from which the situations of social injustice and exploitation it addresses ultimately arise. As Niebuhr writes, 'In its view of man's stature, [Marxism] is forced to deny the depth of spirit in the human personality. It is consequently unable to understand the real character of human evil.'[208]

This theological critique of Marxist anthropology has further consequences for the relationship of Christian to Marxist literary theory. It means that the former cannot accept the Marxist view that literary texts are determined entirely by the socio-economic conditions of their production, or by the dialectical process of history of which such conditions are a given instance. On the contrary, in Christian terms, a literary text is a human work, and the human person who produces it, whilst an essentially social being, is a morally autonomous individual. In Christian literary theory, I would suggest, the author should be regarded as the ultimately determining subject of the work. Furthermore, since, in Christian anthropology, the human person is at once both corporeal and spiritual, both these aspects of the person should be regarded as potential determinants of the literary works he or she produces. Insofar as the author is a bodily creature, the insights of Marxist theory with respect to the determination of literary texts by the material conditions of their production are valid. But, for Christian theory, the author is at the same time a spiritual creature, created by God for a life of love with him and with others, and who bears within him the desire for truth, goodness and happiness that is ultimately fulfilled only in these relationships. As the *Catechism of the Catholic Church* puts it:

> The desire for God is written in the human heart, because man is created by God and for God; and God never ceases to draw man to himself. Only in God will he find the truth and happiness he never stops searching for.[209]

This search for individual and social fulfilment should be regarded in Christian literary theory as a potential determinant of a literary text. As finite and contingent creatures, men and women face the question of the meaning of their existence, and the texts they produce can constitute explorations of this question.

I am now in a position to sum up my conclusions with respect to the consequences of Marxism for the Christian literary theory towards which I am arguing in this book. I have argued that the Marxist critique of religion is logically fallacious insofar as it is taken as an argument for atheism, and that it remains possible meaningfully to use theological language in literary theory after this critique. Whilst Marxism is right to claim that Christian theology has been used in given historical instances to defend unjust social structures, it is wrong to conclude from this that this is necessarily the function of such theology. Properly understood, the latter is a call to precisely the fully human life which is the goal of Marxism. Whilst it remains ethically possible to use theological language in literary theory after the Marxist critique, therefore, this critique also functions as a continual reminder to such theology of the social ethics of the Biblical revelation upon which it is based, and which it is has often failed to reflect. As liberation theology has made particularly clear, these ethics have certain points in common with those of the Marxist critique of capitalism. As a result, I have argued that Christian literary theory can, to the extent that they are supported by the ethics of the Biblical revelation, incorporate some of the principles of Marxist theory. I have suggested that it should accept the principle that literary texts are determined by the economic relations which govern the material conditions of their production, and that it should recognize the Marxist category of ideology, or discourse which promotes the economic interests of powerful social groups. Christian critical practice, I have argued, should, insofar as such economic relations and interests can be shown to be of relevance to a literary text, judge them in the terms of Biblical social ethics. I have also suggested that Christian literary theory should interpret the Marxist category of utopia in terms of the kingdom of God. The desires for the kind of fully human life that does not exist at present, that is, which certain literary texts express, have the life of love with God and others for which men and women were created as their ultimate object. As the Catholic magisterium teaches, the socio-economic terms of historical materialism do not fully account for the moral or spiritual dimensions of the human person, nor for his or her experience of internal conflict. In Christian literary theory, therefore, I have argued that literary texts are ultimately determined by the human person by whom they are produced, and that they are determined by every aspect of the person, physical and spiritual, individual and social.

4
On Psychoanalysis

I will conclude this analysis of those contemporary literary theories which imply a critique of the truth-claim of Christian theology with an examination of psychoanalysis. For Freud, the scientific world-view in which psychoanalysis was conceived prohibited assent to religious beliefs.[1] In this chapter, I will assess the consequences of psychoanalysis, which continues to be influential in many forms in contemporary literary theory, for the Christian theology from which I am proposing to derive a literary theory. I will argue that it remains legitimate to use such theology in literary theory after the psychoanalytic critique of religion, and I will assess the degree to which Christian literary theory and criticism should make use of psychoanalytic principles and practices.

4.1   The psychoanalytic critique of religion

I will begin with an analysis of Freud's views on religion. In *Totem and Taboo* (1912), he offers a genetic account of religious rites, comparing the primitive phenomenon of taboo, in which objects and people are extremely venerated and so considered untouchable, to the symptoms of obsessional neurosis. Psychoanalysts, he writes, are in frequent contact with 'people who have created for themselves individual taboo prohibitions...and who obey them just as strictly as savages obey [their] communal taboos'.[2] They call them obsessional neurotics. Freud summarizes the similarities between the prohibitions involved in this kind of neurosis and those involved in taboo: neither has an apparent motive, both carry a strong sense of obligation, both can easily be displaced onto different objects by a kind of 'infection', and both give rise to the performance of ceremonial acts.[3] Psychoanalysis explains obsessional symptoms as the result of a repressed instinct, typically concerning touching. An obsessional neurotic has a strong unconscious wish for something, and a correspondingly strong conscious disgust for its fulfilment. Freud calls this object-relation 'ambivalent'.[4] The tension caused by this conflict is discharged in a ramifying series of obsessive practices that approach increasingly closely in sense to the originally prohibited activity. Freud applies this diagnosis to the corresponding phenomena of taboo which, he writes, must derive from a series of ancient prohibitions placed upon a generation by its ancestors. 'These prohibitions must have concerned activities towards which there was a strong inclination.'[5] Given that the taboos still persist among primitive peoples, the original desire must also persist. Freud concludes, 'The basis of taboo is a prohibited action, for performing which a strong inclination exists in the unconscious.'[6]

In his essay on totemism, the primitive religious system in which clans are identified by an animal or object which they regard as an ancestor, Freud established that the strongest taboo prohibitions were the two laws not to kill the totem animal and to avoid sexual inter-course with members of the same totem clan. He cites his case-study of 'Little Hans' and a case of child analysis published by Sándor Ferenczi, in which children are seen to display attitudes to an animal comparable to primitive attitudes towards totem animals. These are identification with the animal and ambivalent emotions towards it. Since these are the relations in which men stand to their fathers, according to psycho-analysis, Freud hypothesizes that the totem animal represents the father. It follows from this that the taboos against killing the animal and sexual relations within the totem clan 'coincide... with the two primal wishes of children' which constitute the Oedipus complex, murder of the father and sexual relations with the mother.[7] It is probable, Freud concludes, that 'the totemic system ... was a product of the conditions involved in the Oedipus complex'.[8] He goes on to consider the primitive rites in which the totem animal or a representative of it is sacrificed and eaten by the community in a ceremonial meal. He combines these facts with Charles Darwin's hypothesis in *The Descent of Man* (1871) of the 'primal horde', that is, that the earliest human societies comprised groups made up of an aggressive father who kept all the females to himself and jealously drove away the sons. From these data Freud tentatively elaborates an account of the origin of religion.[9] There came a time when the expelled sons came together and killed the father of the primal horde. Since they were savages they ate their victim. The totem meal represents a joyful commemoration of this ancient crime. As with all sons, the brothers had an ambivalent complex of emotions towards their father, both loving him and hating him, and later felt remorse for their crime. In the process Freud calls 'deferred obedience' they attempted to atone for their crime by forbidding the killing of the totem animal, the representative of the father, and by resigning their claim to the women set free for them by their parricide. The two fundamental taboos of totemism thus arose as a means of allaying the guilt aroused by this ancient crime.

Freud goes on to hypothesize that 'all later religions are...attempts at solving the same problem'.[10] Throughout the development of religion from totemism to monotheism, according to Freud, 'God is nothing other than an exalted father.'[11] He sees the same Oedipal complex of attitudes to the father at work in Christianity. Christ sacrificed himself, and so redeemed the company of brothers (the Christian community) from their original sin. This sin, since it required a death for its atonement, must itself have been a murder. Since the original sin in Christian theology, according to Freud, was one against God the Father, it must have been a murder of the father. He writes:

> In the Christian doctrine...men were acknowledging in the most undisguised manner the guilty primeval deed, since they found the fullest atonement for it in the sacrifice of this one son.[12]

Their rebellious emotions towards the father find expression in the displacement of a religion of the father by a religion of the son, Freud goes on. In communion, the brothers eat and identify with the son just as the totem animal is eaten and identified with in totemism. In *Moses and Monotheism* (1939), Freud applies his theory to Judaism. He argues that the God represented by Moses was revered as a father.[13] Although hostility towards him was largely repressed, the strictness of the Jewish Law, Freud writes, derives from 'the sense of guilt felt on account of a suppressed hostility to God'.[14]

In *The Future of an Illusion* (1927), Freud discusses the value of religious ideas in civilization. He defines religious ideas as those not arrived at by empirical observation and inference but which nevertheless lay claim to our belief. Whilst they are the most potentially useful concepts that civilization provides, he writes, religious ideas are also the least well authenticated. Freud accounts for their persistence by suggesting that they are 'illusions, fulfilments of the oldest, strongest and most urgent wishes of mankind'.[15] By an illusion, he means an imaginary wish-fulfilment. The wishes from which religion arises, according to Freud, derive from the experience of helplessness both of each individual in his early infancy and of the human race in its early stages of development. He writes, 'A store of ideas is created, born from man's need to make his helplessness tolerable.'[16] Civilization is constructed as a means of defending man from the superior power of nature and the disinterest of fate. Religious ideas develop, according to Freud, as a part of this process of civilization. Primitive man tries to overcome his helplessness with respect to natural forces by peopling the world with anthropomorphic spirits and relating to them in religious rites. Human helplessness in the face of nature recalls each individual's helplessness as an infant, when he feared his father but also hoped for and experienced his protection. So primitive men gave their deities the ambivalent character of a father. As religious ideas develop to keep pace with natural science, Freud writes, 'man's helplessness remains, and along with it his longing for his father and the gods'.[17] Judaism eventually allowed men to relate to God precisely as to a father, and was followed in this by Christianity. As in *Totem and Taboo*, Freud concludes that religion is something like 'the universal obsessional neurosis of humanity ... [which] arose out of the Oedipus complex'.[18] We project onto God the precepts of morality that are in fact the result of the process of civilization, in which the pleasure principle is renounced in favour of the reality principle. In Freud's view, science has brought humanity to the point where it is time to mature from the infantile religious attitude, and 'honestly admit the purely human origin of all the ... precepts of civilisation'.[19] In this way, people could understand that these precepts were made to serve them rather than to rule them.

4.2   An assessment of the psychoanalytic critique

In assessing Freud's critique of religion, it should be noted first of all that he qualifies and acknowledges the speculative nature of many of the premises upon which it is based. The argument for the development of religion from an Oedipal complex of emotions enacted in an ancient parricide depends on the identification of the totem animal with the father, which is based on two case studies of neurotic children. Freud does not tell us whether these children's displacement of their attitudes towards their fathers onto animals is typical, and on the evidence of only two studies there is little reason to believe that this is the case. This is especially true since in one of the cases, the boy's 'totemic interests did not arise in direct relation with the Oedipus complex but on the basis of its ... precondition, the castration complex'.[20] Freud writes of his identification of the totem animal with the father that it leads to his conclusions, 'if this equation is anything more than a misleading trick of chance'.[21] He asserts as a result that it is 'probable' that totemism is a product of the Oedipus complex.[22] But even this is an overstatement if the premise on which it is based has no more support than Freud has described. As for the myth of the primal horde from which he derives religion, Freud writes:

> The lack of precision in what I have written...may be attributed to the reserve necessitated by the nature of the topic. It would be as foolish to aim at exactitude...as it would be unfair to insist upon certainty.[23]

Freud points out at various points in his argument some of the inadequacies that force themselves upon him. He acknowledges that in deriving religion from a father-complex he cannot account for the development of mother-goddesses, whose worship may have preceded that of father-gods.[24] Furthermore, his explanation of the Christian Eucharist is awkward. Whilst describing Christianity as a son-religion that displaces the father-religion, and acknowledging that the Christian meal is a consumption of the son, Freud nevertheless asserts, 'The Christian communion, however, is essentially a fresh elimination of the father', like a totem meal.[25] Freud gives no explanation for this transition from eating the son (which is what happens) to eating the father (which supports his argument). Whilst his citation from J.G. Frazer, to the effect that the Christian communion represents an absorption of a pre-Christian ritual, may be true, Freud's own assertion that it represents consumption of a father is difficult to believe. When Freud comes to discuss the phylogenetic assumptions that underlie his hypotheses, he writes, 'It must be admitted that these are grave difficulties...Any explanation that could avoid presumption of such a kind would seem to be preferable.'[26] Freud's confession of presumption is justified with respect to his method of argument. Unsupported speculation underlies many of the fundamental theses of *Totem and Taboo*. As a result, whilst it is compelling for its imaginative quality, it cannot be taken to be a true account of the origin of religion.

We should also note that anthropology and history of religion have not accepted Freud's arguments. Concerning Freud's account of the primal horde, which he constructed from Darwin and J.J. Atkinson, the anthropologist A.L. Kroeber writes, 'The Darwin-Atkinson supposition is only hypothetical.'[27] 'It is a mere guess', he writes, that the earliest organization of human society was so organized.[28] Claude Lévi-Strauss, who is sympathetic to psychoanalysis, nevertheless writes of 'the gratuitousness of the hypothesis of the male horde and of primitive murder', which makes *Totem and Taboo* anthropologically unacceptable.[29] It constitutes a vicious circle, deriving the social state from events that presuppose it. Lévi-Strauss writes, 'The desire for the mother or the sister, the murder of the father and the sons' repentance, undoubtedly do not correspond to any facts or group of facts occupying a given place in history.'[30] The importance Freud attaches to the totem meal is based on W. Robertson Smith's assertion that sacrifice was the essential feature of primitive religion.[31] Kroeber writes:

> Robertson Smith's allegation that blood sacrifice is central in ancient cult holds chiefly for the Mediterraneanoid culture of a certain period...It does not apply to regions outside the sphere of affection by these cultures.[32]

In his book *Anthropology* (1923), Kroeber traced the development of religion among the Californian Indians. The earliest rites he found there were a girls' adolescence rite and a victory dance, which contradicts Freud's premise that the totem meal is the earliest and basic religious rite.[33] In *Structure and Function in Primitive Society* (1952), A.R. Radcliffe-Brown writes of the diversity of totemic rites, and of the impossibility of assigning a single origin to them. He asserts, 'It is clear that the very diverse forms of totemism that exist all over the world must have had very diverse origins.'[34] Any thesis such as Freud's which attempts to speak of an origin of totemism must assume that all its diverse forms are modifications of a single form. Radcliffe-Brown writes, 'There does not seem...to be a particle of evidence to justify such an assumption.'[35] Even if one makes it, he continues, the resulting assertions of what this original form of totemism was, how the existing forms were produced from it, and how it came into existence itself, can be no more than speculation. He writes, 'Such speculations, being for ever incapable of inductive verification, can...have no value for a science of culture.'[36] Radcliffe-Brown asserts that religious rites are symbolic expressions that regulate and perpetuate the sentiments on which the constitution of a given society depends. Religions therefore vary according to the structure of the society in which they function.[37] To account for totemism, and *a fortiori* religion in general, in terms of a universal phylogenetic heritage, as Freud did, Radcliffe-Brown argues, is simply a category mistake.

We should also note that Freud admits that his psychoanalytic account of religion is not exhaustive but rather contributes to an understanding of one of its many determinants. He writes:

> If psychoanalysis is compelled ... to lay all the emphasis on one particular source [of religion], that does not mean it is claiming either that that source is the only one or that it occupies first place [among the many sources].[38]

He points out that in designating religious ideas as illusions he is not concerned with their truth but only with their 'psychological nature'.[39] He writes, 'To assess the truth-value of religious doctrines does not lie within the scope of the present enquiry.'[40] He adds that the analogy he draws between religious and infantile attitudes 'does not ... exhaust the essential nature of religion'.[41] He is right to make these qualifications, since the thesis that religious ideas are wish-fulfilments does not entail a conclusion about their truth-value. Freud's hypothesis that we project onto God our infantile and inherited attitudes to our fathers is indebted to Feuerbach's projection theory, which we have seen also influenced Marx. In *Freud and the Problem of God* (1979), Hans Küng argues that Freud's illusion-theory must be judged in the same way as Feuerbach's projection-theory, as 'a hypothesis which has not been conclusively proved'.[42] It is true that religion can be an expression of neurotic regression to infantile attitudes, as Freud asserts, but it does not follow from this that this is always the case. It is also true that belief in God is structured by a child's attitude to its parents, but it does not follow from this that God has no independent existence. As Küng writes, 'A real God may certainly correspond to the wish for God.'[43] The case cannot be proved either way.

Freud's critique of religion in *The Future of an Illusion* nevertheless has its value. His comparison of religious practices to obsessional neurosis can be taken as a description of the ease with which such practices can slip into automatic and meaningless rituals which do not contribute to a deeper relation with God but are motivated by fear or by guilt. Freud's comment that religious people have 'always known how to externalize the precepts of religion and thus to nullify their intentions' is also fair.[44] He is right to assert that religion can be a means of avoiding a responsible moral life rather than an incentive or encouragement to one. His wish-fulfilment theory similarly reflects the fact that religion can degenerate into a means of avoiding an encounter with the transcendent reality of God rather than constituting such an encounter. Freud's critique of the psychological gratification afforded by religious belief reminds Christian theology that the faith on which it reflects is authentic only to the degree that it exceeds mere wish-fulfilment.

It is clear, however, that Freud's theories are not as incompatible with religion as he himself asserts. His argument that certain Christian doctrines have their origin in an ancient parricide is no more than speculation, and has been rejected as such by anthropology. His thesis that totemism is the original form of religion has also been rejected, upon which his account of the Oedipus complex as the source of religion depended. It does not follow from his claim that religious beliefs are wish-fulfilments that there is no reality to which they correspond. It remains legitimate, therefore, to use Christian theology in literary theory after the critique of such theology posed by psychoanalysis.

4.3 Jung and Fromm on religion

It is well known that Freud's atheism was not shared by many other psychoanalysts. Carl Gustav Jung (1875–1961) points out that Freud's illusion theory is 'based on the rationalistic materialism of the scientific views current in the late nineteenth century'.[45] In *Psychology and Religion* (1938), Jung argues that God is a psychological reality. He defines a religious event in accordance with Rudolf Otto's concept of the 'numinous', that is, as 'a dynamic existence or effect not caused by an arbitrary act of will'.[46] For Jung, religion denotes 'the attitude peculiar to a consciousness which has been altered by the experience of the numinosum'.[47] On this definition, experiences that proceed from the unconscious can be called religious. Jung's unconscious is not the seat of repressed instincts, as Freud conceives it, but 'an illimitable and indefinable addition to every personality'.[48] For Jung, an individual's personality consists of a more or less definable conscious part and an unconscious part about which we only know what we must infer to explain certain psychological facts that cannot be attributed to consciousness. Certain dreams that Jung analyses contain clear and authoritative voices that on waking have the force of an intuition. 'They . . . contain a superior analysis or insight which consciousness has not been able to produce.'[49] For Jung these constitute an 'immediate experience' of the numinous, that is, of an unknown factor that impinges upon consciousness from without. Hence he calls them a 'basic religious phenomenon'.[50]

Certain Christian dogmas, such as those of the Incarnation, the Trinity and the Virgin Birth, Jung sees as such articulations of the unconscious.

They appear so frequently in analysis and in the history of religions that he concludes that they also come to the consciousness of individuals and groups from another source than conscious decision. He writes, 'The dogma is like a dream, reflecting the spontaneous and autonomous activity of the objective psyche, the unconscious.'[51] Jung's unconscious contains collective material as well as individual, whose existence he induces from the repeated occurrence of certain motifs in the mythology and folklore of different peoples. He calls these motifs 'archetypes' and defines them as 'forms or images of a collective nature which occur practically all over the earth as constituents of myths and at the same time as autochthonous, individual products of unconscious origin'.[52] He finds that symbols of quaternity are archetypes of 'a world-creating deity'.[53] This is particularly the case when the number four is combined with the circle form, such as in a quartered circle. Jung supports this assertion by a series of references to ancient and medieval philosophy and theology. God's unity and infinity are symbolized by the circle, and the four elements of creation by the quaternity. Jung writes, 'The four symbolizes the parts, qualities and aspects of the One, . . . a more or less direct representation of the God manifested in his creation.'[54] These comparisons, Jung writes, 'prove the existence of an archetypal image of the Deity', whose frequency makes its existence 'a noteworthy fact for any *theologia naturalis*'.[55] The most complete form of this symbol in Jung's experience is the mandala, a Buddhist symbol of the universe, typically composed of a series of concentric circles surrounding a series of squares. In analysis, Jung found that production of this symbol expressed a feeling of harmony. He writes that it represents an experience of wholeness, of reconciliation of the conscious personality with the unconscious.[56] Before the existence of God was doubted, according to Jung, man would project unconscious experience onto the gods. Nowadays, if he is to achieve mental stability, he must recognize these experiences as part of a greater self than that of which he is conscious. The mandala symbolizes this recognition and hence 'the transformation of man into a divine being'.[57] For Jung, religion proved very often to be a necessity for this kind of internal integration, upon which he saw mental health to depend. In 'Psychotherapists or the Clergy' (1932), he writes:

> Every one [of my patients over thirty-five] fell ill because he had lost what the living religions . . . have given to their followers, and none of them has been really healed who did not regain his religious outlook.[58]

Jung does not directly contradict Freud's thesis that no independently existent reality corresponds to our religious ideas. He asserts primarily that these ideas correspond to a psychic reality. He does not see this kind of explanation as reductive, however. In 'Transformation Symbolism in the Mass' (1954), he writes:

> The modern psychologist is aware that he can produce no more than a description...of a psychic process whose real nature transcends consciousness just as much as does the mystery of life or of matter. At no point has he explained the mystery itself.[59]

Jung remained a Christian to the end of his life, although he thought that Christianity lacked a proper explanation of the unconscious.[60] He makes no judgement on the independent existence of God, since he regards such a judgement to lie outside the field of psychology, but he clearly asserts that his own branch of psychology acknowledges that such existence is possible. It is certainly a psychic reality, acceptance of which in religious belief leads to increased mental well-being, and for some may be a necessary condition of such well-being. In Jung's thought, psychoanalysis neither contradicts the truth-claim of Christian theology nor implies that assent to this claim is a psychic delusion whose reality is to be explained by psychoanalysis.

Erich Fromm (1900–1980) criticizes what he sees as Jung's exclusively psychological perspective on religion. In *Psychoanalysis and Religion* (1951), he attempts to widen the scope of the question by considering the social dimension of the psychology of religion. He defines religion as 'any system of thought and action shared by a group which gives the individual a frame of orientation and an object of devotion'.[61] On this definition, every person needs religion to help him solve the inescapable problem of his existence and to achieve some degree of synthesis of his conflicting energies into a mature social life. There is no-one without religion, according to Fromm. The question is only to which kind of religion a person adheres. Man 'has only the choice of better or worse,... satisfactory or destructive forms of religions'.[62] Fromm discusses several modern religions, such as devotion to a state or to a company, but finds that the basic distinction to be drawn is that between 'authoritarian' and 'humanistic' religions.[63] The former constitutes essentially 'surrender to a power transcending man' which has the right to demand his obedience.[64] Calvinism and totalitarianism are examples of this kind of system. Humanistic religion, on the other hand, is based on 'man and his strength...his relationship to his fellow men and his position in the universe'.[65] Its goal is self-realization rather than obedience. Fromm counts the teachings of Jesus, Socrates, Buddha and Spinoza among this kind of system. He sees church history as a conflict between the two principles. Psychoanalysis is concerned with the 'human reality' underlying religious formulations and practices, according to Fromm. In the humanistic religions this is 'the striving for love, truth and justice', and in the authoritarian religions 'submission to power, lack of love and of respect for the individual'.[66]

Fromm writes that psychoanalytic therapy has two interdependent functions, that of leading the patient to increased social adjustment and that of leading him to greater self-realization. He writes that the latter, which he describes as 'cure of the soul', has 'very definitely a religious function'.[67] He finds that there is 'a core of ideas and norms' shared by the humanistic religions, and that psychoanalytic therapy aims to achieve precisely the attitude they describe.[68] Humanistic religions assert that man must seek the truth about himself and his place in the world. Fromm writes that 'the psychoanalytic process is...a search for truth' also, that of an individual's internal sources of motivation.[69] Fromm continues that psychoanalysis follows humanist-religious thought in linking an individual's search for truth with his attainment of freedom and independence. Fromm thinks that Freud's thought must be '[translated]...from the sphere of sex into that of interpersonal relations'.[70] Where Freud speaks of incestuous instincts, that is, Fromm sees 'the more profound and fundamental desire' to remain a child, attached to protective figures whose prototype is the mother. It is this infantile attitude from which psychoanalysis helps an individual to mature into a morally responsible agent, he writes. In this it agrees with the teaching of humanist religions that man must free himself from 'incestuous' orientations towards gratification and find his humanity in independent moral action. Fromm adds that psychoanalysis follows these religions in asserting that this action is primarily love. He writes, 'Analytic therapy is essentially an attempt to help the patient gain or regain his capacity for love.'[71] He concludes, 'The psychoanalytic cure of the soul aims at helping the patient to achieve an attitude which can be called religious in the humanistic...sense.'[72]

Like Jung, Fromm makes no judgement concerning the independent existence of God. But, as with Jung, he asserts that psychoanalysis is not opposed to religious belief. It is neither false nor harmful, as Freud had argued. On the contrary, in Fromm's thought, Christian belief can be a way to achieve the personally and socially valuable mental orientation which is the goal of psychoanalysis. For Fromm, analytic therapy and

Christianity share similar moral goals. In my examination of Freud's critique of religion, I argued that psychoanalysis does not imply a denial of the truth-claim of Christian theology. The thought of Jung and Fromm shows that, as it developed, various forms of psychoanalysis ceased to assert even that this was the case. Psychoanalysis constitutes an account of human desire which does not contradict the truth-claim of Christian theology. This means that Christian critics can and should use the methods of psychoanalytic criticism where these can be shown to be appropriate.

4.4   Psychoanalysis and Christian tradition

Two significant studies were published in the past decade that argued that psychoanalysis constituted a restatement in modern secular terms of a psychology once formulated by Christian theology. In the first of these, *Why Freud Was Wrong* (1995), Richard Webster argued that Freud's basic concepts are 'not fresh theories of human nature but Judaeo-Christian orthodoxies which have been reconstructed in a secular form'.[73] There are several similarities between the theology of original sin and Freud's concept of the unconscious. Webster notes that both doctrines 'universalized the concept of illness', that is, they attributed a body of negative impulses beyond conscious control to all human beings.[74] Whilst individuals might achieve a certain degree of control over these impulses, they remain endemic. Psychoanalysis recasts the concept of an innate tendency to evil, against which one must struggle in order to live a fully human life, which had been established by the theology of original sin. Just as in Christianity everyone stands in need of grace as a result, so in psychoanalysis everyone needs to overcome the Oedipus complex. Webster also points out that in attributing incestuous and aggressive tendencies to children, Freud did not innovate as radically as is sometimes suggested. He writes that according to the doctrine of original sin, 'children do not come into the world and then learn how to sin, but come into the world bringing their sinful sensuality with them'.[75] In Webster's view, Freud's theory of infantile sexuality represents a restatement of this position.

In *The Religious and Romantic Origins of Psychoanalysis* (1996), Suzanne R. Kirschner situates modern American forms of psychoanalysis in an argument familiar to readers of M.H. Abrams' *Natural Supernaturalism* (1971). Kirschner maps out the 'psychoanalytic developmental narrative', which she finds most clearly and representatively expressed in the work of Margaret S. Mahler (1897–1985). She describes this process as a 'developmental spiral'.[76] The infant is initially aware of a blissful symbiotic 'dual-unity' with the mother, from which he 'individuates' or assumes his own individual characteristics. This leads to a sense of helplessness and vulnerability, which is overcome by forming a sense of relatedness to objects whilst preserving a sense of individual integrity. The initially disappointing existence of self and other must be accepted and integrated, in order that meaningful and satisfying relationships with others can be formed. This trajectory can also be plotted in Freud's theories. As Richard Webster writes, 'Freud saw human history as a difficult upward progress from the realm of the flesh to the realm of the spirit.'[77] The pre-Oedipal infant experiences a series of initially uninhibited gratifications, which his increasing awareness of threats of punishment obliges him to renounce. These renunciations culminate in the repression of the Oedipus complex, and the resulting internal conflict. Nevertheless, this conflict is the precondition for the more valuable attainment of moral maturity and contribution to the process of civilization.

Kirschner compares Mahler's narrative with the patristic tradition of Neoplatonic Biblical exegesis. In Neoplatonic thought, the highest and most fundamental reality is the One, which is also the Good, from which all entities emanate in varying degrees, and to which they strive to return. The soul can achieve this return by turning inwards from the sensible world to contemplate in itself the One that is its source.[78] M.H. Abrams describes the Biblical exegesis influenced by this kind of thought, initiated by Origen (c. 185–254), in which God is conceived primarily as a principle of unity rather than as a father, the Fall is conceived primarily as 'alienation from the source', the original sin as self-centredness, and redemption as a return to lost unity with God propelled by the sustaining energy of his love.[79] Kirschner compares this historical narrative, recast at the individual level by mystics like Jakob Boehme (1575–1624) and the Romantics, to the psychoanalytic developmental narrative. Both describe the same trajectory of 'unity, rupture and division into contraries, higher unity'.[80] She argues that psychoanalysis follows Neoplatonic Christian theology in asserting that 'human selfhood ... originates in and emanates out of an undifferentiated unity', in the former with the mother and in the latter with God.[81] In both systems, 'the recognition of one's estrangement from [this] "source" is associated with self-consciousness ... and suffering'.[82] Freud describes it as being 'cast out of ... paradise'.[83] In both systems, the individual retains a deep yearning to return to the undivided state. Nevertheless, this estrangement constitutes a fortunate fall in both cases, leading to 'higher and more constructive forms of consciousness and relationship'.[84] In

Mahler's version of the psychoanalytic narrative, healthy development results in the capacity to form fulfilling relationships, whose prototype is marriage. For Freud, successful negotiation of the Oedipus and castration complexes results in an adequate and lasting choice of love-object.[85] Kirschner compares this 'higher union' (than with the mother) to the higher union (than the prelapsarian) with God, described by the mystics as the 'divine marriage' of God and the soul.[86]

Webster bases his argument that Freud re-writes certain Christian doctrines on the position that these doctrines had become so unfamiliar in Freud's rationalist *milieu* that he was unaware of his debt to them. Freud's treatment of Christian theology is not detailed, but it is too contrary to his cultural knowledge to suggest that he was simply unaware of the historical significance of the doctrine of original sin. Nevertheless, the similarities between Freud's concept of the unconscious and the doctrine of original sin are as pronounced as Webster claims. Kirschner's thesis that psychoanalysis owes the structure of its developmental narrative to Neoplatonic Christianity by 'cultural genealogy' or 'the redeployment of a pre-existing cultural template to a new context' is more plausible.[87] Put simply, it means that Freud built his theory out of the materials around him. This is true. The psychoanalytic account of human desire is historically indebted to the account of such desire developed by the tradition of Christian theological reflection upon the Biblical revelation. Freud's account of the inner conflict of the human psyche and of the universality of this conflict represents, in certain respects, a psychological reinterpretation of Christian anthropology. The question arises, therefore, of the relative significance of the truth-claim of the psychoanalytic and the theological accounts of the human person.

Webster and Kirschner are in their different ways concerned to show that psychoanalysis is not as based on empirical observation as it claims. In their article 'Christianity and Psychoanalysis' (1984), Paul C. Vitz and John Gartner consider psychoanalysis from an orthodox Christian point of view. They see it as 'a useful theoretical representation of the psychology of sinful humans'.[88] Whilst they do not follow Freud in seeing the Oedipus complex as universal, they write:

> There is no barrier to Christian acceptance of the basic psychology of the Oedipus complex as a ... description of the psychological nature of original sin in the lives of many.[89]

They see the essence of original sin as a tendency towards a fictitious autonomy, and they see the concept of the Oedipus complex as a description of this tendency. 'It is a specific representation of the struggle to become an autonomous ruler of our own and others' lives.'[90] Discussing Freud's argument that religion is a wish-fulfilment, Vitz and Gartner argue that it follows from the logic of the Oedipus complex to think rather of atheism as a wish-fulfilment. The Oedipal child wishes to kill the father and replace him. Freud thinks of God as a substitute for the father, and so the position that He does not exist can be seen as a fulfilment of this wish. If, as in Freud's case, religion is replaced with a system confined to the human sphere, the infantile wish to replace the father with oneself has also been fulfilled. As Vitz and Gartner write, '"God is dead" is ... an undisguised Oedipal wish-fulfilment.'[91] They see this as further reason to think of the Oedipus complex as a description of original sin, which involves rebellion against God. They write, 'Oedipal motivation is the satanic resistance to God deeply stained into human nature.'[92]

This identification of the Oedipus complex and original sin is possible only in the most general sense, however, as we can see from St Thomas Aquinas' formulation of the doctrine in the *Summa Theologiae.* Aquinas defines original sin as a *habitus*, by which he means 'a modification of a nature composed of many elements, according as it bears itself well or ill towards something'.[93] Original sin, he writes, is a 'disordered disposition [*habitudo inordinata*]' of the powers of the soul, which predisposes each person to acts his or her adult conscience would reject.[94] This disorder derives from the primordial turning of the human will from its subjection to the will of God, which constituted original justice, and it can be observed in an 'unruled [*inordinate*] turning to goods that pass away', which Aquinas calls by the Augustinian name 'concupiscence'.[95] In its decree on original sin (1546), the Council of Trent states:

> In the baptized [whose original sin is remitted], there remains concupiscence or an incentive to sin [*fomes peccati*] ... [It] is of sin and inclines to sin.[96]

It is impossible to equate the Freudian theory of the instincts with original sin or with concupiscence so conceived. The disorder of the powers of the soul for Aquinas is understood with respect to their proper order, and original sin is understood as a privation of original justice. The Freudian instincts have no such point of reference. There is no value of which they represent the lack. Whereas original sin and concupiscence are contingent upon something more fundamental, the Freudian instincts are conceived as themselves fundamental.

Nevertheless, there are certain similarities between the two theories. Both describe a drive towards self-gratification that must be overcome in an authentically human life. This is particularly clear in St Augustine's formulation of the doctrine of original sin. In *De Civitate Dei* (413–426), he asserts that the essence of sin is 'to abandon God and to exist in oneself, that is, to please oneself'.[97] The concept of pleasing oneself as opposed to God is similar to Freud's concept of pleasing oneself as opposed to society. Like Freud, Augustine writes that this drive towards self-gratification results in psychological conflict with the adult will. He writes:

> Man's wretchedness is nothing but his own disobedience to himself, so that...he now wills to do what he cannot... [He] is disobedient to himself, while his very mind and even his lower element, his flesh, do not submit to his will.[98]

This conflict of drives, which St Paul describes as that between 'the law of sin' and 'the law of God' (Rom. 7:25), is similar to the conflict Freud describes between the pleasure principle and the reality principle.

We cannot identify Freud's concept of the unconscious with the doctrine of original sin, although there are structural similarities in the two theories. The Freudian instincts are not a description of concupiscence nor *vice versa*. We can say, however, that psychoanalysis is not incompatible with the theology of original sin. There could in principle be both a Freudian unconscious and concupiscence, since Freud describes a psychological conflict of which Christian theology has been aware since St Paul's expression of it at Romans 7:14–25. This means that, as I argued with respect to psychoanalytic accounts of religion, there is no inconsistency implied in the use of psychoanalytic methods in Christian criticism. It is possible to understand human desire in terms both of the theology of original sin and of the psychoanalytic theory of the libido. Christian criticism will interpret the ways in which such desire is represented and expressed in literary texts firstly in terms of the anthropology which derives from Christian theological reflection upon the Biblical revelation. Nevertheless, since the psychoanalytic account of human desire is not inconsistent with this anthropology, Christian criticism can and should use the critical methods of psychoanalysis where this can be shown to be appropriate.

I am now in a position to summarize my conclusions with respect to the significance of psychoanalysis for Christian theology and for the literary theory which I am proposing to derive from it. I have argued that it remains legitimate to use Christian theology in literary theory after the psychoanalytic critique of such theology. Freud's theory of the origin of religion is, as he acknowledges himself, a speculation that cannot be proved. Furthermore, anthropology and the history of religion no longer support the premises upon which it is based. As with the Marxist claim that religious beliefs are reflections of the social conditions in which they are held, Freud's claim that such beliefs are infantile wish-fulfilments, insofar as it is taken as an argument for atheism, is based on a logical fallacy. It does not follow from the influence of psychological factors on religious beliefs that their content is either true or false. It does not follow from the fact of the wish for God that there is no reality to which this wish corresponds. It remains legitimate, therefore, to use Christian theology in literary theory and criticism after the critique of such theology posed by psychoanalysis. The work of Jung and Fromm, in which psychoanalysis is no longer held to contradict the truth-claim of Christian theology, supports this claim. I have argued that the psychoanalytic account of human desire is historically indebted to the tradition of Christian anthropology, as a result of which there are similarities between the theology of original sin and the psychoanalytic theory of the libido. These two interpretations of human desire cannot be identified, in the sense that the one could be held to constitute an explanation of the other, because of the fundamental differences that also exist between them. Nevertheless, the psychoanalytic theory of the unconscious does not imply any contradiction of Christian anthropology. From the perspective of Christian theology, the psychoanalytic theory of human desire could in principle be true. This means that Christian criticism can, where it can be shown to be appropriate, use the principles and methods of psychoanalytic criticism in interpreting the representation and expression of desire in literary and cultural works.

5
Hermeneutics

In the previous chapters, I have responded to the critique of Christian theology constituted by the most influential forms of contemporary literary theory. In this chapter, I will argue for the legitimacy of Christian literary theory on the basis of another mode of contemporary theory, hermeneutics. I will examine some of the most influential work in hermeneutics, and assess its significance for Christian literary theory. I will argue firstly that the point of view of Christian faith, from which I am proposing to construct a literary theory, is, insofar as it is based upon an interpretation of the Biblical text, a rational point of view in the light of contemporary theories of the text. As a result, I will argue, literary theory and criticism practised from this point of view are legitimate forms of these discourses, even in the postmodern culture which calls it so widely into question.

5.1 Gadamer's hermeneutics

I will begin with an examination of the work of Hans-Georg Gadamer (b. 1900). In *Truth and Method* (1960), Gadamer argues that interpretation in the human sciences cannot be understood in terms of the concept of method which guides the production of knowledge in the natural sciences. Since Descartes, he writes, science has been based on the principle that the methodologically disciplined use of reason can safeguard the scientist from error. The inductive method of the natural sciences, in which laws are induced from the results of experiments subjected to procedures of verification, and predictions made on the basis of these laws, has remained the model in whose terms the human sciences have, more or less explicitly, understood their own mode of inquiry. This reliance on the concept of method has led to inconsistencies in the best attempts to justify the truth-claim of the human sciences, Gadamer argues, because it fundamentally misrepresents both the nature of their investigation and the kind of knowledge produced in it. He writes, 'The experience of the socio-historical world cannot be raised to a science by the inductive procedures of the natural sciences.'[1] Such disciplines as philosophy, history and literary criticism, that is, produce a kind of know-ledge that, although not verifiable by the methods of natural science, nor even by an analogous method, has a claim to truth nevertheless. It is in setting out to describe the nature of this truth that Gadamer develops his theory of interpretation in the human sciences.

The first philosopher to formulate a concept of understanding in whose terms the knowledge produced in the human sciences can be rightly explained, in Gadamer's view, was Heidegger. In *Being and Time*, the latter described understanding as an 'existential', that is, as a char-acteristic of human existence as such, shifting the concept thereby from a methodological to an ontological level.[2] Understanding is not fundamentally something that a human being achieves, that is, through the application of this or that scientific method, but rather something that he is always already engaged in, simply by virtue of being human. Furthermore, Heidegger argues that understanding, like the human being of which it is constitutive, is temporal in structure. It is a projection of what one can be, determined by what one has already been. He describes this as the 'fore-structure' of understanding. When we understand something as something, or interpret it, he argues, this fore-structure means that an interpretation is always determined by the experiences, perceptions and concepts that we bring to it in advance. He writes:

> Whenever something is interpreted as something, the interpretation will be founded essentially upon fore-having, fore-sight and fore-conception. An interpretation is never a presuppositionless appre-hending of something presented to us.[3]

As Heidegger recognizes, this is an existential description of the hermeneutic circle, the paradox of textual interpretation according to which one understands the whole of a text in terms of its parts, and the parts in terms of the whole. It is because of this circular structure of textual interpretation that the human sciences are regarded by the natural sciences as less rigorous, and indeed, as Gadamer demonstrates, have themselves thought that it would be ideal if this structure could be avoided. But this is a misunderstanding, for Heidegger. He writes, 'If we see this circle as a vicious one and look for ways of avoiding it, even if we just "sense" it as an inevitable imperfection, then the act of understanding has been misunderstood from the ground up.'[4] If we are to interpret rightly at all, he argues, we must first recognize the conditions under which interpretation can be performed. This is what he means when he says, 'What is decisive is not to get out of the circle but to come into it in the right way.'[5] The right way is to recognize that the fore-structure of understanding, as a characteristic of human being as such, is the structure of all understanding and interpretation whatever. The experiences, perceptions and concepts that we bring to an interpretation in advance, therefore, are not obstacles to a right understanding of what is to be interpreted, but rather conditions of it. The point, in good interpretation, is not to attempt to avoid these advance determinants, but to understand them as fully as possible. Gadamer bases his hermeneutics on an application of Heidegger's existential description of understanding and interpretation to the specific acts of textual interpretation on which the human sciences are based. He describes the process as follows:

> A person who is trying to understand a text is always projecting. He projects a meaning for the text as a whole as soon as some initial meaning emerges in the text. Again, the initial meaning only emerges because he is reading the text with particular expectations in regard to a certain meaning. Working out this fore-projection, which is constantly revised in terms of what emerges as he penetrates into the meaning, is understanding what is there.[6]

This dialectical concept of understanding, Gadamer writes, constitutes a recognition that 'all understanding inevitably involves some prejudice'.[7] It is only during the Enlightenment, he argues, that the concept of prejudice (*Vorurteil*) acquires the negative connotation that it has at present. Logically, the term denotes a judgement reached before all the determinants of the situation to be judged are examined. In German legal terminology, Gadamer points out, it still refers to a provisional verdict before the final verdict is reached. It is only with the rationalist critique of religion in the Enlightenment, he claims, that the term's meaning is limited to the sense of an unfounded judgement, inasmuch as the absence of a methodological justification of a judgement is taken to be the absence of any foundation whatever. Gadamer writes, 'This conclusion follows only in the spirit of rationalism. It is the reason for discrediting prejudices and the reason scientific knowledge claims to exclude them completely.'[8] A proper reflection on the nature of understanding, however, shows that this claim is false, and that the Enlightenment's demand that the interpreter should reject all prejudices is itself based on a prejudice, 'the prejudice against prejudice itself, which denies tradition its power'.[9] The Enlightenment critique was primarily directed towards the religious tradition of Christianity, Gadamer argues, and therefore became concerned with hermeneutics insofar as it contradicted the dogmatic interpretation of the Bible. It aimed to interpret the Bible and Christian tradition without prejudice and under the authority of reason alone. In Gadamer's view, this is itself a prejudice, a judgement in advance against the historical determinations which limit the operations of human reason. He writes:

> The overcoming of all prejudices, this global demand of the Enlightenment, will itself prove to be a prejudice, and removing it opens the way to a appropriate understanding of the finitude which dominates not only our humanity but also our historical consciousness.[10]

The interpreter's situation in traditions is not an obstacle to his freedom, that is, subjecting him to prejudices which reason must overcome, but rather the condition of all human being and therefore of interpretation as such. Reason itself, Gadamer argues, depends upon the historical conditions in which it operates. He writes, 'The idea of an absolute reason is not a possibility for historical humanity.'[11] This is why 'the prejudices of the individual, far more than his judgements, constitute the historical reality of his being.'[12]

In order properly to understand the acts of understanding and interpretation, Gadamer argues, the Enlightenment's discrediting of the concept of prejudice needs to be overturned, and the positive aspect of the concept to be rehabilitated. He writes, 'If we want to do justice to man's finite, historical mode of being, it is necessary fundamentally to rehabilitate the concept of prejudice, and acknowledge the fact that there are legitimate prejudices.'[13] There are such things as legitimate prejudices, that is, which produce knowledge, as well as the illegitimate ones which prevent it, and which critical reason must overcome. The fundamental question for hermeneutics, therefore, is that of the ground of their legitimacy. Gadamer begins to answer this question by examining the positive value of the Enlightenment's critical theory of prejudices. In the first place, he argues, the Enlightenment rejected authority as a source of truth, on the basis that assent to authority and the free use of one's own reason are mutually exclusive. Gadamer recognizes the legitimacy of this distinction, but argues that it does not follow that authority is therefore never a source of truth. In opposing it to reason, he writes, the Enlightenment misunderstood the concept of authority as blind obedience. In fact, he writes, to recognize an authority is not to abandon the use of one's own reason but 'an act of acknowledgement and knowledge – the knowledge, namely, that the other is superior to oneself in judgement and insight and that for this reason his judgement takes precedence'.[14] To acknowledge that, in a given case, another is better informed or has a greater capacity for judgement than oneself, is a free act of reason, based on a recognition of one's own limitations. Hence Gadamer writes, 'Authority has not to do with obedience but rather with knowledge.'[15] It is essential to this concept, therefore, that an individual could, in theory, come to verify for himself what he accepts on authority. As Gadamer puts it, 'What the authority says is not irrational or arbitrary but can, in principle, be discovered to be true.'[16] This is the way in which authority rightly understood differs from authoritarianism. The latter demands obedience alone and rejects rational criticism. The prejudices implanted by the former, Gadamer writes, 'effect the same disposition to believe something that can be brought about in other ways – e.g., by good reasons'.[17] This is the kind of authority granted to a teacher or to an expert in a given field. Although it can be a source of prejudice in the negative sense, Gadamer concludes, proposing for belief statements that critical reason rightly judges untrue, authority can also be a source of the legitimate prejudice which is a constitutive precondition of understanding and of interpretation as such.

One of the most important sources of authority to be criticized by the Enlightenment, Gadamer argues, was tradition. Both the Enlightenment critique and the subsequent Romantic defence of this concept, he writes, again fundamentally misrepresent it, as the opposite of free self-determination through the use of reason. In Gadamer's view, 'there is no such abstract opposition between tradition and reason', since to affirm and therefore to preserve a doctrine in a tradition is as much an act of the reason as to reject it.[18] He writes:

> Even the most genuine and pure tradition does not persist because of the inertia of what once existed. It needs to be affirmed, embraced, cultivated. It is, essentially preservation, and ... preservation is an act of reason, though an inconspicuous one.[19]

The choice to assent to a traditional doctrine, that is, is as free and rational as the choice to reject it. Indeed, not only did the Enlightenment and

Romantic periods misunderstand the concept of tradition as such, Gadamer argues, but they also misunderstood its place in the hermeneutics of the human sciences. In fact, he writes, 'Our usual relationship to the past is not characterized by distancing and freeing ourselves from tradition. Rather we are always situated within traditions.'[20] We do not study a text from the past, that is, as an object from which we as interpreters are independent, disinterested subjects of knowledge, but rather as a part of the very process of tradition by which our thinking, and all that which structures our interpretation in advance, is determined. Gadamer writes, 'The abstract antithesis between tradition and historical research, between history and the knowledge of it, must be discarded.'[21] It is impossible to interpret the past, in short, without already having been affected by it, in a way that determines both what one interprets and how. This is why the human sciences cannot be thought of on the model of the natural sciences, since the latter's object-in-itself simply does not exist in them. In the human sciences, Gadamer writes, 'The particular research questions concerning tradition that we are interested in pursuing are motivated in a special way by the present and its interests', which themselves are determined by elements of precisely that tradition into which we are inquiring.[22] Understanding, that is, is 'less a subjective act than a participating in an event of tradition', in which the past and the present mutually determine one another.[23]

Gadamer calls the effect of history on our understanding of history *Wirkungsgeschichte*, or 'history of effect'. A good interpretation will be one in which the interpreter realizes as fully as possible the ways in which his interpretation is determined by this history. Gadamer calls this *wirkungsgeschichtliches Bewusstsein*, or 'historically effected consciousness', and he defines it in the first place as consciousness of the 'situation' in which one interprets.[24] Since we are historical beings, we always understand and interpret within a given situation, outside which we cannot stand and so cannot know objectively. Since we are finite beings, this situation limits the possibilities of our understanding. Gadamer calls these limits an interpreter's 'horizon', which he defines as 'the range of vision that includes everything that can be seen from a particular vantage point'.[25] The historicist hermeneutics of the nineteenth century, he argues, thought of good interpretation as a process in which the interpreter reconstructed the horizon of the text and then transposed himself into that horizon, understanding the text from within its limits. This is what Schleiermacher meant when he claimed that the aim of interpretation was to understand a writer better than he had understood himself. This concept of interpretation suspends the claim to truth of the text, Gadamer points out – he compares it to a conversation in which one listens to one's partner in order only to understand the meaning of his words. It does so because it is based on a misunderstanding of the nature of the horizons within which the text is written and the interpretation is carried out, according to which these are closed and determinate possibilities for understanding. Since we are historical beings, however, the horizon of the present, within which we interpret texts from the past, is never closed but rather constantly in the process of being formed. Gadamer writes, 'Horizons change for a person who is moving.'[26] Clearly, this is also true of the horizon of the past, which was also once that of the present. The horizon of the interpreter's present situation and that of the past situation of the writer of the text are in fact only separate phenomena in the first phase of understanding. The horizon of the present is constituted by the prejudices which determine an interpretation in advance. But these prejudices are not a 'fixed set of opinions and valuations', Gadamer argues, but are rather continually in the process of being tested, above all by the act precisely of interpreting texts from the past. Gadamer writes:

> The horizon of the present is continually in the process of being formed because we are continually having to test all our prejudices. An important part of this testing occurs in encountering the past and in understanding the tradition from which we come. Hence the horizon of the present cannot be formed without the past.[27]

He calls this the 'fusion of horizons' of the past and the present, which initially appear to exist by themselves, and argues that all understanding whatever consists in this fusion of horizons. He still calls it a fusion of two horizons rather than the formation of one because of the testing of prejudices that occurs in the process of interpretation. He writes, 'Every encounter with tradition that takes place within historical consciousness involves the experience of a tension between the text and the present.'[28] This tension consists in the experience of being 'pulled up short' by the text, in which the validity of the prejudices in whose terms one interprets it are called into question by the text. In an encounter with a text from the past, that is, one can become aware of the prejudices of the present, and come consciously to accept or reject them as such. In this way, the horizon of the present, which determines the way in which we encounter the past, it itself determined by precisely that encounter.

Gadamer's theory of interpretation in the human sciences is the theory in whose terms the legitimacy of the concepts of Christian literary theory and criticism is best understood. It follows from his concepts of understanding and interpretation that literary theory and criticism from the point of view of Christian faith and theology are not essentially more dogmatic or authoritarian than any other mode of literary theory or criticism. They do not necessarily constitute an imposition of individual beliefs upon texts which would be better understood in their own terms or in the terms of more culturally dominant beliefs. As I have made clear, Gadamer's hermeneutics is based upon Heidegger's insights that the structure of interpretation is always a fore-structure, and that the hermeneutic circle thus constituted is universal. These propositions are true, and Gadamer expounds their significance well for interpretation in the human sciences. It is true that all interpretation is determined by the prejudices, or pre-conceptions and pre-judgements, that an interpreter brings to the text in advance from the historical situation within which he necessarily interprets. This is, as Gadamer claims, a universal truth of interpretation. Good interpretation is not that which avoids prejudices, therefore, but rather that which makes as many of the interpreter's prejudices as possible conscious, and therefore open to rational acceptance or rejection. Most important for the concept of Christian literary theory is Gadamer's insight that authority and tradition, when rightly understood, can constitute sources of legitimate prejudice, or advance determinations of an interpretation which produce understanding rather than preventing it. Clearly, assent to the truth-claim of the Bible and to the articles of Christian faith, which determines the standpoint of Christian faith from which I am proposing to construct a literary theory, means that one accepts the Bible and the church's interpretation of it as authoritative. These texts and their interpretation constitute a tradition whose authority Christians accept, and which determines their subsequent understanding. Now, as Gadamer shows, accepting the authority of the Bible and of the church's tradition of interpretation of its message in this way is not an act of blind obedience or of submission, but rather a free act of reason based on an acknowledgement of one's own finitude. Given that an individual understands the totality of his experience to only a limited extent, that is, he decides that it is this tradition which allows him to understand it to the greatest extent, and believes its message to be true, accepting it as an authority. Furthermore, as Gadamer also shows, to accept the authority of Christian tradition in this way is not a merely passive act, in which one subordinates present concerns and interests to what was taught in the past, but rather a dialectical process, in which an individual interprets the tradition in the light of these present concerns, and reinterprets and develops it. Indeed, it is precisely in this constant process of reinterpretation that Christian tradition, like all other traditions, consists. The significance of Gadamer's hermeneutics for the concept of Christian literary theory is that this process of accepting the authority of a tradition, which determines an individual's subsequent thinking, does not negate the validity of his cultural interpretations but is rather a universal condition of interpretation. The difference between literary criticism practised from a point of view determined by Christian faith, that is, and literary criticism practised from points of view which claim to be rationally determined alone, is ultimately that the former recognizes the situatedness in tradition which both in fact share and which determines both more explicitly. The latter is also determined by the interpreter's situation in tradition but recognizes as much less clearly. The situation is in fact more complex than this – literary criticism from a Christian perspective is determined not only by the interpreter's Christian faith but also by his situation within many other cultural traditions as well, of which he may be more or less aware, and which affect his understanding of Christian tradition itself. An interpreter is always situated at a conjunction of many traditions, that is, of which some are dominant and others in the background of his historical situation, and which may even conflict and contradict one another. The Christian critic, therefore, is still obliged to become as conscious as possible of his prejudices in terms of the texts he interprets, a process that, as in all interpretation, is never complete. It is a consequence of Gadamer's concept of the fusion of horizons that the prejudices of the Christian literary critic, including all the theological views he holds on the authority of the Christian tradition, are constantly called into question and tested by his criticism. Many of the literary theorists I will examine in the next chapter make precisely this point, arguing that literary texts can criticize Christian theology even as they are understood in its terms. The most important consequence of Gadamer's hermeneutics, however, remains his demonstration that, since situation within traditions which determine the interpretation is a condition of all interpretation, Christian literary theory and criticism have the hermeneutic structure of all literary theory and criticism. Christian literary theory, that is, is not an irrational or unethical concept in postmodern culture, as that culture would seem to suggest, since the prejudices which determine it are of precisely the same kind as those which determine all literary theory whatever.

5.2   The Gadamer–Habermas debate

The most significant critique of Gadamer's hermeneutics with respect to its significance for Christian literary theory has been that of Jürgen Habermas. In *On the Logic of the Social Sciences* (1967), Habermas argues that the social sciences need to supplement the empirical methodology which was then the dominant concern in the philosophy of science with hermeneutic considerations, since these sciences are concerned not only with observable facts but also with intentional actions, whose meaning needs to be understood and interpreted. Gadamer's hermeneutics is therefore a useful tool for the self-understanding of the social sciences, teaching them that 'a pre-understanding of historical situations is inevitably incorporated into the fundamental assumptions of [their] theories'.[29] Nevertheless, he is wrong, in Habermas' view, to claim that the scope of this hermeneutics is universal. Whilst Habermas accepts Gadamer's critique of historicism, for which the object of investigation is held to be independent of the investigating subject, he argues that the concept of method should not therefore be rejected in the social sciences. He writes, 'This accurate critique of a false objectivistic self-understanding cannot, however, lead to the suspension of the methodological distancing of the object that distinguishes a reflective understanding from everyday communicative experience.'[30] It is by methodical procedures alone, that is, that the social scientist can raise his understanding of the linguistic data of his investigation to the level of scientific reflection upon them. Truth should not be simply opposed to method, for Habermas, since, beyond the objectivistic concept of truth which both he and Gadamer reject, it can be attained precisely through methodical reflection upon the linguistic data of a given tradition. Although hermeneutics legitimately criticizes the dominance of the methodology of the natural sciences, Habermas writes, 'this does not relieve it of the business of methodology as such – this claim, we must fear, will be effective either *in* the sciences or not at all'.[31] For Habermas, the characteristic interest of the critical social sciences is the emancipation of the human subjects about whom it forms hypotheses, and this end can be achieved only through the methodical process of reflection upon these hypotheses and the data on which they are based.[32] Gadamer's rejection of method in favour of understanding works against the emancipation which, for Habermas, is the purpose of the social sciences.

Habermas criticizes Gadamer's claim that interpretation is always determined by the interpreter's situation in tradition. Against this claim he opposes 'the insight that the reflective appropriation of tradition breaks the quasi-natural substance of tradition and alters the position of subjects within it'.[33] Habermas denies that interpretation necessarily constitutes a development of the tradition within which the text and the interpreter both stand, claiming rather that an interpreter can reflect critically upon the prejudices that derive from his situation in tradition, and thereby alter them. He writes, 'The structural affiliation of understanding with the traditions it continues to develop through appropriation does not, however, justify the conclusion that the medium of tradition has not been profoundly transformed as a result of scientific reflection.'[34] He accepts Gadamer's claim that interpretation is determined by the prejudices that follow from an interpreter's situation in tradition, but he argues that this situation can and should itself become an object of critical reflection. In this way, understanding can be determined not by unacknowledged prejudices but rather by rational reflection upon these prejudices. Habermas writes, 'When reflection understands the genesis of the tradition from which it proceeds and to which it returns, the dogmatism of life-praxis is shaken.'[35] Gadamer's view of tradition constrains us to think and act within its limits, whereas, for Habermas, critical reason, reflecting on precisely these limits, can lead us to think and to act differently.

Habermas denies that any form of prejudice can have the positive role in understanding to which Gadamer restores it. He asks, 'Does it follow from the unavoidability of hermeneutic anticipation that there are legitimate prejudgements?'[36] Gadamer claims that authority can be legitimate source of prejudice, when it is accepted on the basis of an acknowledgement that another is better informed or has greater insight than oneself, as when a student accepts what he is taught on the authority of his teacher. Habermas denies that this is the case. In the first place, he argues, the student accepts the view of the teacher not only on the basis of rational acknowledgement of the teacher's greater knowledge but also 'under the potential threat of sanctions and with a view to gratifications'.[37] In the second place, even when the student comes to reflect upon what he has been taught in the light of later knowledge and experience, his reflection changes this material from a source of prejudice to an object of judgement. Habermas writes, 'Made transparent, the prejudgement structure can no longer function as prejudgement.'[38] Nevertheless, he argues, this is what Gadamer implies. As the student matures and reflects upon the prejudices he has acquired through his acceptance of the authority of the teacher, he does so in terms of the prejudices he has acquired through his situation in tradition, of which his education was a part. This means that, in reflection, the collective authority of tradition replaces the individual authority of the teacher as the source of the prejudices which determine understanding. Habermas comments, 'It would remain authority, for reflection would be able to move only within the facticity of what was handed down.'[39] He concludes that Gadamer fails to acknowledge the critical power of reflection with respect to the claims of authority and tradition. He writes:

> Gadamer's prejudice in favour of prejudices validated by tradition is in conflict with the power of refection, which proves itself in its ability to reject the claim of traditions.[40]

Gadamer limits reflection to consciousness of the situation within which we interpret, Habermas argues, whereas in fact we can reflect on this situation in such a way as to criticize and reject those prejudices by which it is characterized. He writes that reflection 'not only confirms but also breaks dogmatic forces'.[41] He accepts that understanding is in the first instance structured in advance by the prejudices which follow from our situation in traditions, but argues that critical reason can reflect back upon this situation and judge the validity of these prejudices. In this way, he writes, 'Authority can be stripped of that in it which was mere domination and dissolved into the less coercive forces of insight and rational decision.'[42]

Ultimately, for Habermas, Gadamer's concept of tradition does not acknowledge the social forces upon which cultural traditions are dependent. He writes, 'Hermeneutics comes up against the limits of the context of tradition from the inside. Once these limits have been experienced and recognized, it can no longer consider cultural traditions absolute.'[43] For Habermas, the critical social sciences must recognize that social action is 'the combined result of reactive compulsions and meaningful interactions', that is, the product both of the conscious intention of social subjects and of unconscious motivations whose objective causes must be induced from empirical observation.[44] The hermeneutics of tradition, whose object is human discourse, can recognize only the former. Gadamer does not acknowledge that 'this meta-institution of language as tradition is dependent in turn on social processes that cannot be reduced to normative relationships' expressible in the language of social subjects.[45] Language, seen in the light of these social processes, Habermas writes, is '*also* a medium of domination and social power. It serves to legitimate relationships of organized force'.[46] The objective context in which social actions can be fully understood, for Habermas, is 'constituted conjointly by language, labour and domination'. Whereas hermeneutics recognizes and wrongly universalizes only the first of these contexts, Habermas argues that critical sociology must 'make tradition as such, and tradition in its relationship to other moments of the social life context, comprehensible, so that we can indicate the conditions external to tradition under which transcendental rules of worldview and action change empirically'.[47] If social subjects are to be free from the potentially exploitative force of tradition, that is, and to orient their understanding and action towards this freedom, tradition must be seen in its place within the social whole. In this way, Habermas writes, 'it becomes possible to understand the functions that cultural tradition serves in the system as a whole, without them being expressed *in it* and *as such* – ideological relationships, in other words'.[48]

There are several fundamental respects in which Habermas has misrepresented Gadamer's views in the course of these arguments. In the first place, he is wrong to oppose to Gadamer's concept of the role of tradition in understanding the claim that an individual can reflect upon the prejudices which follow from his situation in tradition, and reject them in the light of critical reason. This is itself Gadamer's view, as I have made clear in the previous section. The historically effected consciousness for which Gadamer argues is precisely a process of reflecting upon the prejudices which structure our understanding and interpretations in advance, and accepting or rejecting them in the light of this reflection. Gadamer claims that the prejudices which derive from our situation in traditions *can* be legitimate, that is, that when we have rationally reflected upon them, we choose to affirm them. Equally, he argues, we may choose to reject them. It is in precisely this process of judgement that the legitimacy or illegitimacy of a prejudice becomes clear. It is true that Gadamer claims that the act of reflection occurs in the context of a series of given traditions, but it does not follow from this that an individual cannot reject any prejudice which derives from this context when it becomes an object of his reflection. On the contrary, Gadamer claims that this is the case. When Habermas asserts that reflection can break the dogmatic force of tradition, that it can alter the position of subjects with respect to their judgement of trad- itional propositions, and that their understanding and action can be altered as a result, these are all assertions with which Gadamer would agree. With respect to Gadamer's example of the prejudices inculcated into the student by the teacher, Habermas also misrepresents Gadamer's position. Although the student, on reaching maturity, remains situated within traditions, for Gadamer, he 'can – but need not! – adopt on the basis of insight that which he adhered to on the basis of obedience alone'.[49] The prejudices accepted on authority in Gadamer's example are legitimated by the reflection of critical reason. Although this reflection itself occurs within a context of traditions, it is not these traditions but the act of rational judgement by which the prejudices are legitimated, if they are legitimated at all. For Gadamer, one can reject that which is taught on authority in the light of critical reason as well as accept it. Hence, when Habermas argues that reflection can strip authority of that in it which was mere domination and understand its contents from the perspective of rational decision, Gadamer justifiably comments, 'I no longer know what we are arguing about.'[50]

In 'Rhetoric, Hermeneutics and the Critique of Ideology' (1967), Gadamer responds to Habermas' critique. With regard to the latter's fundamental criticism that hermeneutics does not recognize the social context upon which cultural traditions are dependent, Gadamer writes that hermeneutics is 'unjustly restricted when its limits are defined in terms of a conjunction between all motives for action and their under-stood meaning'.[51] Habermas had argued that hermeneutics is oriented towards only the linguistic medium of cultural tradition, and that it cannot account therefore for the objective reality of social forces and relations in which this medium exists. Gadamer responds that hermen-eutics is oriented towards understanding whatever can be understood, and that this includes social forces and relations. He writes, 'It abridges the universality of the hermeneutical dimension when a realm of understandable meaning ("cultural tradition") is set off against other determinants of social reality, identifiable solely as concrete factors.'[52] In the case of ideology, he argues, it is not only the internal sense of a discourse that can be understood but also the sense in which it is an expression of class interest. The concrete factors of work and dominance, insofar as they are understood, are articulated linguistically in the consciousness of those whose understand them, and therefore become the object of hermeneutics in the same way as the discourse which arises in their context. Indeed, when we see through prejudices or unmask pretences which disguise the truth, Gadamer writes, 'there most of all we "understand".'[53] Finally, Gadamer responds with a critique of Habermas' own position. He argues that the latter does not adequately recognize the consequences of the fact that reflection upon traditions itself occurs within a situation in traditions. He writes, 'Habermas' concept of reflection and bringing to consciousness seems heavily burdened by its own dogmatism', insofar as it is based upon the premise that that which is reflected upon can become an object independent of the reflecting subject.[54] Gadamer denies that this is the case, and argues that, since the position is not self-evident, Habermas must hold it precisely as result of his situation in traditions. In fact, he argues, 'The one who does the understanding can never reflect himself out of the historical involvement of his hermeneutical situation so that his own interpretation does not itself become a part of the subject at hand.'[55] Although reflection upon prejudices in the light of critical reason is the ground of their legitimacy, Gadamer argues, this reflection itself occurs within traditions and constitutes a development of them.

In 'The Hermeneutic Claim to Universality' (1971), Habermas continues to deny that hermeneutics can give an adequate account of the social forces by which the discourse to which it is oriented is determined. In this essay, he argues from the example of psychoanalysis that Gadamer's claim that hermeneutics orients itself to everything which can be understood, and that this understanding occurs in the medium of language, is false. He asks, 'Can there be an understanding of meaning in relation to symbolic structures formulated in everyday language that is not tied to the hermeneutic pre-supposition of context-dependent processes of understanding?'[56] He means that, if there are examples of discourse which cannot be understood within a process of dialogue, but only on the basis of a pre-formulated theory of discourse, then Gadamer's claim that all understanding occurs within a process of dialogue can be disproved. He finds such examples in the speech of the neurotic subjects treated by psychoanalysis. The expressive acts characteristic of neurotics are incomprehensible according to the ordinary rules of communication, even to the subjects themselves. They are examples of what Habermas calls 'systematically distorted communication', that is, acts of communication whose meaning can be understood only in terms of the conditions of its production.[57] In psychoanalysis, a theory has been developed to explain these conditions of production and hence the meaning of the otherwise incomprehensible speech and acts of neurotics. The psychoanalyst's understanding of his patient's discourse, Habermas writes, 'is distinguishable from the elementary hermeneutical understanding of meaning by its explanatory potential', that is, it makes the meaning of ordinarily incomprehensible expressions accessible through an explanation of their origin.[58] Habermas calls this kind of interpretation 'depth-hermeneutics', and argues that it transcends the capacity of hermeneutical understanding insofar as it is not merely an application of communicative competence but 'presupposes a theory' of such competence.[59] Again, he emphasizes that the purpose of his critique of Gadamer's concept of understanding is that the latter does not adequately account for the social context of that which is understood. The example of psychoanalysis, he argues, shows that acceptance of the prejudices which derive from authority or tradition may seem to constitute a rational agreement with the latter but may in fact be the result of precisely the kind of distorted communication with which the psycho-analyst is faced. He writes, 'Every consensus, as the outcome of an understanding of meaning is, in principle, suspect of having been enforced through pseudo-communication.'[60] Hermeneutics, that is, describes as an act of rational choice what may in fact be a capitulation to social force. Habermas concludes:

> The dogmatic recognition of tradition, and this means the acceptance of the truth-claims of this tradition, can be equated with knowledge itself only when freedom from force and unrestricted agreement about tradition have already been secured within this tradition.[61]

To a large extent, this criticism has already been anticipated by Gadamer's previous claim that hermeneutical understanding is not limited to the conscious intention of the author of the discourse an interpreter aims to understand. Habermas' concept of depth-hermeneutics cannot be opposed to Gadamer's concept of interpretation, but is in fact an example of such interpretation. For Gadamer, understanding is a continual process of dialogue, with interlocutors past and present. The kind of interpretation Habermas describes, which is structured in advance by theoretical principles that the interpreter has come to accept on the basis of previous interpretive dialogues, is precisely an example of interpretation as Gadamer describes it, rather than a counter-example, as Habermas asserts. In his 'Reply' (1971) to Habermas' essay, Gadamer makes this point, denying Habermas' claim that hermeneutics is 'concerned, both originally and exclusively, with colloquially constituted and trans-mitted culture', and arguing that it is precisely the task of historically effected consciousness to 'impede and undermine all attempts to understand the tradition in terms of the most tempting, seductive opportunities which are being actualized'.[62] He goes on to argue that the analogy on which Habermas' critique is based, between the psychoanalytic dialogue and that which occurs between social subjects as such, does not hold. He claims, 'The emancipatory power of reflection to which the psycho-analyst lays claim . . . has its limit – a limit which is defined by the larger social consciousness of which analyst and patient alike understand themselves, along with everyone else.'[63] The psychoanalyst's interpretation of his or her patient's discourse both explains the meaning of this discourse and liberates the patient from the forces which rendered it inexplicable within the context of the specific social roles played by the doctor and the patient. There is no justification, Gadamer claims, for thinking of the author of any given discourse as 'ill' in an analogous way to the patient, since there is no equivalent in the dialogue between social subjects as such to the patient's understanding that he is ill and conse-·quent submission to the analyst's interpretation of his discourse. Gadamer writes, 'In the case of psychoanalysis the patient's suffering and desire to be cured is given as a supporting foundation for the therapeutic activity of her doctor.'[64] In the case of the interpretation of the discourse of one social subject by another, he writes, there is no such foundation for the kind of depth-hermeneutics which Habermas describes. Gadamer asks, 'With respect to which self-interpretation of social consciousness...is covert questioning and deception, as might be found in the revolutionary desire for change, not out of place, and with respect to which is it out of place?'[65] By this he means ultimately that to interpret a discourse in the light of a theory of ideology is to do so from within precisely the kind of situation in tradition by which all understanding and interpretation are characterized. A theory of ideology is an example of the kind of pre-understanding which determines interpretation in advance, rather than a meta-theory of interpretation as such, as Habermas asserts.

Habermas enters into debate with Gadamer concerned primarily to defend the emancipatory significance of the critical social sciences against what he sees to be the compromise of the function of critique represented by Gadamer's hermeneutics. This concern is legitimate. Habermas is right to argue for the necessity of critical interpretation of ideological discourse, especially against a view which seems to encourage the acceptance of that which is taught by authority and tradition. He is also right to argue that the texts of a given tradition are adequately understood only in the light of the context of the social relations in which they are written and read. Nevertheless, neither of these claims can be legitimately opposed to those of Gadamer's hermeneutics, as Habermas does, since they are already part of that hermeneutics. It is an essential aspect of Gadamer's claim that the pre-understandings which derive from tradition are legitimated, if at all, by critical reflection upon them, on the basis of which reflection an interpreter chooses rationally whether to accept or to reject them, and to what extent. His argument is that tradition can be a source of legitimate prejudice, but not that the prejudices which derive from tradition are always or necessarily legitimate. On the contrary, he recognizes that there are equally prejudices deriving from authority and tradition which 'it is the undeniable task of critical reason to overcome'.[66] Furthermore, Gadamer's claim that understanding is always situated in traditions does not entail the position that it is oriented towards cultural traditions alone, so that it takes no account of the social context in which these traditions occur. On the contrary, Gadamer argues that understanding is oriented towards all that can be understood, and this includes the social context of cultural traditions. Habermas is wrong, therefore, to claim that Gadamer's hermeneutics is conservative, validating that which is taught by authority and tradition without adequate critical reflection on the social and political context in which it is taught. In fact, Gadamer does not privilege authority and tradition, as if these sources of prejudice in themselves legitimated the prejudices which derive from them. On the contrary, he recognizes that authority and tradition can equally be sources of illegitimate prejudice, making claims which appear to be freely accepted but which are in reality socially enforced. Gadamer does not describe a mode of interpretation to which the critique of ideology can be opposed as an alternative, therefore, but one of which the latter is precisely a part. He disagrees most fundamentally with Habermas over the theory of interpretation insofar as he claims that the critique of ideology is, like all other modes of interpretation, situated in tradition and determined by this situation. This is true. As Paul Ricoeur points out, there is a tradition of critique, to which Habermas demonstrably belongs and which he develops.[67] When Gadamer describes Habermas' claims for reflection as dogmatic, this is what he means, that the critique of ideology is itself an interpretive practice developed within a series of traditions, and not a meta-theory of the interpretation of tradition as such.

This means that the claims I have made for the concept of Christian literary theory in the light of Gadamer's hermeneutics cannot be criticized on the grounds that they are conservative. This is an important point, because it is precisely on the grounds of their supposed conservatism that Christian faith and theology are most widely rejected in postmodern theory. In the previous section, I argued that Christian literary theory and criticism, insofar as they are determined by an acceptance of the claims of a given tradition, participate in the conditions of all literary theory and criticism, and are therefore legitimate forms of those discourses. I can now add that this is not a claim which fails to recognize the potentially ideological function of that which is taught by authority and tradition. On the contrary, as I have already argued, an individual assents to the truth-claim of the Bible and to the Christian tradition of interpretation of its message on the basis of a process of rational judgement. It is on the basis of precisely this process that those traditional claims which he judges to be ideological are also rejected. As Gadamer has rightly pointed out, it is in this process of reinterpreting the claims of a tradition in the light of the concerns of the present that tradition as such consists. As he puts it in his reply to Habermas, 'Tradition exists only in constantly becoming other than it is.'[68] To defend the legitimacy of a literary theory formulated from the point of view of Christian faith, therefore, on the grounds that this point of view is determined by a situation in tradition shared by all forms of literary theory, is not to ignore the potentially ideological function of tradition in general or of Christian tradition in particular. On the contrary, to be situated within a tradition, in the way that Christian literary theory and criticism are situated, is precisely to subject the claims of this tradition to the kind of reflection on whose basis that which can be judged to be ideological in them can be rejected. Indeed, as I have already argued, the interpretation of literary and cultural works from the perspective of Christian faith may constitute a practice which necessitates precisely this kind of reflection. I will conclude this section by pointing out that such reflection is also the task of literary and cultural interpretation practised from the point of view of critical theory.

5.3   Ricoeur's hermeneutics

During the 1970s, Gadamer's project of a philosophical hermeneutics was developed most influentially by Paul Ricoeur (b. 1913). The first principle of Ricoeur's theory of textual interpretation is that the linguistic code or system which was defined by Ferdinand de Saussure as the object of linguistics, as opposed to speech or utterance, does not exhaust the phenomena of language available for investigation. For Saussure, linguistic structure – *langue* as opposed to *parole* – was the only aspect of language in whose terms it could be studied as the object of an independent science.[69] As Ricoeur points out, however, once structuralism began to apply the model of structural linguistics to linguistic entities larger than the sentence, such as myths and literary texts, in many cases language came to be posited as a self-sufficient system of inner relationships, as a 'world of its own' without reference to the external world.[70] In 'Introduction to the Structural Analysis of Narratives' (1966), for example, Roland Barthes claims, '"What takes place" in a narrative is from the referential (reality) point of view literally nothing;

what happens is language alone, the adventure of language, the unceasing celebration of its coming.'[71] As soon as this kind of claim is made, Ricoeur argues, in which the autonomy of a text is taken to imply the abolition of its referential dimension, structural analysis becomes what he calls 'structuralist ideology' or 'ultra-structuralism', whereby 'a methodological choice becomes a dogmatic decision'.[72] In fact, Ricoeur argues, 'To say with de Saussure that language is a system of signs is to characterize language in just one of its aspects and not in its total reality.'[73] In order to understand the concept of the text rightly, Ricoeur argues, we need to account not only for the system of language but also for its concrete instance in the form of discourse. Following Benveniste, he argues that the 'linguistics of language', that is, structural linguistics, whose object is language in the form of a system made up of signs, needs to be complemented by a 'linguistics of discourse', whose object is language in the form of a work made up of sentences.[74] He calls these sciences 'semiotics' and 'semantics' respectively. They constitute distinct sciences, since the fundamental units of language with which they are concerned, namely the sign and the sentence, are different in kind and must therefore be described in different terms. Although made up of signs, that is, a sentence is not a larger or more complex sign, but a 'new entity', with properties irreducible to those of the signs which comprise it. An adequate theory of textual interpretation, Ricoeur argues, must recognize that the object of interpretation is in the first instance a discourse, a linguistic work whose properties cannot be understood in terms of those of the structure of language.

In several different essays, Ricoeur describes the properties of discourse as such. It is a dialectical phenomenon, he argues, which can be considered fundamentally in terms of a dialectic of event and meaning. He writes, 'If all discourse is actualized as an event, all discourse is understood as meaning.'[75] On the one hand, that is, discourse is an event of language – it is the actual instance of someone speaking, temporally realizing the language-system whose existence, by contrast, is virtual and outside of time. As Ricoeur writes, 'Discourse grounds the very existence of language since only the discrete and each time unique acts of discourse actualize the code.'[76] This ontological priority would be without consequence, however, if discourse were merely a temporal event, which vanished as soon as it appeared. On the other hand, Ricoeur argues, discourse has a content which can be identified and re-identified as the same, so that it can be said again, or in different words, or even in another language. He writes, 'Through all these transformations, it preserves an identity of its own which can be called the propositional content, the "said as such".'[77] This is the meaning pole of discourse, according to which, if discourse is realized as an event, it is one which is 'eminently repeatable', because its meaning or propositional content can be identified and re-identified as the same.[78] According to what Ricoeur calls the dialectic of event and meaning, that is, discourse is actualized as a temporal event, but the temporal character of the event is superseded by the ideal character of the meaning in whose terms it is understood.

A significant characteristic of the meaning pole of discourse, Ricoeur argues, which again cannot be understood in the terms of structural linguistics, is that it can be understood, in Frege's terms, both as sense and as reference, that is, both in terms of what is said and that about which it is said. It is only at the level of the sentence that this distinction arises, since, when language is considered as a system of signs, the signs relate only to other signs in the system. In the sentence, however, language is also directed beyond itself towards the world. Ricoeur writes, 'Whereas the sense is immanent to the discourse, and objective in the sense of ideal, the reference expresses the movement in which language transcends itself.'[79] The sense derives from the internal relations of the signs within the sentence; the reference is its claim to be true. The two are dialectically related, he argues, inasmuch as it is precisely through the construction of sense within language that the statement's reference passes beyond language to the world.

Since interpretation is ordered primarily towards discourse in the form of a written text, Ricoeur inquires into the effects on discourse of the transition from speech to writing. Although it initially appears that the function of writing is merely to fix the message, in opposition to the transitory character of the event of speech, in fact, Ricoeur argues, it effects the detachment of event and meaning in discourse, which is apparent in only a nascent form in speech, thereby rendering the dialectic of these two aspects of discourse fully explicit. This is what he means when he writes that 'writing is the full manifestation of discourse'.[80] When discourse is inscribed directly in writing, without passing first through speech, Ricoeur argues, the 'dialogical situation' in which two interlocutors speak to, understand and reply to one another face to face, is exploded. This means that 'the relation between writing and reading is no longer a particular case of the relation between speaking and hearing'.[81] In the first place, the author's intention and the meaning of the text cease to coincide. In spoken discourse, the speaker's intention is only accessible through the meaning of his utterance, specifically through its indicators of personality and subjectivity, but because he belongs to the situation of interlocution, the reference of his utterance back to him appears immediate. Since an author does not belong to such a situation, however, his intention and the meaning of his text can no longer be identified in this way, and the one must be construed in terms of the other. Ricoeur writes, 'The text's career escapes the finite horizon lived by its author. What the text means now matters more than what the author meant when he wrote it.'[82] He calls this the 'semantic autonomy' of a text. It also pertains to the relation between a text and its reader. Whereas speech is addressed to the person or persons determined in advance by the face-to-face situation of dialogue, most texts are addressed to an unknown reader and all texts are potentially addressed to anyone who knows how to read. Ricoeur calls this the 'universalisation of the audience' of discourse effected by writing.[83] The kind of criticism which assumes that the meaning of a text is determined by the horizon of understanding of its original addressees wrongly reduces the extent of its meaning, therefore.

Most importantly, for Ricoeur, the referential function of discourse is altered by the passage from speech to writing. In spoken discourse, he argues, 'the ultimate criterion for the referential scope of what we say is the possibility of showing the thing referred to as a member of the situation common to both speaker and hearer'.[84] Spoken discourse always occurs in a given situation, that is, the elements of which can be shown most simply by pointing. The discourse itself performs this ostensive function, Ricoeur argues, with deictic indicators – demonstratives, personal pronouns, adverbs of time and place, and so on – which refer the discourse back to the situation in which it is spoken. Furthermore, definite descriptions can be established by the dialogue, so that the same referent can be identified by both interlocutors. In this way, reference is again related back to the situation in which the speakers perform this identification. In speech, Ricoeur argues, reference is ultimately a kind of pointing. He writes, 'The ideal sense of what is said turns towards the real reference, towards that "about which" we speak. At the limit, this real reference tends to merge with an ostensive designation where speech rejoins the gesture of pointing.'[85] The shared situation on which the ostensive character of reference depends disappears in writing, since the writer and reader are indefinitely distanced from one another. In writing, Ricoeur argues, reference continues to function 'as if' to the circumstances of a surrounding situation, but these are no longer in fact the circumstances of the reader. A text opens up to the reader a situation in which he is not himself present, thereby enlarging the scope of his experience from that of his situation to that of an indefinite number of possible situations. Ricoeur writes, 'Thanks to writing, man and only man has a world and not just a situation.'[86] A text, that is, frees reference from the limits of the situation in which speech occurs, and opens up to the reader a 'world', which comprises 'the ensemble of references opened up by texts'.[87] At this stage, Ricoeur is still thinking of what he calls the 'first-order' reference of texts, that is, that of those which claim to describe reality. These texts, he writes, 'provide the reader with an equivalent of ostensive reference in the mode of "as if"', that is, they refer to a real situation as if the reader were in it.[88] In poetic and fictional texts, however, this claim is not made. In these texts, Ricoeur points out, not only is reference non-ostensive, but it is also non-descriptive, that is, it does not refer to an externally given reality. Poetic and fictional discourse, he writes, do 'not directly augment our knowledge of objects'.[89] This does not mean that their referential function is abolished, Ricoeur argues, but rather that their abolition of first-order reference opens up a 'second-order' reference to 'aspects of our being in the world that cannot be said in a direct descriptive way'.[90] This kind of reference, Ricoeur argues, is to a level of existence which precedes our opposition as subjects to a world of manipulable objects, and which Husserl spoke of as the 'life-world' and Heidegger as 'being-in-the-world'. Poetic texts, that is, refer not at the level of externally given objects, but at the more fundamental level of our belonging-to or participation-in the world in which we exist. They propose a possible world, Ricoeur writes, 'which I could inhabit and wherein I could project one of my ownmost possibilities'.[91] Just as descriptive texts open up a 'world' to the reader, which extends beyond his immediate situation, so fictional and poetic texts propose a world in which a reader can dwell at the level of his lived experience. This is what Ricoeur means when he says that poetic texts 'intend being, not under the modality of being-given but under the modality of power-to-be'.[92] They propose a possible world, into which I can project myself, and thereby enlarge my experience of being in the world in general. As Ricoeur writes, 'Through fiction and poetry, new possibilities of being-in-the-world are opened up within everyday reality.'[93] The meaning of a text, therefore, is not to be understood as something concealed 'behind' it, in the form of the author's intention, but rather as the possible world proposed 'in front of' it by its non-ostensive and, in the case of fiction, non-descriptive references.[94]

The concept of the world of the text is the central concept of Ricoeur's hermeneutics. It is this possible world which is the object of textual interpretation, he argues. It is true that structuralist and other formalist modes of interpretation confine their analyses to the internal ways in which sense is constructed in a text. This is a legitimate approach, Ricoeur argues, since texts suspend situational reference. Nevertheless, unless we are to conclude that the referential function of discourse disappears altogether in a text, it remains possible to interpret at the level of the reference as well as at that of the sense of a text. Indeed, it is an essential element of discourse, Ricoeur argues, that it has a referential function. Although there are limiting cases, discourse in general is said by someone to someone else about something. To think of it otherwise would be to reduce it to a natural rather than a man-made object, committing what Ricoeur describes as the 'fallacy of the absolute text'.[95] In fact, he argues, formalist or immanent analyses of the sense of the text can be understood in a dialectical way as contributing to the elucidation of the reference, which occurs precisely through the construction of sense. In this way, the two concepts of interpretation which Dilthey opposed to one another, explanation and understanding, can be thought of as the two points of a 'hermeneutical arc' or 'arch', which moves from the ideal sense of the text to the lived experience of the reader, in a single, dialectical process.[96]

It is in this sense that the referent of the text, the world proposed in front of it, is the object of interpretation for Ricoeur. He calls interpretation so conceived 'appropriation', that is, a process by which the reader 'makes his own' what was initially alien, because of the distance between writer and reader. To appropriate the meaning of a text is to actualize in the present the possible world it proposes. This is not to say that an interpreter submits the meaning of the text to the finite capacities of his own understanding. Rather, in projecting himself into the possible world opened up by the non-ostensive references of the text, he submits his own understanding to the possibility of being developed by the text. Ricoeur writes:

> Far from saying that a subject already mastering his own way of being in the world projects the *a priori* of his self-understanding on the text and reads it into the text, I say that interpretation is the process by which disclosure of new modes of being . . . gives the subject a new capacity for knowing himself.[97]

To understand a text, therefore, is to 'understand oneself in front of the text'.[98] In actualizing the possible world proposed in front of a text, the world of the reader's lived experience is enlarged. Since, in Ricoeur's view, we do not fully understand ourselves by self-reflection alone, but by 'the long detour of the signs of humanity deposited in cultural works', to increase our experience of the world in this way is to increase our understanding of ourselves.[99] This is what he means when he writes, 'The reader is enlarged in his capacity of self-projection by receiving a new mode of being from the text.'[100] Ricoeur contrasts this developing 'self' which emerges from the interpretation of text with the fixed and stable 'ego' which claims to precede and determine it. He writes, 'It is the text, with its universal power of unveiling, which gives a *self* to the *ego.*'[101]

Ricoeur's hermeneutic theory is significant for the concept of Christian literary theory in several ways. In the first place, his theory of discourse constitutes a basis on which the Christian belief in the truth-claim of the Scriptures can be justified against post-structuralist theories of the text, in which the play of signification is held to disrupt the relationship between signs and things. Like structuralism, post-structuralist analysis works at the level of the sign, understanding a text as an open play of signifiers irreducible to a previous or corresponding signified. For Barthes and de Man, the internal play of language in a text implies the eclipse of its external reference. Even for Derrida, the reference of a text can only be to the other which emerges after its sense has been shown to collapse into contradiction. In each case, the analysis works at the level of the relationships of the signs in the text and its context. Ricoeur rightly shows, however, that language can be analysed not only as a system or as a play of signs but also as discourse, as an event in which someone says something to someone else about something. Whilst it is possible to analyse the play of signification in the Biblical texts, that is, it would be wrong to conclude from any such analysis that this play exhausts the meaning of those texts. Ricoeur is right to argue that discourse has an event character, that it is addressed by someone to others, and that it has both sense and reference, that is, that something is said about something. The play of signification within the Biblical texts, therefore, is only one aspect of their reality. The event in which a reader makes sense of the Biblical texts, appropriating their meaning in his own situation, is another aspect, and it is at this level – given to 'semantic' rather than to 'semiotic' analysis – that his or her choice to believe in their truth-claim can be understood.

Ricoeur's theory of the referential function of literary texts is in many respects true. He is right to argue that a text has a semantic autonomy with respect to its author's intention, which is no longer accessible in the same way as that of an interlocutor in dialogue, but must be construed from the sense of the text. He is also right to argue that the referential function of written discourse remains in the absence of the dialogical situation. Except in limiting cases where the referential function seems to be intentionally undermined, a text remains something said about something. This means that texts either refer to the real world, opening up precisely that world as we understand it before them, or that, in the case of literary texts, which make no claim to be true, they refer analogously to a quasi-world. I agree with Ricoeur that literary texts refer by analogy to a world that exists in a different way than that of the objects of perception or science, and in which the reader dwells as he imaginatively actualizes the text's meanings. It follows from this proposition that to dwell during reading in the world proposed by a literary text is to increase one's experience of the world as a whole in which one dwells and in whose terms one understands oneself. Ricoeur is right, therefore, to say that to understand a literary text is to further one's self-understanding, according to a dialectic in which the initially new experience of the world of the text is incorporated into the reader's experience of the world as a whole. Reading a literary text could be said to constitute the negative stage of a dialectic of self-understanding, in which a reader's understanding of the world of his experience is shown to be incomplete insofar as the world of the text constitutes a new experience, but is raised to a higher level by the incorporation of this experience into his reconstituted experience of the world as a whole. The extent of this negativity, in my view, contributes to a reader's judgement of the value of the text.

5.4   Ricoeur's Biblical hermeneutics

This account of interpretation as the opening up of a world to the reader holds true of Biblical interpretation. Before I draw conclusions from my analysis of Ricoeur's general hermeneutics for Biblical hermeneutics, however, it will be necessary to examine his own work on precisely this subject. In 'Philosophical Hermeneutics and Biblical Hermeneutics' (1975), Ricoeur works out the implication of each stage of his general hermeneutic theory for Biblical interpretation. Firstly, he examines the significance of his claim that discourse is always structured in a certain form, as a 'work' of a given genre. With respect to the Bible, he writes, this means that 'the "confession of faith" that is expressed in Biblical documents is inseparable from the forms of discourse – by this I mean the narrative structure of, for example, the Pentateuch and the Gospels, the oracular structure of the prophesies, parables, hymns and so on.'[102] The theological content of a Biblical discourse, that is, is determined by its literary form. Narrative, for example, is not a rhetorical device independent of the content it conveys, but rather a specific determinant of that content.

Ricoeur writes, 'Not just any theology could be tied to the narrative form but only a theology that announces Yahweh as the great actant in a history of deliverance.'[103] By speaking of God in the form of a narrative, in which characters and their actions progress through history, the Old Testament narratives determine God precisely as a character who acts in the salvation history of Israel. In the same way, the form of prophecy determines God as one who interrupts this history, and who threatens to explode it in the coming 'day of Yahweh'. Indeed, Ricoeur argues, not only does the meaning of the Biblical texts arise from their literary forms in this way, but it also arises from the contrast between these forms. He writes, 'The same history which narration founds as certain is suddenly undercut by the menace announced in the prophecy.'[104] He hypothesizes that 'an exhaustive enquiry ... would perhaps reveal that all the forms of discourse together constitute a circular system and that the theological content of each of them receives its meaning from the total constellation of the forms of discourse'.[105]

Ricoeur points out that the distanciation effected by writing is a characteristic of the Biblical texts as such, as well as of the tradition of their interpretation. This means that it is the world of the text, determined by its sense, towards which Biblical interpretation is directed. He sets out the significance of his theory of the world of the text for Biblical interpretation. In the first place, he writes, the world projected by the Biblical text is mediated through its sense. This means that exegesis, analysis of the ways in which this sense is constructed, is a necessary stage in understanding the reference of the text, and therefore in understanding oneself in terms of this referent. Secondly, he argues, the concept of revelation can no longer be understood in terms of a psychological theory of the inspiration of Scripture, according to which God dictates to the author of the text, causing him or her to write what he wills that he or she should write, in the form of 'something whispered in someone's ear'.[106] Although this is the model of revelation suggested by prophetic discourse, Ricoeur argues, it cannot be applied so appropriately to the other forms of discourse in the Bible, such as narrative, especially when those narratives are viewed in terms of their redaction history, since in this genre it is 'the force of what is said that moves the writer'.[107] In the second place, it follows from his concept of the semantic autonomy of the text that, if the Biblical texts are revealed by God, this revelatory power must be a property of the world proposed by those texts, since it is this world to which they refer and which we appropriate for ourselves in the present in interpreting them. Ricoeur writes:

If the Bible can be said to be revealed, this is to be said of the "thing" it says, of the new being it unfolds. I would then venture to say that the Bible is revealed to the extent that the new being that is in question is itself *revealing* with respect to the world, to all of reality, including my existence and my history.[108]

If the Bible mediates God's self-revelation to us, according to Ricoeur's theory of the text, it can do so only through the possible world it opens up to us, that is, to the extent that this possible world seems to me actually to explain and to ground the world of my experience as I understand it thus far.

Thirdly, Ricoeur argues that the Bible is the same kind of text as 'literary' texts, poetic and fictional, whose projected world is distanced from that of everyday reality. The world of a literary text is not that of the familiar objects of perception or those determined by scientific standards of measurement. This is also true of the world of the Biblical text, Ricoeur claims. He writes, 'The new being projected by the Biblical text opens its way across the world of ordinary experience and in spite of the closed nature of that experience.'[109] This means that the Bible is a 'poetic' text, in the strong sense of the word defined by Ricoeur, a redescription of reality at the level of our lived experience of it, opening up a reality of the possible 'across the ruins of the intraworldly objects of everyday existence and of science'.[110] It is in this sense that Ricoeur can call the Bible 'one of the great poems of existence', and assert that 'it is by listening to this book to the very end, as to one book among others, that it can be encountered as the word of God'.[111]

Nevertheless, the Biblical texts are not only a species of poetic texts, for Ricoeur. In a long essay on New Testament interpretation, 'Biblical Hermeneutics' (1975), he argues that the Biblical texts he considers display certain characteristics which determine them as religious language. He argues that 'religious language *modifies* poetic language by various procedures such as intensification, transgression, and going to the limit'.[112] Ricoeur calls these procedures 'limit-expressions', by which he means that they take a given form of expression beyond its ordinary limits. He examines Jesus' parables, proverbial sayings and proclamatory sayings, and in each case argues that these discourses are characterized by a kind of internal 'transgression', by which they are made to 'point beyond their immediate signification toward the Wholly Other'.[113] In Jesus' proclamatory sayings, for example, he uses the apocalyptic form of discourse, and at the same time transgresses the boundaries of that form. Apocalyptic, Ricoeur argues, pertains to chronological order, and addresses the question of when the end of the present order will come. When Jesus proclaims that the kingdom of God is 'close at hand' and 'in the midst of you', however, he refuses to 'calculate the time' or to 'interpret the symbol of "the coming kingdom" in terms of literal temporality'.[114] The apocalyptic form of which he makes use, therefore, is 'simultaneously employed, transgressed and upset by its new usage'.[115] In the same way, Ricoeur argues, the 'extravagance' of the parables, that is, their portrayal of the 'extraordinary within the ordinary', simultaneously employs and transgresses the conventions of the realistic story form. He writes, 'The parables tell stories that could have happened..., but it is this realism of situations, characters and plots that precisely heightens the eccentricity of the modes of behaviour to which the kingdom of God is compared.'[116]

In religious discourse, Ricoeur argues, these limit-expressions are characterized by a process that, following Ian Ramsey, he describes as that of 'models and qualifiers'.[117] In *Religious Language* (1957), Ramsey argued that theological language, especially in formulating attributes and characteristics of God, functions by positing a 'model' in whose terms human experience can be understood, and then by 'qualifying' that model. So, in negative theology, if God is said to be 'immutable', a model, according to which 'everything changes', is posited, only to be qualified by the concept, 'but not everything'. The qualifier suggests that 'something more' can be developed from the model – in this case, the fact that everything changes can be understood in such a way that there is one thing which does not – so that 'the logical meaning gives way to a *disclosure*'.[118] It is precisely this logic of model and qualifier that Ricoeur argues is at work in the Biblical forms of discourse he has considered, and which determines them as religious discourse. In each case, he writes, the discourse functions as a model in whose terms reality can be conceived, in the sense that it redescribes reality in the mode of fiction. This model is qualified, in the case of Jesus' sayings, by the term 'the kingdom of God', which is the common referent of the parables, the proverbs and the proclamatory sayings. The redescription of reality which they effect as limit-expressions, that is, is further developed by their being related back to the referent 'the kingdom of God'.

It is this qualification of the model constituted by a poetic discourse – in the Bible as a whole, it is the term 'God' which functions as the qualifier to which all the literary forms are related back – that constitutes it as religious discourse, for Ricoeur. The referent of such discourse, he argues, insofar as it constitutes a limit-expression, is to be found in the 'corresponding characteristic of human experience that we can call a limit-experience', that is, experience which transcends the limits of ordinary experience.[119] Religious language, he writes, opens up a distinction 'between ordinary experience, considered globally, and the discernment worked by this language at the heart of this ordinary experience'.[120] Just as the qualifier 'God' disrupts and reorients the model in whose terms human experience as a whole can be understood, so its referent is precisely that kind of experience which disrupts and reorients our ordinary experience. Ricoeur writes:

> The characteristic qualifier of religious language dislocates our project of making a whole of our lives – a project which St. Paul identifies with the act of 'self-glorification' or, in short, 'salvation by works'.[121]

Religious language, that is, conceived as a limit-expression which works on the basis of model and qualifier, refers ultimately, through its qualifier, to those limit-experiences in which the whole of our experience and our understanding of it is disrupted and reoriented.

Ricoeur's final application of his hermeneutics to Biblical interpretation concerns the significance for the latter of his concept of appropriation. He argues that religious faith, insofar as it is engendered by the Biblical message, is constituted by the new world proposed by the text. He acknowledges that faith is also 'an *act* irreducible to all linguistic treatment', but adds that it 'cannot be separated from the movement of interpretation that raises it to the level of language'.[122] If it were not for the discursive constitution of a world into which I could project my ultimate concern, that is, this concern would 'remain a weak and inarticulated feeling'.[123]

Ricoeur is right to claim that the Bible is read as one text among others, and that his theory of interpretation holds true for Biblical interpretation. He is right, therefore, to point out that the reference of the Biblical texts is determined by their sense, which is itself determined in part by their form. He is also right to claim that the world proposed by the Biblical texts is experienced in the same way as that of all texts, and that it opens up the reader's experience of the world as a whole according to the dialectic of self-understanding in whose terms I described literary texts above. Ricoeur does not seem to me adequately to account for the truth-claim which distinguishes the Biblical from literary texts, however, inasmuch as he presupposes the assimilation of the referential function of Bible to that of poetic, or non-descriptive, texts. His reason for doing this is that the most characteristic elements of the world proposed by the Bible, insofar as these are supernatural, are not elements of the world of ordinary perception or of science. Whilst this is true, the world of given objects is suspended in a different way in the Bible than in literary texts, inasmuch as many of the Biblical texts nevertheless claim to be descriptive, that is, to refer at the level of the world of given objects, in a way which literary texts do not. Indeed, the Biblical texts are constituted by a complex interaction between what Ricoeur calls first-order and second-order reference, inasmuch as they refer to supernatural objects, which are given neither to ordinary perception nor to science, as existing in and interacting with the world precisely of ordinary perception and of science. This is the essence of the evangelical accounts of the miracles, for example, or of the resurrection – events which are not given in ordinary experience are described as events precisely of such experience. In this sense, Ricoeur is right to say that religious language is distinct from poetic language inasmuch as it refers, by way of limit-expressions characterized by the logic of model and qualifier, to limit-experiences, that is, to aspects of human experience which transcend the limits of that experience as it is ordinarily understood. The world proposed by the Biblical texts, that is, is distinct from those proposed by literary texts inasmuch as it claims to constitute the ground of the world of the reader's experience in general.

5.5   Fish: interpretive communities

In *Is There a Text in This Class?* (1980), Stanley Fish develops a theory of interpretation based on the concept of interpretive communities. In 'Literature in the Reader', the first essay in the collection, Fish states the case for a method of criticism which attends not to the objective structure of the text but to the process in which the reader responds to the text. He calls this method 'affective stylistics', that is, analysis of the effect upon the reader of the style in which the text is composed. It is a mode of criticism which asks 'What does this word, phrase, sentence, paragraph, chapter, novel, play, poem, *do*?', rather than, 'What does it mean?', since, for Fish, the latter question can be answered only fully by asking the former. The meaning of a text, that is, is not reducible to its logical content, but consists in the reader's complex experience of response to the text as he reads it. Meaning, for Fish, is not an objective property of an utterance but an event, in which someone makes sense of an utterance. The value of reader-response criticism, which describes precisely this process of making sense, he writes, is 'predicated on the idea of *meaning as an event*, something that is happening between the words and in the reader's mind'.[124] Such criticism can therefore be defined as 'an analysis of the developing responses of the reader in relation to the words as they succeed one another in time'.[125]

Fish conceives of reader-response criticism as a corrective to the formalism of the New Criticism, which was still influential during the period of his early work. Formalism, he argues, takes no account of the experience of the reader which is in fact constitutive of the meaning of a text. This is what he means when he writes that 'commentators and editors have been asking the wrong questions and that a new set of questions based on new assumptions must be formulated'.[126] In 'Interpreting the *Variorum*', Fish states his opposition to the assumptions on which formalist criticism is based, 'the assumptions that there is a sense, that it is embedded or encoded in the text, and that it can be taken in at a single glance'.[127] As he reflects upon his own method of criticism, however, he comes to realize that it too is based on a set of assumptions, and therefore cannot claim that the phenomena to which it attends have any more objective a mode of existence than those to which formalism attends. In the first part of the essay, he writes, 'I argue that a bad (because spatial) model had suppressed what was really happening, but by my own declared principles the notion "really happening" is just one more interpretation.'[128] Everything in a text, Fish comes to argue, whether its formal features, its author's intention or the patterns of response it invites in a reader, appears to the reader as a result of the interpretive strategies that he puts into action in reading it. This is what he means when he writes, of a previous reader-response analysis, 'I did what critics always do: I "saw" what my interpretive principles permitted or directed me to see, and then I turned around and attributed what I had "seen" to a text and an intention.'[129] In fact, Fish claims, everything that a reader perceives in a text is a result not of its objective existence there but rather of the ways in which the reader is predisposed to perceive it. He concludes with the thesis that 'the form of the reader's experience, formal units and the structure of intention are one, that they come into view simultaneously', as the reader performs the act of interpretation.[130]

Clearly, this raises the question, what is textual interpretation an interpretation *of*? Fish writes, 'I cannot answer that question, but neither, I would claim, can anyone else', since there are no terms in which one could describe that which precedes interpretation which are not themselves already interpretations of it. However critics may describe the objective data of interpretation, Fish argues, these 'do not lie innocently in the world but are themselves constituted by an interpretive act, even if, as is often the case, that act is unacknowledged'.[131] He writes, 'The choice is never between objectivity and interpretation but between an interpretation that is unacknowledged as such and an interpretation that is at least aware of itself.'[132] This position raises further questions, which lead Fish to the concept of interpretive communities. Firstly, if no objectively available phenomena precede the act of interpretation, why is it that readers often agree on the form or meaning of a text? Secondly, why does the same reader perform different acts of interpretation when interpreting different texts? Both facts seem to derive from the priority of the text. In fact, Fish argues, this is not the case. Rather, they derive from the priority of the interpretive strategies the readers use in each instance. In the first place, if two readers agree on the interpretation of a single text, this is not because they are both recognizing objectively existent features of that text, for Fish, but because they are both using the same methods of interpreting it. The history of literary criticism makes clear that different readers respond in very different ways to what is apparently the same text according to the interpretive principles they use as a result of their different historical situations. In the second place, Fish argues, if a single reader performs different interpretive acts when interpreting different texts, this is again not because of any objectively recognizable differences in the texts, but because the set of interpretive rules he employs demands that different texts be interpreted in different ways. Fish points out that there are many critical methods, including his own, which read many apparently different texts in the same way.

Why then should two or more readers ever come to agree on the meaning of a text by using the same interpretive strategies to make sense of it? Fish argues that it is because such strategies are not the product of individual choice but the shared conventions of social groups or communities. It is by virtue of an individual's membership of a given set of such communities that he acquires the principles in whose terms he interprets texts. Fish calls such groups 'interpretive communities', that is, communities whose defining characteristics determine the ways in which their members are predisposed to interpret texts. He writes, 'Interpretive communities are made up of those who share interpretive strategies not for reading (in the conventional sense) but for writing texts, for constituting their properties and assigning their intentions.'[133] If two readers interpret the same text in the same way because they share the same interpretive strategies, this is not because they have both chosen the same strategies but because they are members of the same interpretive community. Again, if two readers interpret what is apparently the same text in different ways, it is because they belong to different interpretive communities. We are all members of numerous interpretive communities, for Fish, since we are all members of numerous distinct social groups. In *Doing What Comes Naturally* (1989), he writes, 'Each one of us is a member of innumerable interpretive communities in relation to which different kinds of belief are operating with different weight and force.'[134] Fish lists some of the numerous social roles he himself occupies – he is white, male, a teacher, a literary critic, a member of a law faculty, a Jew, a Democrat, and so on – and argues, 'In each of these roles...my performance flows from some deeply embedded (I don't have to consult or apply it) sense of an enterprise, some conviction by which I am (quite literally) grasped concerning the point and purpose of being a member of the enterprise.'[135] The convictions shared by each of the various communities of which one individual is a member may of course come into conflict in that individual, in which case he will interpret a given text on the basis of a negotiation between these conflicting principles. Fish writes, 'One is often "conflictually" constrained, that is, held in place by a sense of a situation as requiring negotiation between conflicting demands that seem equally legitimate.'[136] The conventions shared by each community, Fish argues, which determine the ways in which its members are predisposed to interpret, are not fixed laws but are continually being developed through the practice of interpretation. New data appear that the existing conventions do not seem adequately to account for, and interpreters develop new methods out of the existing set in order to explain them. Fish writes, 'A new interpretive strategy always makes its way in some relationship of opposition to the old, which has often marked out a negative space (of things that aren't done) from which it can emerge into respectability.'[137] Furthermore, each interpretive community contains a complex network of sub-communities, each of which is characterized by conventions which determine the interpretive strategies of its members. The institution of academic literary criticism is Fish's initial example of an interpretive community, and he thinks of the various schools of critical theory within it as sub-communities.

In 'Is There a Text in This Class?', Fish illustrates his argument that the meaning of an utterance or text is determined by the interpretive strategies shared by interpretive communities rather than by the utterance or text itself. He gives an example of a student's question to a colleague of his, asked on the first day of a literature class, 'Is there a text in this class?'. Initially, the lecturer understands the utterance to mean, 'Is there a set text in this class?', but the student corrects him, since she really means, 'Do we believe in the independent existence of texts in this class?' What this example shows, Fish argues, is that the sentence in question has neither one normative meaning nor an indefinite plurality of meanings. It has in fact 'two literal meanings', one in the lecturer's first interpretation of it, another in his second.[138] In the first instance, he interprets it in terms of his knowledge of what occurs on the first days of literature classes, and in the second in terms of disputed issues in literary theory. In both cases, Fish argues, the meaning of the utterance is determined by the structure of assumptions and beliefs within which it is interpreted. Both interpretations, he writes, are performed on the basis of publicly available norms, which make communication possible; 'it is just that these norms are not embedded in the language (where they may be read out by anyone with sufficiently clear, that is, unbiased eyes) but inhere in an institutional structure within which one hears utterances as already organized with reference to certain assumed purposes and goals'.[139] The lecturer and the student quickly come to understand one another because they are both members of the interpretive community of academic literary criticism. The structure of beliefs and assumptions in whose terms the student intended her question to be understood was precisely the structure within which the lecturer came to understand it. In the first instance, he interpreted the question within a basic structure of assumptions determined by his situation in an interpretive community, and in the second case within a more precise structure of assumptions determined in the same way. 'He has not misread the text', Fish writes, but 'mis*pre*read the text, and if he is to correct himself he must make another predetermination of the structure of interests from which the question issues'.[140] He is able to do so without the necessity of a long explanation because he already has the set of assumptions at his disposal within which the question was intended to be understood, and this is because he is a member of the same interpretive community as the speaker. Fish writes, 'The hearer is already in a situation informed by tacitly known purposes and goals, and . . . he ends up in another situation whose purposes and goals stand in some elaborated relation (of contrast, opposition, expansion, extension) to those they supplant.'[141]

The conclusion to be drawn from this analysis, Fish argues, is that 'meanings come already calculated, not because of norms embedded in the language but because language is always perceived, from the very first, within a structure of norms'.[142] This structure is social in nature, and therefore changes from one interpretive community to another. Clearly, this means that there are as many norms and standards of interpretation as there are interpretive communities, and that there are no transcendental norms and standards by which to judge between them. Fish writes, 'The positing of context- or institution-specific norms surely rules out the possibility of a norm whose validity would be recognized by everyone, no matter what his situation.'[143] Nevertheless, he argues, whilst this may be generally true, 'it is beside the point for any particular individual, for since everyone is situated somewhere, there is no-one for whom the absence of an asituational norm would be of any practical consequence'.[144] Although there are no interpretive standards that are not those of a particular interpretive community, that is, since everyone is a member of a complex set of interpretive communities, there is no-one for whom this fact could be a limitation of the validity of his or her interpretive standards. This is what Fish means when he writes that 'no one can *be* a relativist', that no-one is in fact indifferent to the beliefs and values which he holds, however much he may recognize that others hold and have held very different beliefs and values. It is true that one can change one's beliefs, but even then the new beliefs continue to have the same normative force as convictions that the previous beliefs had. Fish writes, 'There is never a moment when one believes nothing, when consciousness is innocent of any and all categories of thought, and whatever categories of thought are operative at a given moment will serve as an undoubted ground.'[145] If the theory of interpretive communities is not relativistic, Fish argues, it is not solipsistic either. As we have already seen, it is not Fish's claim that the categories of an individual's thought are the product of individual choice, so that each individual would remain in the circle of his own beliefs, unable to communicate with others on the basis of shared beliefs. In fact, Fish argues, an individual's assumptions and opinions are, in one sense, not his own at all. He writes, 'He is not their origin (in fact it might be more accurate to say that they are his); rather it is their prior availability which delimits in advance the paths that his consciousness can possibly take.'[146] It is the interpretive communities within which individuals are situated which determine the categories in whose terms they interpret utterances and texts. The lecturer and the student communicate on the basis of shared interpretive strategies, but these strategies are their own, Fish writes, only in the sense that 'as actors within an institution, they automatically fall heir to the institution's way of making sense, its systems of intelligibility'.[147] Hence he can claim that interpreters do not act as individuals but as 'extensions of an institutional community'.[148] Indeed, he argues, 'the self does not exist apart from the communal and conventional categories of thought that enable its operations (of thinking, seeing, reading)'.[149] Insofar as the interpretive communities of which we are members fashion the ways in which we think, that is, they can also be said to fashion us. Fish writes, 'To the list of made or constructed objects we must add ourselves, for we no less than the poems and assignments we see are the products of social and cultural patterns of thought.'[150]

The concept of the interpretive community is not precisely defined in Fish's work, largely because he develops it in addressing specific hermeneutic problems rather than in constructing a general hermeneutic theory. As it stands, there are flaws in his theory of interpretation. In the first place, he overstates the case for the total determination of the meaning of an utterance by the interpretive strategies an interpreter uses. It is true that utterances have different senses according to the different contexts in which an interpreter understands them to have been uttered, but interpretation remains interpretation of an utterance, and the selection and combination of the linguistic units of this utterance determine an interpreter's strategies as well as *vice versa*. For example, I have learnt to interpret novels and history books in different ways as a result of the interpretive communities in which I am situated, but, within this situation, it is on the basis of textual signals that I recognize the difference between a novel and a history book. Furthermore, it is in part precisely because of these textual signals that the communities in which I am situated have come to believe in the differences between novels and history books in the first place. There is a dialectical relationship, that is, between the meaning of texts and the ways in which communities of interpreters are predisposed to interpret them. It is because he does not acknowledge this relationship that Fish does not answer the question why an interpretive community should share the particular set of interpretive strategies by which it is characterized, as opposed to another set, at any given time. This is the major objection to his claim that meaning is entirely determined by the interpretive strategies shared by interpretive communities. He acknowledges that these strategies change throughout history, but does not give a convincing account of why they do so. Such an account would have to recognize that changes in social, political and cultural history determine the nature of the beliefs and values characteristic of historical communities. These historical changes are themselves mediated to and throughout communities by language, which is to repeat the point that the interpretive strategies of a community are determined by the language of historical communities as well as *vice versa*, as Fish claims.

Given that Fish's concept of interpretive communities needs to be supplemented by an account of the determination of their characteristic interpretive strategies, the concept is an important one in the formulation of a Christian literary theory. Fish is right to claim that everyone is a member of numerous distinct social groups, each of which determines the beliefs and values in whose terms he or she is predisposed to interpret texts. We are always already members of a complex set of interrelated communities and sub-communities, by each of which our interpretive principles are predetermined. These principles may conflict, and they may change, but there is no act of interpretation which does not take place in a social context which structures it in advance. These propositions have several consequences for Christian literary theory. In the first place, the church constitutes an interpretive community, with a complex network of sub-communities and relations to other communities with similar concerns. The church interprets the Bible as a text inspired by God, and therefore as a text in whose truth-claim one can believe. Those of its members who interpret it in this way do so because of the beliefs and values they have acquired through membership of the Christian community. Fish's theory of interpretive communities makes clear that this is not an exceptional way to interpret a text, but a case of the way in which texts are always interpreted, that is, pre-structured by the beliefs and values of the communities in which the interpreter is situated. Although many of the sub-communities of the practice of literary theory and criticism deny the truth-claim of the Bible, their members do so on the basis of the beliefs and values by which their sub-communities are characterized, that is, in the same communally deter- mined way as that in which Christians assent to its truth-claim. The belief of many of the current sub-communities of literary theory and criticism that the Bible is untrue, that is, is no more universally valid than the belief of the Christian community that it is true. Whilst it may be more normal for a member of the community of literary studies to deny the Bible's truth-claim than to assent to it, therefore, since many of its sub-communities share this denial, it is not a necessary condition of the practice of literary theory or criticism.

In fact, there is nothing intrinsic to the practices of literary theory or criticism which prevents a critic interpreting literary texts in terms determined by his membership of the Christian community as well as of the community of literary scholarship. Clearly, such interpretations will be only recognized as valid by the latter if they conform to its conventions. Nevertheless, members of many of the contemporary sub- communities of literary theory interpret texts in terms determined by the conventions both of academic literary criticism and of a given philosophical, psychological or political sub-community. There is no reason why Christian literary theory and criticism should not constitute a literary sub-community in the same way, interpreting texts according to the principles both of academic literary criticism and of Christian theology. Indeed, one objection that Fish's theory rightly removes is that the principles of the Christian community are articles of faith, that is, are believed by that community to be true. Fish rightly claims that this is the case with the principles of every interpretive community, including the contemporary sub-communities of literary theory, that they are not supra-historical truths but are rather believed to be true by that historical community.

I am now in a position to sum up my conclusions with respect to the significance of contemporary hermeneutics for the concept of Christian literary theory. I have argued that Christian literary theory and criticism are legitimate contemporary modes of literary theory and criticism, even in the postmodern culture in which the truth-claim of the Bible is largely denied. On the basis of Gadamer's hermeneutics, I have argued that Christian literary theory and criticism, insofar as they are determined in advance by an individual's acceptance of the claims of a given tradition, participate in the conditions of all literary theory and criticism, and are therefore legitimate forms of these discourses. I have further argued that this is not a conservative claim, in the sense that one could object that it fails to recognize that traditions, including Christian tradition, can be sources of ideology. On the contrary, tradition is an active process of reinterpreting the claims of the past in the light of the concerns of the present, and *vice versa*, based on precisely the kind of rational reflection upon these claims by which they can be judged ideological. The Christian critic, like all critics, is continually obliged to reflect upon his prejudices and to bring as many as possible to conscious acceptance or rejection. Nevertheless, the fact that many of his prejudices derive from a tradition does not necessarily mean that he has accepted as if true claims which are in fact ideological, but only that he shares a situation in tradition, which determines his criticism in advance, with all forms of literary theory and criticism.

I have further argued for the legitimacy of Christian literary theory and criticism on the basis of Fish's theory of interpretive communities. Every interpreter is a member of a complex and inter-related series of interpretive communities, or social groups whose defining characteristics determine the ways in which their members interpret texts. To interpret the Bible in the terms of the beliefs of the Christian community is not an exceptional way to interpret a text, therefore, but precisely an example of the way in which all texts are interpreted. Indeed, the denial of the truth-claim of the Bible by many contemporary schools of literary theory is an interpretation in terms of the characteristic beliefs of those communities in precisely the same way as the Christian affirmation of its truth-claim. To interpret literary texts from within the Christian as well as the literary community is again an example of the way in which literary texts are always interpreted, from within the complex series of communities of which any given interpreter is a member. Christian literary theory and criticism, that is, are not exceptional forms of these discourses, since they are characterized by a situation in a series of interpretive communities shared by all forms of literary theory and criticism whatever.

On the basis of Ricoeur's hermeneutics, I have formulated certain principles of literary theory. I have followed Ricoeur in claiming that discourse as such has a referential function. Literary texts, therefore, which do not claim to refer to the world of given objects, refer to a quasi-world of their own, in which the reader dwells, at the level of his or her lived experience, whilst he or she reads. To experience the world of a text in this way is to increase one's understanding of the world of one's experience as a whole. Reading a literary text constitutes the negative stage in a dialectic of self-understanding, according to which the new experience of the world of the text is incorporated into the reader's greater understanding of his experience of world as a whole. The extent of this negativity is an index of its value to the reader. I have argued that the Bible, which is experienced in the same way as other texts, shares with literary texts this property of opening up a new world to the reader, but differs from literary texts insofar as it claims that this world constitutes not only a new experience but the ground of the world of the reader's experience as a whole.

6
Christian Literary Theory

The interdisciplinary study of religion and literature, begun in the twentieth century by Christian critics such as T.S. Eliot and Helen Gardner, became an established discipline in the United States in the 1950s, and has continued to flourish up to the present day. In this section, I will examine some of the most important work in this area written in the past 20 years. The field is very diverse, and I will be examining the work both of theologians and literary critics, almost all of whom approach the question of the relations between religion and literature in different ways. My purpose is to analyse the ways in which contemporary scholars have argued that literature can be conceived and analysed from the perspective of Christian theology, and to assess the validity of these arguments for the theological literary theory towards which I am working in this book.

6.1 Christian theology and postmodern theory

Many scholars in recent years have been concerned with the nature of the truth-claim that can be made for Christian theology in the light of the critique of such theology posed by postmodern literary and cultural theories, especially deconstruction. In this section, I will examine the work of three literary critics who ask the question of the significance of postmodern theory for religious and theological language, whose potential use in literary theory and criticism they do not wish to abandon.

In his book *Justifying Language* (1995), Kevin Mills expounds St Paul's thought in the light of contemporary hermeneutics, in particular that of the debate between Ricoeur and Derrida, and argues that it constitutes the foundation of a hermeneutics based upon faith, hope and charity.

In doing so, he writes, he intends to affirm 'the viability of a critical belief which is cognizant of the array of philosophico-linguistic objections to its existence, and yet understands why faith, hope and love are able to remain in the face of this onslaught'.[1] Mills takes as his primary text 1 Cor. 13:13, 'And now these three remain [*menei*], faith, hope and love. But the greatest of these is love.' The concept of the remainder, he argues, is central to postmodern theory, denoting that which resists every attempt prior to such theory to conceive of reality in a total or systematic form. For Paul, what remains in this life, until full knowledge of reality is given in the beatific vision, are faith, hope and love. Mills sets out to expound the meaning of this concept of remainder for contemporary hermeneutics. He argues that in structural linguistics, in which language is conceived of as a closed system whose elements each acquire meaning through their difference to all the other elements, a 'prevenient faith' in the conventions by which meaning is so distributed is necessary before a speaker can make use of the system. This fact of use of the language-system, Mills points out, is the point at which Ricoeur's hermeneutics dialectically supersedes deconstruction, whose analysis remains at the level of the sign. To interpret a text, for Ricoeur, is not only to 'distanciate' oneself from it in order to construe it as a linguistic object but also to 'participate' in a linguistic event. It is at this level of participation in language, the point at which an interpreter enters the hermeneutic circle, that Mills locates what he calls 'linguistic faith', or 'the trust we place in a language we did not choose and cannot control but which binds us to its other users in a joint investment'.[2] In order even to begin the process of understanding the speech or text of another, that is, a faith in the conventions by which his utterance is constructed is necessary. Mills writes, 'To enter the hermeneutic circle is to keep faith; to refuse it is to return language to a closed system of signs, or a process of endlessly deferred signification.'[3] At Rom. 10:17, Paul writes, 'Faith comes from hearing the message, and the message is heard through the word of Christ.' Mills points out that in order for a message to be heard as the word of Christ, faith is again necessary, and so concludes that 'Paul's theorem of faith is intimately connected with the hermeneutic circle.'[4] In Paul's formulation, he writes, this means that 'faith and language constitute each other, ground each other, and will not be parted'.[5] In Ricoeur's words, 'I must believe in order to understand, and understand in order to believe.'[6]

If faith underlies every act of interpretation, Mills argues, it does so in the light of hope, namely a hope that such interpretation will lead to a genuine understanding of the meaning of a text. He writes, 'The faith which produces linguistic meaning brings along with it a hope that such meanings are justified.'[7] Mills locates the hope that understanding will take place among the 'pre-understandings' identified by Heidegger and Gadamer, which structure interpretation in advance. Its function in the hermeneutic circle as he has defined it is 'to ensure that this circle is not a vicious one', that is, to keep the act of interpretation open to possibilities of meaning not yet determined by its context.[8] Mills sets this hermeneutic principle in a cosmological context, which he derives from Moltmann's theology of hope, according to which the Resurrection is the sign of a promise that history is progressing towards an end that radically transcends the present. Mills writes, 'The futurity of the promise means that it contradicts present reality and creates a tension, an interval of hope.'[9] Christian hope in this context is what Moltmann calls 'crucified hope', that is, hope in the promise of resurrection in the face of the present reality of crucifixion. Mills identifies this hope with that of Abraham, of which Paul speaks at Rom. 4:17, in the God who 'calls things that are not as though they were'. In the light of this kind of hope, he writes, 'the appearance of the world is not allowed to totalize the future. That is to say, present reality can be read in terms of the possibility of a different kind of knowledge which it does not yet admit'.[10] In hermeneutic terms, he argues, this hope 'limits the power of tradition to determine understanding', and allows interpretation to be 'a reading for the future'.[11] The paradigm of this kind of interpretation is that of the text of one's own life in the light of conversion, which 're-orients hermeneutics ... and sets up a resistance to received ideas by virtue of an eschatological sense which unsettles the totality of presence and its determination by the past'.[12]

Mills departs from Ricoeur and the Heideggerian tradition as he expounds the meaning of Pauline charity for hermeneutics. He looks for a model of reading that results neither in Heideggerian authenticity nor the revised self-understanding of Ricoeur, but is rather 'communal, socialized and directed towards the other'.[13] In Mills' Pauline hermeneutic, language is 'a social phenomenon which is not possessed nor enclosed by any individual, nor ultimately totalizable by any élite'.[14] Mills argues that, like faith and hope, charity is implied in every act of interpretation insofar as an acknowledgement of the other precedes every such act and structures it in advance, so that 'self-understanding is subordinated to interaction'.[15] Rejecting the interiority of Augustine's concept of charity, he proposes a 'revised concept of charity', which is 'not just directed towards the other, but [remains] open to the otherness which limits and defines it'.[16] He derives such a concept from Bakhtin, who thinks of language as the product of heterogeneous, competing voices. For Bakhtin, language is irreducibly social in nature, and every utterance is determined by its speaker's social context and point of view. Mills writes, 'Meaning will thus be determined by the speaker and his/her orientation to the hearer', rather than by the system of elements posited by structural linguistics.[17] In Bakhtin's theory of language, 'To come to consciousness I must share meaning, must find myself as part of the interactive linguistic environment.'[18] Every act of interpretation, Mills argues, in the light of this theory, presupposes a commitment of charity to the other whose very otherness determines the utterance or text as such. He relates this principle to Paul's preference for prophecy in the church, which is publicly comprehensible, over speaking in tongues, which is not. Charity, or commitment to the other, is the principle by which Paul makes this judgement: 'He who speaks in a tongue edifies himself, but he who prophesies edifies the church' (1 Cor. 14:4). Mills writes, 'Language, for Paul, is encounter with the other; locution is interlocution. Charity is the foundation of interpretation, the condition of its possibility.'[19] As a hermeneutic principle, he argues, charity underlies both utterance and interpretation as acts essentially structured in advance by the encounter with the other which they constitute.

It is difficult to accept Mills' claim that these hermeneutic principles derive from Paul's letters. It is true, as he points out, that Paul is frequently concerned with textual interpretation, performing many complex readings of the Old Testament, each of which implies an unstated theory. Nevertheless, it is difficult explicitly to identify such a theory with Paul's concept of the virtues of faith, hope and charity. Hence, when Mills claims that 'contemporary literary theory, for all its rhetorical sophistication, has not progressed beyond Paul's first-century hermeneutic', I do not agree that the hermeneutic principles Mills develops can be attributed as such to the intention of Paul.[20] Given that his thesis represents a contemporary meditation upon faith, hope and charity rather than an exegesis of Paul himself, however, Mills develops the work of Gadamer and Ricoeur on the fundamental conditions of interpretation well. His concepts of faith, hope and charity elucidate aspects of the fore-structure of understanding in textual interpretation that the latter have not made explicit as such, and which make clear that the Christian practice of these virtues remains a rational activity in postmodern culture. We have already seen Derrida recognize the faith that underlies the interpretation of scientific discourse, which is written with the implied promise that its author is speaking truly, and Mills is right to add that a similar faith in the communicative function of language underlies every act of textual interpretation, whether of 'trust' or 'suspicion'. He is also right to add that this kind of faith is accompanied by the hope that the interpretation is justified. The faith with which the Christian reader of the Scriptures believes that he or she is hearing the word of God, therefore, is not an ideological imposition upon the text, but an example of the kind of pre-understanding which all textual interpretation presupposes. Faith in the function of language does not involve the existential commitment of Christian faith, of course, but, like the latter, it is an attitude of provisional trust in that which one cannot objectively verify. Whilst Mills does not make the difference between 'linguistic' and religious faith as clear as he might, he is right to assume their family resemblance. It is the same with hope. Christian hope in God is not of the same kind as the pre-understanding of hope that a textual interpretation is justified. Nevertheless, the former, insofar as it derives from an interpretation of the Scriptures, is an example of an attitude that underlies every act of textual interpretation, that the unverifiable object of one's faith will prove to exist, as one believes. What Mills' study shows most clearly is that hermeneutics, even in the anti-hermeneutic culture of postmodernism, continues to imply the theological categories of a cultural tradition once dominated by the Christian Scriptures.

In contrast to Mills, the work of Brian Ingraffia, although also indebted to the thought of Ricoeur, does not claim that the Biblical message contains the basis of a contemporary hermeneutics, but rather that postmodern theory has misunderstood and misrepresented that message. In *Postmodern Theory and Biblical Theology* (1995), Ingraffia argues that, if the message of the Bible is correctly interpreted, as in the tradition of the theology of the cross represented by Luther, Pascal, Kierkegaard, Barth and Moltmann, then 'an either/or must be proclaimed to the present age: either biblical theology or postmodern theory'.[21] There is no possibility of synthesizing the Biblical message with postmodern theory, for Ingraffia, because the latter at no point acknowledges this message as such, but rather assimilates it into the metaphysical category of onto-theology. In the modern period, the God whose existence Descartes proves, in the *Meditations on First Philosophy*, is 'the god of metaphysics' rather than the God of Biblical revelation, which Ingraffia writes is 'always the product of human reason, is always the result of humanity's attempt to formulate an understanding of god rather than the result of God's revelation towards us'.[22] From Feuerbach onwards, Ingraffia claims, modern and postmodern thought has defined itself against a concept of God which is in fact this rationally constructed object of onto-theology, but which it has wrongly identified with the God of Biblical revelation. He writes:

> The rejection of Christianity in both modernism and postmodernism has been for the most part based upon a profound misunderstanding of biblical revelation. Christian faith has all too easily been conflated with ontotheology in modernism and then criticized for being onto-theology in postmodernism.[23]

Ingraffia's view is that 'a Christian tradition can be identified which resists the influence of Greek and modern metaphysics', and which is based on the ultimately Hebraic categories of the Biblical message.[24] He sets out to differentiate these two theological traditions, and to show that the anti-theological attitudes of Nietzsche, Heidegger and Derrida are properly adopted only towards the metaphysical discourse of onto-theology and not towards that of Biblical revelation.

In Nietzsche's case, he argues, although Christian theology is presented as the fundamental object of critique, Nietzsche misrepresents such theology as 'Platonism for the people', that is, as a system which condemns the material, temporal world in order to privilege an ideal, eternal world which transcends it. On the contrary, Ingraffia writes, 'The distinction between this world and the world to come in the Bible is not metaphysical, but rather *eschatological*.'[25] In the first place, he argues, the Bible thinks of the world as God's creation, which he judges to be good. 'God is separate from the *kosmos* [world]', he writes, but also 'related to his creation in love and concern for his creatures'.[26] Nietzsche's condemnation of Christianity as a religion which devalues the world simply fails to take this Biblical doctrine into account. Furthermore, Ingraffia argues, although there is a sense of the New Testament term *kosmos* which has the negative connotation of humanity in rebellion against God, this implies 'no gnostic dualism in which the physical world or the physical body is inherently evil, a prison for the pure, divine soul'.[27] Rather, the 'two worlds' of Biblical doctrine refer primarily to 'a temporal, eschatological separation between the present age and the age to come'. This eschatological hope is designated by several terms, the 'age to come', the 'new heaven and new earth' and also the 'kingdom of God'. In each case, Ingraffia argues, the opposition is not a metaphysical distinction between the material and the ideal, but rather a theological one between those who have been reconciled with God and those who remain alienated from him. So, in Rom. 8:19–23, Paul writes that 'the creation itself will be liberated from its bondage to decay and brought into the glorious freedom of the children of God'. He does not speak of the redemption *from* the creation, as Nietzsche represents Christian doctrine, but rather of the redemption *of* the creation, including 'our bodies'. Again, in Phil. 3:20–21, he writes that Christ 'will transform our lowly bodies so that they will be like his glorious body'. Ingraffia concludes, 'Rather than constructing metaphysical dualisms, Paul is actually arguing against... both a cosmological and an anthropological dualism.'[28] Hence, with respect to Nietzsche's attack on the other-worldly emphasis of Christian doctrine, he writes that it 'cannot be used to condemn biblical theology, for Paul attacks the same type of other-worldly philosophy'.[29]

It has long been recognized that Heidegger, particularly in the period up to and including *Being and Time*, drew upon the categories of Christian theology, and particularly those of Pauline anthropology, to articulate the existential structures of human being. Ingraffia argues that Heidegger modifies these categories in such a way that they can no longer be recognized as Biblical. He finds a clear example of such modification in Heidegger's 1920–1921 lecture course, 'Introduction to the Phenomenology of Religion', in which the latter expounds the concept of authentic temporality from St Paul's letters to the Thessalonians. Paul writes that, with respect to 'times [*chronoi*] and dates [*kairoi*]', the Thessalonians 'know very well that the day of the Lord will come like a thief in the night' (1 Thess. 5:1–2). Heidegger comments that the question as to when Christ will return is not answered by 'any reference to objective time':

> Rather the question is, as it were, bent back and referred to factical life-experience... The question of temporality in Christian religious experience becomes a matter of how one lives one's facticity.[30]

The authentic temporality of original Christian experience, for Heidegger, is an attitude taken up with respect to existence here and now rather than a historical expectation of Christ's return. Clearly, this is to emphasize only a part of Paul's eschatology. Ingraffia writes:

> By interpreting *parousia* in Paul's letters as referring not to a future event but to the time of an existential decision, Heidegger has turned the historical, temporal term of Paul's Judaeo-Christian thought into an a-historical, a-temporal Greek term.[31]

Under the influence of liberal theology, Ingraffia argues, for which belief in a life after death was part of the anachronistic, mythical world-view of the New Testament, Heidegger addresses the Hebraic eschatology of the Bible as if it were a Greek philosophy of present existence.

In the analysis of *Dasein* in *Being and Time*, Heidegger continues to use the formal structures of the categories of Biblical anthropology in order to describe the elements of fundamental ontology. Although he claims that such formal indications are theologically neutral, Ingraffia argues that they distort the meaning of the Biblical concepts beyond recognition as such. He writes:

> While the language of *Being and Time* does reflect the influence of Judaeo-Christian theology in Heidegger's *Dasein*-analysis, the distortions of Christian theology belie not a theological but rather an anti-theological motivation.[32]

The fundamental distinction between modes of human existence in Paul's thought is that between a life grounded in God and a life grounded in oneself. This is the meaning of the Pauline distinction between 'flesh' and 'Spirit', Ingraffia argues, 'those who live by their own being and those who live for God'.[33] This opposition does not correspond to Heidegger's fundamental distinction between authentic and inauthentic modes of human existence, since the authentic self in Heidegger is precisely one's own, and even results from a call from one's own self. In Paul's thought, by contrast, the Christian can say, 'I have been crucified with Christ; and it is no longer I who live, but Christ who lives in me' (Gal. 2:20). As Ingraffia comments, 'The ego of the old life has been crucified with Christ, and the "I" of the new self is ... the surrender of the self to the lordship of the crucified and resurrected Jesus Christ.'[34] For Heidegger, the inauthentic self has 'fallen' from relationship with the authentic self, and become subject to 'the They', whereas in Paul's concept of the life of the flesh, the self has fallen from relationship with God and become subject to sin. Heidegger takes mankind's relationship to God out of the structure of the Biblical concepts of man, and as a result, Ingraffia argues, entirely alters their significance. In Heidegger's concept of authentic existence, one lives according to the commands of one's own self, above all accepting one's death as one's own. In Paul's thought, by contrast, living according to one's self is a characteristic of the life of the flesh, of the *sarkikos anthrôpos*, whereas it is by contrast a mark of life in the Spirit, of the *pneumatikos anthrôpos*, to hope to participate in the Resurrection of Christ. Hence Ingraffia concludes:

> Although he bases much of his analysis on insights gathered from the New Testament, Heidegger's hermeneutic of Dasein's authentic self must be rejected by Christian theology because his ontological structures ... are incompatible with the Biblical conception of faithful existence.[35]

Finally, in tracing Derrida's concept of theology, Ingraffia focuses on the concept of logos which he uses to articulate the notion of logocentrism as a characteristic of the Western metaphysical tradition. He argues that Derrida 'has only recognized the Johannine logos as it has been distorted through Greek and Hegelian conceptuality', that is, as a metaphysical category which grounds the self-presence of the subject.[36] The Biblical concept, by contrast, precisely questions the validity of any philosophy which would ground truth and meaning in the individual human subject. Whilst the author of the fourth gospel draws upon the metaphysical senses of the Hellenic term 'logos', that is, his incorporation of the term into his distinctive Christological assertions gives it a new sense altogether, whose difference from the Stoic and Middle Platonic uses of the term Derrida does not acknowledge. Derrida makes what Ingraffia calls a 'leap of unfaith' in concluding from the deconstruction of the concept of self-presence in the theory of consciousness, and so of the category of logos which expresses that self-presence, that he has thereby deconstructed the Biblical and Christian concept of Christ as the Logos of God. In fact, he has done no such thing, Ingraffia argues. Indeed the autonomous concept of the self, which is the object of deconstruction, is a feature of precisely the Enlightenment rationalism with which the modern critique of Christian theology can be said to begin. Commenting on Derrida's view that 'God is the name and element of that which makes possible an absolutely pure and absolutely self-present self-knowledge', Ingraffia writes:

> The God written about in the Bible is completely different from this man-made god. The God revealed in the Bible does not make possible, but rather makes impossible an absolutely pure and absolutely self-present self-knowledge.[37]

As I argued in Chapter 2, Derrida, especially in his earlier works, identifies the concept of God as it functions in systems of rationalist and idealist metaphysics with the God of Biblical revelation and Christian theology in an untenable way. In fact, as Ingraffia emphasizes, the God of the Biblical revelation, far from functioning as the ground of the autonomy of the self, judges precisely such autonomy as an illusion and as sin.

Ingraffia's central claim with respect to the postmodern critique of theology in general, and of Christian theology in particular, that is, that it is largely based on a misrepresentation of that theology, is true. As we saw in the discussion of Derrida's concept of theology in Chapter 2, the latter's critique is in fact applicable only to onto-theology, or to the concept of God as it is used to ground certain metaphysical systems, although it is on the whole presented as if it applied to Christian theology as a whole. Ingraffia's arguments with respect to Nietzsche, the founder of postmodern thought, and Heidegger are well made, and supplement this case. He rightly shows that Nietzsche's critique of Christian theology cannot be said to apply to a recognizably Biblical theology, since the Bible does not express or even imply a dualistic metaphysics in which the spiritual realm is privileged over against the material. One might add that it was against precisely such dualistic systems that Christian theology early defined itself as such against both Gnosticism and Manichaeism. He is also right to argue that the categories which Heidegger derives from the structure of New Testament thought, whether explicitly, as in his lectures on Paul's epistles, or implicitly, as in *Being and Time*, are so secularized as no longer to represent the distinctive content of the Biblical categories from which they are derived. Despite the influence of existentialist theology, therefore, it would be difficult to use Heidegger's thought as a framework in which an authentically Biblical theology can be expressed. Ingraffia thus carves out a space for Christian theology in postmodern culture insofar as he shows that the fundamental critiques of such theology do not apply to the Biblical revelation as such, but only to the assimilation of that revelation into onto-theology. The difficulty with his approach rests in his use of the term 'Biblical theology', by which he means the message of the Bible itself, which he thinks of as fundamentally Hebraic, as opposed to interpretations of that message in the terms of Greek philosophical first principles. Whilst one can certainly distinguish between the onto-theologies of metaphysics and the Biblical gospel, one cannot absolutely distinguish between the Biblical text and its interpretations, which are necessarily structured in advance by the interpreter's beliefs and first principles. Ingraffia writes from a broadly Reformed perspective, and identifies the tradition through which he comes to the Bible as 'the theology of the cross . . . recovered in the great tradition of theology represented by thinkers such as Luther, Pascal, Kierkegaard, Barth and Moltmann'.[38] Whilst I agree that the contents of Ingraffia's 'Biblical theology' are indeed authentically Biblical, it must be added that this theology cannot be thought of simply as the self-evident meaning of the Bible, as opposed to later interpretations of that meaning in terms of non-Biblical philosophies, since, as Ricoeur has rightly argued, any interpretation of the Bible must necessarily use such an extra-Biblical hermeneutic framework. Whilst 'Biblical theology' remains a rationally legitimate way in postmodern culture of thinking about the world and the place of men and women in it, this cannot be conceived as the pure message of the Bible as opposed to its interpretations in terms of philosophical principles vulnerable to the postmodern critique, but rather as the theological reflection upon and the proclamation of that message in the contemporary community of Christian faith. This is perhaps a minor point with respect to the significance of Ingraffia's insight that the postmodern critique of theology has so far failed to address Christian theology as such, but worth spelling out nevertheless. What remains an intellectually legitimate world-view after Nietzsche, Heidegger and Derrida is not the view present in the Biblical text alone, but that proclaimed by the Christian church as it reflects upon and interprets that text in contemporary society.

A third approach to the relationship of Christian theology to the postmodern critique of such theology it is that of Valentine Cunningham, in the final chapter of his *In the Reading Gaol* (1994). The argument of the book is that the use of language, especially in literature, implies the existence not only of a system of intra-linguistic relations, as both structuralism and post-structuralism have stressed, but also a relationship between language and the external world. In the final chapter, Cunningham argues that post-structuralist theory, despite appearing to constitute a radical critique of theology, is in fact deeply indebted to the Christian theological tradition, insofar as the latter constitutes a culturally dominant framework in whose terms much contemporary theory is still expressed. He writes, 'Our linguistics, our critical theory, our writing, are all performed under the shadow of our traditional Graeco-Christian metaphysics.'[39] In the first place, postmodern theories continue to negotiate with religious questions and texts. In *The Truth in Painting*, for example, Derrida argues that, in Kant's *Religion within the Limits of Reason Alone*, religion functions as the characteristically deconstructive supplement or 'parergon' of reason. Indeed, the role of 'transcendent exteriority' which Kant ascribes to religion in that work is a category with which deconstruction continually negotiates. In a similar way, Roland Barthes devotes considerable attention to Scriptural texts, recognizing even as he analyses them in the exclusively linguistic terms of structuralism and post-structuralism that they themselves insistently postulate a referential function. Indeed, the very concepts of the text and of writing, Cunningham argues, are indebted to the privileged position assigned to the Biblical text in the history of Western thought (the French term *écriture*, as we have seen, denoting both 'writing' and 'Scripture'). The concept of the infinitely meaningful text resurfaces in postmodernism as the dream-text in Freudian theory and as the text of *Finnegan's Wake*. As Cunningham points out, Joyce's desire that the latter should constitute a kind of rival Scriptures has been very much respected by his postmodern critics, such as Derrida. Even Derrida's concept of the double-bind of deconstruction, in which metaphysical language is necessarily used in order to deconstruct precisely such language, he argues, can be found in the Bible. Derrida's 'two interpretations of interpretation', that of the rabbi on the one hand, who seeks a text's final signifieds, and that of the poet on the other, who delights in the play of signifiers, are both at work in the revelation that Judaeo-Christian tradition discerns in the Bible, which on the hand reveals the truth of God and the presence of Christ, but at the same time reveals God precisely as absent and unknown. Derrida argues that there is no question of a choice between the two interpretations, just as the Bible reveals God as both present and absent, as both made known and hidden by the text. Cunningham writes, 'Silence, puzzle, *aporia*, blankness, stuttering, are as much part of Biblical theology, of Scriptural logocentrism, as their opposites.'[40] This is what he means when he says that 'Biblical logocentricity is already deconstructionist', and so that 'the "challenge of deconstruction" has been the challenge of theology'.[41] Postmodern theories of language continue to operate within the terms of the tradition of Christian theological reflection upon the Bible. Cunningham also argues that a process of 'repression', that is, of deliberately effacing the traces of this influence can be discerned in such theory, as in the readings Derrida and de Man give of Walter Benjamin's concept in 'The Task of the Translator' of the interlinear version of the sacred text as the 'model or ideal of all translation'.[42]

Cunningham is right to emphasize that it is theological questions above all with which post-structuralist theory negotiates and against which it defines itself. Heidegger's view that 'since the beginning of and throughout the modern age [Christianity] has continued to be that against which the new freedom – whether expressly or not – must be distinguished' remains true of post-structuralist theory, perhaps most clearly so in Derrida's critique of logocentrism. He is also right to point out that certain concepts which originate in the Western theological tradition, such as that of the infinitely meaningful text, continue to play a significant positive role within such theory. Perhaps the most significant theological idea repeatedly to resurface in the theory of the postmodern period is that of the other beyond language, which is a concern of numerous post-structuralist and other Continental philosophers. It would be wrong to conclude from this cultural debt of post-structuralist theory to the dominance of Christian theology in Western cultural history that there is a consequent logical debt. Postmodernism is not theology in disguise, although it is formulated in its shadow. Cunningham's most significant point is that there are aspects precisely of the postmodern critique of theology that, on a more careful consideration of the nature of the theology in question, do not apply to it as such. So, the double bind of deconstruction does not displace the possibility of theological language in general or even of Christian theology in particular, as may initially appear to be the case, but rather to articulate a problematic that was already theological. The Christian theological tradition cannot be represented as the kind of naïve or even oppressive logocentrism beyond which postmodern theory progresses, since it has in fact already formulated much of the latter's apparent critique of that tradition.

6.2 Literature in theology: Jasper and Wright

The study of literature and theology has been pursued most influentially in recent years in Britain by David Jasper, who writes as a theologian concerned to develop the significance of literary criticism and theory for the interpretation of the Bible and the practice of theology. In his first work, *Coleridge as Poet and Religious Thinker* (1985), Jasper traces the relationship of Coleridge's theological thought to his theory and practice of poetry, arguing that the two cannot fully be understood independently of one another. Basing his analysis on the belief that 'art and aesthetics can illuminate and refresh the religious life', Jasper examines the close relationship in Coleridge's thought between the nature of divine revelation and that of poetic inspiration and creativity.[43] Not only can literature not be understood apart from theology, in Coleridge's Romantic aesthetics, but 'theology begins to find a new language in literature'.[44] Jasper places Coleridge's thought in the context of European Romanticism, in which poetry is conceived of as a channel of divine revelation, and the poet as one inspired to communicate this revelation to mankind. He analyses the ways in which Coleridge understands this process to occur, in the imagination, in the symbol, and above all in the structure of 'polar logic', in which opposing phenomena can be seen to participate in a higher unity which incorporates them both. In all these ways, poetry is understood as the expression of an inspired vision into the divine unity which underlies the multiplicity of experience. Jasper writes:

> In the poem, the human and the non-human world meet at the point of visionary consciousness, and by the imaginative act of the poet, the finite is opened momentarily onto the infinite.[45]

He calls this the 'theological task of the poetic imagination', and argues that it is precisely through reflection upon its function that Coleridge's own theology, even in its later most orthodox forms, was developed. For Jasper, this represents an important insight into the practice of a theology 'free from platitude or sterile doctrine', and he concludes with an analysis of Austin Farrer, whom he argues represents a working out of Coleridge's manner of understanding divine revelation through reflection upon the poetic imagination. In *The Glass of Vision* (1948), Farrer argues that revelation takes place primarily through the images used in Scriptures, which are taken from finite experience but refer in an inspired manner beyond that experience. It is precisely in the poetry of his message, for Farrer, that the Biblical prophet communicates his divine revelation.

Jasper follows through the logic of these ideas with respect to New Testament interpretation in *The New Testament and the Literary Imagination* (1987). In this book, he argues that the New Testament texts should be read primarily as literature, and that it is precisely as such, as structured and symbolic works of the imagination, that they reveal the mystery of the ultimate realities with which they are concerned. 'By a close attention to what the evangelists and apostolic writers wrote, we may draw a little closer to the mystery which inspired them.'[46] Rejecting the possibility of reconstructing the facts of the New Testament narratives as historical documents in the light of the failure of the 'quest of the historical Jesus', but not prepared finally to abandon the significance of the historical life of Jesus for Christian faith, Jasper argues that the true significance of New Testament accounts of the life of Jesus is the role he plays in the *literary* framework of the salvation history which they construct. Jasper conceives this history primarily as a genre of narrative, and so describes the New Testament as 'mythical literature rather than as history', whose function as such is to 'explore the relationship and rupture between the finite and the infinite'.[47] It is in the imaginative response to this literature, in reading the Bible and in liturgical worship, that we encounter Jesus Christ as the point of this relationship and rupture. On the basis of this understanding of revelation, Jasper conducts a thorough investigation of the literary techniques of the New Testament and the manner in which they mediate issues of ultimate concern to us. The images and metaphors it employs, for example, whether the apocalyptic imagery of Revelation or the Pauline concept of adoption, are 'finally irreducible and untranslatable, but are alive with inexhaustible significance'.[48] Again, the hyperbolic devices in the parable of the Prodigal Son, in Jasper's analysis, contribute to a 'style that is stretched to the point where the images of human life break through into a perception of a greater love and a greater forgiveness', that speaks more profoundly to the imagination than doctrinal abstractions from the story.[49] Jasper goes so far as to suggest that 'the resurrection is a truth of the imagination', insofar as the Biblical narratives of the event speak more profoundly to the human imagination than to historical reason. 'The poetry of the description liberates our imaginations to reflect upon the moment of inspiration' which produced it. Each individual, rather than any ecclesiastical or academic institution, must make the decision for himself as to whether such poetry is divinely inspired, based upon whether it carries his imagination beyond the poetry itself into the presence of the ultimate concerns which it intimates. Jasper concludes:

> Our primary response must be to [the Scriptures] as language, as structures of words which may indicate to us, without finalising, the meaning of the mysterious event of Jesus Christ.[50]

In *The Study of Literature and Religion* (1989) and subsequent works, Jasper brings contemporary literary theory, especially deconstruction, to the analysis of Scriptural and theological language in the way that he had previously used more traditional categories of literary criticism. Jasper surveys a wide range of traditional and contemporary ways in which the relationship between literature and religion has been conceived, with the broad intention of a 'revisitation of theology, returning to it through literature and recovering something of those uncomfortable ... qualities of a lack of definition, of mystery and fluidity'.[51] In an essay on 'The Limits of Formalism and the Theology of Hope', he argues that, whilst the formalist critical theories of the early and middle parts of the century emphasized an exclusive attention to the text alone, they were obliged to ground their interpretations in a series of extra-textual theoretical principles, some of which are explicitly ethical, and even theological. He concludes, 'The aesthetic value of literary autonomy is not necessarily in conflict with the theological value of relevance.'[52] He argues that these two aspects of criticism are best understood by the dialectical hermeneutics of Paul Ricoeur, and relates this dialectic to Moltmann's theology of hope, claiming that it is precisely in and through the rigorous attention to the text characteristic of formalism that its transcendent ethical and religious dimensions may appear. It is in deconstruction that he sees the greatest significance for theology, however, and for the theological understanding of literary texts, since Derrida's concept of writing means that, in any text, literary or theological, 'there are no answers, only extreme scepticism, and a continuing evasion of the self-enclosed systematising of texts by which we long to find meaning'.[53] The dogmatic interpretation of literary texts, including those of the Bible, for Jasper, which a Coleridgean view of the imagination had initially displaced, is rendered profoundly problematic by deconstruction. In a deconstructive analysis of the textuality of the discourse of theodicy, he argues that a post-structuralist concept of textuality is a way of 'releasing us from the false assumptions and presuppositions of a theological absolutism, out of which we may deconstruct our sense of the divine workings into a new sense of freedom and a new discernment of the mystery'.[54] Perhaps the most significant aspect of his analysis of theodicy as a text which necessarily deconstructs the metaphysical principles by which it is also constructed is that such analysis, preventing rational certainty concerning the problem of evil, leads to the necessity of faith. He writes, 'We need to pass beyond the fictions of finite human understanding into greater honesty, a greater commitment of faith.'[55]

The fundamental insight of Jasper's literary theory is that literature conveys theological meaning, and this is true, in several ways. I do not agree that the Biblical texts should be read primarily as literature, even in the sense that their truth is apprehended primarily by the imagination, since in the interpretive community of the church, they are granted a truth-value that fictional and imaginative texts are not. Nevertheless, Jasper is right to point out that the Bible and even Christian theology signify in similar ways to literary texts, and that the tools of literary hermeneutics can therefore be used to elucidate their meaning. The Bible uses numerous literary genres and devices to express its message, and, as Farrer says, it is precisely through these genres and devices that we apprehend the message. Literary analysis, as Jasper demonstrates, can bring out some of the multiplicity and complexity of the sense of a Biblical metaphor, symbol or narrative, for example, that would escape a logical or theological analysis. It is true, in short, that the Bible, like literary texts, speaks to the imagination and to the emotions as well as to the reason, and that literary analysis is especially suited to elucidating the ways in which it does so. Jasper is right to claim, in his study of Coleridge, that the converse is also true, that literary texts are well suited to the expression of religious and even theological insights. Typically, for Jasper, they function as critiques of orthodox or institutionalized theology, and this indeed one of their theological functions, although not, in my view, the only one. This is certainly the function of deconstruction, however, as Jasper also claims. As I have argued, one of the values of deconstruction for Christian theology is that it insists that the meaning of the Biblical texts is never finally exhausted or closed, but must continually be reinterpreted in the light of contemporary concerns and discourses, as in the light of the ultimate incomprehensibility of its referent. As Jasper says, deconstruction reminds Christian theology that it is a discourse based on faith rather than certain knowledge, and, as I have argued in Chapter 2, it follows from its logic that this is also true of every other positive discourse.

Another influential work which surveys some of the ways in which the relationship between literature and religion has been and can still be conceived is T.R. Wright's *Theology and Literature* (1988). Writing as a literary critic, Wright argues that literary works 'can express important theological truths', in a way that makes of them a significant complement to theological reflection as such, since they 'recognize more fully [than such reflection] their own limitations as constructs of imagination and ideology'.[56] Wright sets out to examine 'the literary forms adopted by faith', that is, the ways in which theological insights are conveyed through such forms. Wright suggests that most critics would agree that a literary work is one whose meaning is not susceptible to paraphrase without loss – that it 'says something about life which cannot be said in any other way'.[57] On the basis of this axiom, he argues that, insofar as literary forms are used in theological discourse, including the text of the Bible, they express theological insights that cannot be conveyed in any other way. He writes, 'It is because no language is completely transparent upon reality, providing unambiguous "names" for clear-cut "things", that the indirect mode of reference employed in literature constitutes some of the most effective theology.'[58] This is not to reduce the referential dimension of theological language, he stresses, but rather to argue that it is precisely through 'literary' devices and techniques, such as metaphor, symbol, narrative, and so on, that theology can refer most truly to the ultimately incomprehensible reality which is its object. Wright begins by applying this insight to the texts of the Bible, not in order to refuse its claim to be a revelation of God's action in history which demands a human response, but rather 'to appreciate how [these claims] are made'.[59] After surveying the recent exegetical approaches to the Bible that have drawn upon the insights of formalism, structuralism and deconstruction, Wright offers literary analyses of the texts of Genesis and St Mark's gospel. He examines the methods of characterization, especially the elliptic series of intimations by the narrator of the psychological states and motivations of Adam and Eve in the story of the Fall, in order to draw the conclusion that, by these methods, 'readers are positively encouraged to fill the psychological gaps imaginatively, ... involving them in the process of exploring sinful human nature'.[60] Again, with respect to the apparently abrupt ending of St Mark's gospel in the most ancient manuscripts at Mk. 16:8, 'for they were afraid', Wright argues that the effect of this ending is that readers are forced to supply their own ending to the story. Mark's original readers, like us, must have been familiar with the tradition of resurrection appearances, Wright argues, but 'any reader is forced at this point to leave the world of the story for the "real" world of history'.[61] The ending of the gospel, especially abrupt in the Greek construction *ephobounto gar*, makes of it something like a self-consuming artefact, a story which finally points beyond its own represented world to the historical world to which it refers, so that its readers are confronted with the call to 'follow for themselves the difficult road of discipleship' with which it is concerned.[62]

Wright goes on to examine the theological significance of the most fundamental of literary forms, narrative, poetry and drama. Drawing upon narrative theology, he analyses religious autobiography, showing how, in works such as Bunyan's *Grace Abounding to the Chief of Sinners*, 'literary forms fashion religious experience, providing the structures through which believers make sense of their lives'.[63] The theology of conversion in the works of Luther and Calvin, as well as the Pauline texts on which such theology is based, form a series of intertexts in whose terms Bunyan constructs the narrative of the meaning of his life. This narrative itself becomes an intertext of Carlyle's pseudo-autobiographical account of the conversion of Professor Teufelsdröckh in *Sartor Resartus*. The common rhetorical devices and structures of religious autobiographies, Wright argues, derive from their authors' shared literary conviction that 'it is through the reconstruction of the self, meditation on the past and recognition of its meaning, that faith in God finds its most coherent and convincing expression'.[64] Continuing his examination of narrative, Wright offers an interesting analysis of the Catholic novels of Evelyn Waugh, Graham Greene and Flannery O'Connor. He argues that the realism of the nineteenth-century novel, most clearly in the work of George Eliot, is 'deeply ideological', the product of a specific, liberal humanist, way of understanding the world. He writes, 'Such realism is formal and philosophical at the same time, describing in meticulous detail the only objects believed to be accessible to definite knowledge, the "facts" of human experience.'[65] Many modern critics, as Wright points out, have argued that the presentation of this positivist philosophy as the natural or self-evident way of understanding the world is a product of the liberal humanism which dominates the culture in which the realist novel was produced in the nineteenth and the first half of the twentieth centuries. In the terms of this world-view, religion is primarily a human phenomenon, representing the highest point of development of human feelings or morality. So, in George Eliot, Christianity is presented in the humanistic terms she derived from Strauss and Feuerbach, and in D.H. Lawrence, Biblical language functions as a series of metaphors for human experience. In the work of the Catholic novelists Wright considers, however, an 'alternative ideology, a theology' is expressed, in which the reality of the supernatural is affirmed. In both *Brideshead Revisited* and *The End of the Affair*, the initially secular, rationalist narrators come to recognize the limits of their world-view, and the need for a supernatural and even divine dimension to their lives. In the latter, Sarah's 'other' lover is of course God himself, and Greene introduces divine intervention and even miracle into the conventions of realist narrative. Again, O'Connor uses the grotesque and the abnormal in order to question the validity of the secular, rationalist assumptions of many of her characters. In all three cases, Wright writes, 'readers are challenged to abandon the secular assumptions of their age, to admit the depth of evil in themselves and the world, to acknowledge their need of redemption'.[66]

Wright goes on to argue that the characteristic features of poetic language can also constitute significant modes of theological expression. Metaphors in particular, he writes, 'provide perhaps the most important means by which language is stretched beyond the literal in order to talk of God'.[67] Ricoeur has stressed the cognitive aspect of metaphor, by which the trope generates new meanings from the logical tension between its constituent elements. It is in this sense, Wright argues, drawing on recent studies of metaphor and religious language, that metaphor functions in Scripture and in theological language, as a means of indicating something about God which could not be said otherwise, in literal language. Wright analyses the function of the metaphors in devotional poems by Hopkins and Herbert, arguing that the poets' accretion of metaphors in describing religious experience allows their readers to understand such experience in a way which exceeds literal propositions, and thereby 'to glimpse and to encounter a reality which they cannot fully understand'.[68] He also examines the theological significance of symbols. Most significantly, he analyses the Romantic concept of the symbol, in which the poetic imagination sees in the phenomena of the natural world symbols of the deeper, divine reality which underlies them. The Romantic symbol, Wright argues, is a 'poetic form of natural theology', a way of expressing the traces of God that can be discerned in the creation, whose complex play of meanings cannot be reduced to the dogmatic formulations of academic theology.[69] He traces the development of this concept into T.S. Eliot's exploration of the theological meanings of traditional Christian symbols in 'Little Gidding'. In both cases, he writes, 'It is the freedom such symbols provide to explore their plurality of meaning which makes them so much more rewarding for poetry than dogma.'[70] This is not to say, with liberal theology, that poetic symbolism constitutes an alternative to Christian doctrine, but rather that it is a 'complementary mode of theological reflection', exploring the mysteries of the Christian faith in a more personal and existential manner than the rational discourse of theology as such.[71]

Although Wright is more concerned with what he calls a 'poetics of faith', analysing the way in which Scripture and theology convey their meanings through devices associated with literature, than with a 'theology of poetry', in which literature is understood from the perspective of Christian faith, his work contains some important arguments for the Christian literary theory I am working towards. Wright approaches the question of the literary qualities of the Bible in a balanced way, focusing critical attention on the ways in which its meanings are constructed without negating the claim to truth made for it in the church. He respects both the truth-claim of the Bible and the insights concerning the construction of its meanings that can be derived from applying the methods of literary criticism to it, acknowledging that, from a Christian perspective, its texts are *both* of the kind institutionally regarded as literature *and*, unlike the rest of those texts, divine revelations. Perhaps the most important aspect of Wright's work, however, is the existential form of criticism that he practises, analysing numerous literary texts in terms of the world-view expressed in them, or the nature of the fictionally constructed 'world' they present to the reader, and relating this to the world as it is understood from the perspective of Christian faith. We saw this with respect to his analyses of realist and Catholic novels, and he analyses Renaissance drama, metafiction and the theatre of the absurd in a similar way. He writes, 'All these portraits of reality...are both ideological and theological, deeply imbued with value-judgements about the nature, purpose and origin of a world either sustained or abandoned by God.'[72] This is true, and the principle is an important one for Christian critical practice. A fundamental way of understanding literary works from a Christian perspective is to analyse the nature and characteristics of the fictional 'worlds' they present, and to compare this view of the world with that of Christianity. In particular, as with Wright's analyses of Vonnegut and Beckett, a Christian critic might be concerned with role of religious concepts and desires in the ideology of the text.

6.3   Theology in literature: Edwards and Fiddes

The most original and constructive work of Christian literary theory in the past 20 years has been Michael Edwards' *Towards a Christian Poetics* (1984). Edwards is less concerned to bring Christian theology into dialogue with contemporary modes of criticism and interpretation than to expound the meaning of Christian theology for literary criticism in general. His first principle is that 'we do not understand literature without a theory of language, and we do not understand either without a theory of life'.[73] On the whole, this is true. Whilst a theory of language is not necessarily implicit in understanding literary texts, a 'theory of life' – a collection of first principles and beliefs about the way the world is and how to live in it – is certainly implicit in interpreting such texts, and to a certain extent governs such interpretations. Edwards asks how literary texts can be understood and interpreted on the basis of a Christian world-view, or 'specifically, in the light of biblical teaching, what literature and language mean'.[74] He takes a dialectical view of the fundamental articles of Christian faith, following Pascal in emphasizing the paradox that human beings constitute according to those articles. On the one hand, men and women were created by and in the image of God, and from this creation derives their goodness, value and dignity – which Pascal calls the *grandeur*, or 'greatness' of the human being. On the other, as a result of the original sin of Adam, we now exist in a state marked by conflict, suffering and death – which Pascal calls our *misère*, or 'wretchedness'. In Jesus, whom Edwards calls the 'supreme paradox', the greatness and wretchedness of the human condition are united in his two natures, divine and human, in order that the latter can be resolved into a higher mode of the former. 'By the extreme greatness of his extremely wretched death, he overcomes wretchedness, and initiates a renewed greatness.'[75] Edwards argues that every aspect of human life, according to Biblical revelation – cosmology, history, anthropology and theology – is governed by this 'ternary process' or 'strong dialectic', in which an initially positive state is negated, and that negation itself negated into a higher positive. Edwards emphasizes that we live in the second stage of this dialectic, the state of wretchedness brought about by original sin, a state in which there are nevertheless traces of our former greatness and, most importantly, of the future redemption of our wretchedness. These latter traces comprise what Edwards calls 'possibility' – the possibility of the redemptive transformation of our present existence which the gospel promises – and this is the key term of his literary theory.

It is in the terms of this dialectical structure, which Edwards conceives as the fundamental structure of Christian history, that he thinks of the way in which language and literature function. He writes, 'Language allows us to become aware of the process; literature is a privileged means of enacting it, and especially of contesting the Fall and of reaching towards possibility.'[76] He thinks of Adam's acts of naming the animals as the first, positive term of the dialectical history of language according to Biblical revelation, in which the word had some kind of necessary connection with the thing it named. The serpent's words in tempting Eve, 'You will not die' (Gen. 3:4), he identifies as the negation of this positive, bringing ambiguity and obscurity – a disjunction between words and the world – into language. Just as Jesus claimed that the devil is the 'father of lies' (Jn. 8:44), Edwards writes, 'The serpent's phrase is the beginning of semantic obscurity, and since it was effective it has left us a world in which meaning is no longer evident, and a language equally uncertain, as we interpret it and as we use it.'[77] Now, the Biblical passages on Adam's naming do not speak of a prelapsarian language, which fell, along with Adam's original sin, into an arbitrary relationship to the world. It is true that the Bible speaks of a fall and redemption of the entire creation, and not just of humanity (Rom. 8:19–22; Gen. 3:17–19), but it gives us no reason to think that language is not essentially arbitrary, or was once naturally related to the world it named. Edwards' most interesting claim is his next one, that in language as we use it now, with its arbitrary and uncertain relationship to the world, and its irreducible potential for ambiguity and obscurity, there are equally irreducible possibilities of naming and imagining a new world, one not limited to the nature and qualities of the given world. He writes, 'Explored, language becomes a domain of suggestions, fragments of a novel reality emerging with fragments of a novel speech.'[78] Just as words can always fail to relate truly to the external world, that is, constructing complex references to other worlds that they have as it were brought into being, so they suggest precisely the possibility of which the Biblical revelation speaks, the coming of a new world into this one. Edwards writes, 'Language, by hints of its own renewal, adumbrates no less than the renewal of reality, of ourselves, of the disrupted harmonies. As it witnesses to Edenic creation and the Fall, so it witnesses to re-creation.'[79]

It is in literature above all, Edwards argues, that the dialectical structure of this theology of language can be seen at work most clearly. He writes, 'Literature occurs because we inhabit a fallen world. Explicitly or obscurely, it is part of our dispute with that world, and of our search for its and our own regeneration.'[80] He expounds this claim in several ways. First, and most importantly, he argues that narrative fiction is, as he puts it, 'dialectical in itself', that is, that it functions within the structure of creation, fall and redemption which governs his theology. By this he means that 'the need for story comes with the exile from Eden', that is, that it is from our experience of the manifest imperfection of the world in which we live and of its constant failure to match our idea of a good, happy or just world, that we invent and tell stories as a means of reaching for another, better world than this one. Clearly, the subject-matter of many stories – the happy endings of comic plots, for example – directly counters the fallen situation in which they are written, but Edwards means more than this. Even if the world of a given story is more unjust, painful or grotesque than this one, he writes – the world of *Nausea* or of *American Psycho*, for example – it still, as a narrated world, represents a 'desirable otherness'. He writes:

> We tell stories in a fallen world. By their matter they may lament and counter that fall . . . The strange power of story, however, is also to achieve those ends simply by being itself. Whatever its 'content', it opens a story-world, where everything coheres infrangibly and is impeccably.[81]

Narrative fiction in itself, that is, whatever the nature of the world narrated, opens up a new world to the reader with many of the desirable characteristics that the fallen world of his everyday experience lacks. Edwards lists several of these characteristics. Firstly, stories offer us the experience of a new beginning, an aesthetic version of the 'new creation' of which St Paul speaks. The start of a narrative opens up a new world for the reader, one not already determined like his own by an original sin or by the conflict and suffering which derive from it. Edwards writes, 'The start of a story is so fresh that it occurs in another dimension than our own, which replaces ours in the twinkling of an opening sentence.'[82] Secondly, the world of a story, unlike that of our own lives, has an ending, which Edwards describes as 'a form of salvation, substituting, for mere addition, finality and climax, and concentrating time into a shape'.[83] The lives of the characters, the events of the time-period, and ultimately the entire world of a story come to an end, and every aspect of that world assumes a retrospective significance, a pattern of meaning that can be discerned only from the perspective of that end, a perspective that we never achieve in our own lives. Frank Kermode has argued in *The Sense of an Ending* (1966) that literary narratives answer at the imaginary level to the desire of human beings born and dying in the middle of time to give meaning to their lives by seeing them from the perspective of the end of time. Edwards recasts this argument in the terms of his theology, claiming that in a fallen world, in which we can imagine and desire a world more perfect than this one, we create stories, whose endings give to the worlds they project a guarantee of coherence and of comprehensibility that we do not experience in our own. Thirdly, and most importantly, he writes that 'personae in story lived charmed lives in comparison with persons in reality'.[84] In a narrative, that is, the lives of the characters are invested with meaning at every point, progressing logically as well as merely temporally towards a guaranteed ending. The life of a narrative character, Edwards writes, has 'its moments caught up into significance and its whole governed by the logic of final causes' – it has, in short, precisely the kind of meaningful story that we desire but are not guaranteed in our own lives, and that, even for the Christian, is a matter of faith. Hence Edwards can write that narrative characters inhabit the 'glory of form', and that story is the 'fiction of a fallen world remade'.[85]

It is not only in the phenomenon of narrative that Edwards sees literary works to embody the dialectic upon which his theology is based. He also argues that, in certain fundamental forms, especially tragedy and comedy, literary works can be seen to articulate this dialectic at the level of their plot. In tragedy, he argues, the hero is typically an exceptionally great man. He is usually a ruler, endowed with exceptional qualities that are praised to the point of divinity, and yet he is often presented as representative. Edwards suggests, 'The hero seems a bid, more or less obscure, to conceive Adam, the uniquely eminent and special, representative man, the pitch and lord of creation.'[86] As well as his extreme greatness, of course, the tragic hero is also extremely wretched, becoming the guiltiest, the most unfortunate and the unhappiest of human beings, emphatically embodying therefore the paradox of the human being according to Edwards' Christian anthropology. Furthermore, there is usually a 'fall' from the one condition to the other – as Chaucer's monk says, 'Tragedie is to seyn a certeyn storie . . . Of hym that stood in greet prosperitee/And is yfallen out of heigh degree/Into myserie.'[87] At the same time, the two remain dialectically related – it is precisely the hero's greatness that makes his wretchedness so extreme. Edwards writes, 'Tragedy is the place in literature where the interaction of the two truths of our double condition is most clearly operative.'[88] It is because of this interaction, he argues, that the dialectic progresses to its third stage, since, in the death in which the fall into wretchedness culminates, the greatness embodied by the hero survives in a new and regenerative mode. The vision of the dead hero may inspire excessive celebrations of his worth, or some new hope of prosperity for his city or kingdom may arise after the event of his death. In the *Oresteia*, the misery of the house of Atreus culminates in Athene's prophesy of a glorious future for Athens, and in the Furies' promise of beneficence towards the city of the hero they had cursed. Again, in *Romeo and Juliet*, the death of the two lovers brings peace to Verona and ends the feud that caused that death. Tragedies like these, Edwards claims, articulate the entire dialectic upon which Christian theology is based, expressing the paradox of the greatness and misery of the fallen human condition, and hinting at a future transformation of that misery into a new and lasting greatness.

In comedy, he argues, a similar negotiation with a fallen world and fictive transformation of it can be observed. Edwards is able to make this case less generally and less consistently with respect to his theological paradigm than in his analysis of tragedy, but one or two points are worth mentioning. Firstly, he observes, many of the negative characteristics of the characters of comedy – egoism, lust, crime, violence, and so on – function as depictions of the condition of fallen humanity. Furthermore, insofar as these characteristics are presented at the light and inconsequential level of humour, they lose the genuinely negative qualities and effects that they have in the real world. Edwards calls this 'showing and fictively purging the fall'.[89] This is especially true of the figure of the clown or fool, he argues, who functions something like a scapegoat, experiencing to an excessive degree our own failings and fears, and raising this experience to a level of play in which their negativity is transformed into an occasion for laughter. The fool, Edwards writes, 'suffers ridicule and perhaps violence in our place; and he enables us to enter an aesthetic world of hilarious possibility. He is both a diminished and an enlarged image of ourselves'.[90] A second important point he makes concerns the marriage with which many comedies end. He writes, 'This basic plot of comedy is also a plot against a fallen condition.' On the one hand, it usually represents the overcoming of certain negative conditions of the fallen world, such as an avaricious father or a deceitful rival. On the other, it has a theological significance with respect to that world. Edwards relates the comic marriage to the pre-lapsarian relationship of Adam and Eve. At Gen. 2:23, the man describes the woman as 'flesh of my flesh', and the Yahwist comments, 'Therefore a man leaves his father and his mother and clings to his wife, and they become one flesh' (2:24). Edwards writes, 'To marry, it seems, is to recover something of that primal unity that preceded the Fall.'[91] He also points out that, in St Paul's interpretation of this passage in Eph. 5:31, marriage is held to be symbolic of the relationship between Christ and the church. From this perspective, he writes, 'the marriage of the lovers, which is the success of the comedy, looks towards the supreme success, the end of the dialectic, insofar as that too is a marriage, both spiritual and eternal.'[92]

Edwards' work contains several significant contributions to Christian literary theory. In my view, he overstates the case for the dialectical pattern by which the fundamental articles of Christian faith are structured. Whilst his literary theory fits consistently into his theology, the dialectical structure on which this theology is based does not underlie every fundamental aspect of Biblical revelation or of Christian theology in the way that he seems to suggest. The progression from creation to fall to redemption constitutes the structure of Christian history, but there is no Biblical justification for extending this structure to theological reflection upon 'all turns of our experience'.[93] Even the structure of Christian history is more complex than that of Edwards' dialectic – redemption, for example, begins in the past with the death and resurrection of Christ, continues in the present in the believer's faith, baptism and life in Christ, and is finally completed only in the future at the Parousia. I disagree with Edwards, therefore, that a Biblical theology of language should think of the latter in terms of the dialectic of creation, fall and redemption. As I have already argued, the Bible does not suggest that language has fallen with humanity from a natural to an arbitrary relationship to the world. Nevertheless, Edwards is right to point out that it has the capacity to refer independently of the external world and so to refer to new worlds that it, as it were, brings into being. It is above all in literary texts that this occurs, and Edwards' theological reflection upon this fictional potential of language is sound. It is a significant part of the pleasure of reading a story that one inhabits during the time one reads a better and more satisfying world than that of one's everyday experience. Like Kermode, Edwards identifies some of the qualities which make the worlds of narrative fiction desirable in comparison to the reader's own, most important among which are their comprehensibility and the certain significance of the lives of the characters within them. I would add to these characteristics the beauty which derives from the aesthetically formed quality of a narrated world, the permanence which derives from the fixed form of the text, and the freedom from practical concerns, personal failings and the consequences of human evil that derives from the reader's distance from the narrated world. What is the theological significance of this account of the pleasure of fiction? Edwards is surely right, from a theological perspective, to claim that we read stories, and inhabit the more satisfying worlds that they project, in response to the conditions of our own world that Christian theology explains with the doctrines of the fall and of original sin. The new worlds of narrative fiction answer, in the ways I have listed, to the desire of human beings who live in a world characterized by original sin and its effects for a new, better and redeemed world, and for a new, better and redeemed life in it. This may or may not be a conscious aspect of the pleasure of fiction, but it is the meaning of the latter deducible from Christian theology. That we tell and read stories, which project worlds in certain ways more desirable than the fallen world of our own experience, is, in my view, a phenomenon to be accounted for in terms of St Paul's doctrine that the whole creation awaits and strains towards its redemption – 'We know that the whole creation [*ktisis*] has been groaning in labour pains [*sustenazei kai sunôdinei*] until now; and not only the creation, but we ourselves, who have the first fruits of the Spirit, groan inwardly [*en heautois stenazomen*] while we wait for adoption, the redemption of our bodies' (Rom. 8:22–23). Whilst the world of a story is a temporary and imaginary experience, and does not actually constitute the redemption of the world promised by the Christian gospel, it nevertheless can be understood as an expression of the desire for that redemption which St Paul attributes both to fallen human beings and to the created world itself.

Edwards is also right, in my view, to argue that some literary works articulate at the level of their plot or subject-matter the conditions of the fallen world and the human desire for redemption that arises from those conditions. As I have already argued, there is no Biblical justification for thinking of the progression from creation to fall to redemption as a universal structure of Christian theology, and hence there is no intrinsic theological reason for thinking of tragedy, comedy or any other literary genre in terms of this progression. Whilst Edwards on the whole fits his account of tragedy plausibly into the structure of his theology, there are aspects both of individual plays and of the generic characteristics one can induce from them that do not seem to derive from this structure. For example, whilst he is right to point out that many tragedies end with a suggestion that the world of the play will be set right again, this is often so little emphasized that it does not seem to represent a dialectical progression beyond the misery which has been its main subject in the way that he claims. So, in *King Lear*, although Albany returns to restore order, the play ends with the meaningless death of Cordelia, the painful death of Lear, and a funeral march. The play's final words, 'We that are young/Shall never see so much, nor live so long', do not seem to indicate a dialectical progression beyond misery in the way that Athene's speech does in the *Oresteia*, but rather mere recovery from the fall of Lear and its effects. Although tragedy cannot in general be said to articulate the entire progression from creation to fall to redemption in the way that Edwards suggests, however, he is right to claim, from a theological perspective, that tragedies portray with particular depth and intensity the conditions of human life in the fallen world. The tragic flaw in the hero represents precisely the kind of moral disorder within the individual that Christian theology explains with the doctrine of original sin. Other characters, such as Cordelia or Iphigenia, suffer injustice and die, through no fault of their own, but through the evil actions of others, experiencing, as Edwards rightly says, the moral evil of a fallen humanity. The world of tragedy is characterized by precisely the kind of disjunction between our sense of how the world ought to be and how it is that Christianity explains with the doctrine of the fall. Theologically, Edwards is right to claim that tragedy represents a portrayal of the fallen world, and to suggest that the disjunction in the tragic world implies the possibility of precisely the kind of redemption or transformation that the Bible promises with respect to this one. With respect to comedy, Edwards is less able to fit his observations into the dialectical structure of his theology, and, as I have made clear, I see no reason for attempting to do so. The most valid theological reflection he makes is that the marriage with which comedies typically end, whilst it might have historical roots in fertility ritual, represents a symbolic expression of the desire for completion and consummation felt by human beings in a world that both lacks and tends towards precisely such consummation.

The most detailed theological response to Edwards's literary theory has been that of Paul Fiddes, in *Freedom and Limit* (1991). He follows Kermode and Edwards in arguing that the world offered to the imagination by narrative fiction '[consoles] us with the assurance of order in an everyday world that appears random and chaotic', and he adds that the novelty of the story world satisfies the reader in a world that 'appears dulled by routine'. In this way, he argues, stories respond to the same 'double problem of reality' with which Ecclesiastes struggles, that is, that the world seems on the one hand impenetrably complex and on the other repetitive and meaningless.[94] He adds, rightly, that poetry – even lyric poetry – has the same capacity to project a new world in front of the text, and he argues that it is in its metaphors and imagery that this capacity is most fully realized. 'Unexpected imagery . . . seems to dissolve the world as we know it, to disintegrate the familiar in preparation for a new order.'[95] Fiddes argues that the capacity of literary texts to project the kind of new world I have been discussing does not lead to the satisfaction merely of escapism, but rather to a sense that 'the text is reaching out beyond itself to something of "ultimate concern" to us'.[96] In poetry, for example, the complex play of meanings generated by metaphorical language exceeds the limit of the author's intention and of the reader's ability to interpret in univocal language. Again, some narratives dramatize precisely the process of seeking the meaning of one's life in the form of a narrative that constitutes one of our fundamental motives for reading and enjoying them. Fiddes writes, 'In poetry, drama and novel, the imagination thus reaches out towards mystery, towards a reality that is our final concern but which eludes rational investigation and bursts empirical concepts.'[97] He rightly recognizes that there are other ways of interpreting this 'mystery', this sense of that which exceeds all that can be empirically observed and logically discussed, than the theological view that God exists in a manner which transcends that of his creation, but he asks 'how someone who *does* take such a view might relate imaginative literature to the doctrinal statements which he makes'.[98] In the first place, he observes, the fundamental movement that he sees in literary works, in which language is used to point beyond itself to that which exceeds our experience, is, as it were, reversed in theology, in which 'the Final mystery has actually disclosed himself to us, and human images and stories take their place in witnessing (however imperfectly) to this encounter'.[99] Literature, for Fiddes, moves from language to mystery; Christian theology from mystery to language. On the other hand, Fiddes argues that there is also a close parallel between theology and imaginative literature, insofar as the former can be described as a response to the self-revelation of God, translating this personal event into narrative and propositions. From a theological perspective, Fiddes argues, a similar description can be applied to literary texts. He draws on the theology of grace to argue that our search for the mystery of God is itself a result of God's prior gift of himself to us. In Rahner's thought, for example, human 'openness to mystery can never be separated from God's own openness to us in gracious self-communication'.[100] If this is the case, Fiddes argues, then the movement towards mystery he discerns in literary texts is, as a way in which this search or openness is expressed, also motivated by God's reaching towards us. He writes, 'The work of the creative imagination is in fact one kind of response to revelation.'[101] More specifically, it is a response to what Fiddes calls 'general revelation', by which he means that 'God is present in his world to disclose *himself* within nature and human life.'[102] This is not to suggest that creative writers necessarily understand themselves to be writing in response to divine revelation, but rather a theological interpretation of their work. Whereas Christian theologians, for Fiddes, respond to the 'special' self-revelation of God in the events of the history of Israel and the life of Jesus Christ by developing a context of concepts and propositions within which to interpret this encounter, creative writers respond to his general self-revelation in nature and human life by expressing in some way the mystery at the heart of their experience of the latter.

Fiddes' theological view of the similarity he discerns in creative writing and theology is that both discourses, in their different ways, open up the senses of order and of novelty that seem to be lacking in the everyday world of their readers' experience. He writes, 'The two [sets of] stories [and images] interact in the ever-present grace and the universal self-revelation of God.'[103] He proposes a critical method, in which literary texts are interpreted from the perspective of Christian theology and *vice versa*, so that a mutually informative dialogue takes place between the two. He conceives this dialogue in Gadamer's terms as a 'fusion of horizons' between the literary text and the theological context in which it is read. On the one hand, 'theological ideas can be influenced by an imaginative presentation of the themes with which both theology and literature deal and of the symbols they share', and on the other, 'Christian belief and doctrine can provide the reader...with a perspective for interpretation of literary texts.'[104] In order to stage a dialogue with literary texts in terms acceptable to contemporary readers, Fiddes argues, the traditional structure ascribed to what he calls 'the Christian story' must be reconceived. Focusing on the view of Northrop Frye, he writes that whilst the narrative structure of the Bible has traditionally been interpreted as a 'U-shaped curve', from paradise through its loss to its restoration, this view needs to be challenged. It corresponds very imperfectly to a reading of the Bible itself, in which the sin of Adam is explicitly mentioned as the cause of the human predicament only once (Rom. 5:12–21). In the Old Testament there is not a single direct reference to the story of Adam and Eve after Genesis 3, although many of its authors are exercised by the problems of human sin and evil. 'The form that the Christian story should take now', Fiddes argues, which will represent both a closer reading of the Bible itself and a narrative more closely related to contemporary concerns, is that of a 'line of tension' between human freedom and human limitation, the result of which is anxiety. Comparing the two creation accounts in Genesis, in which man is made on the one hand from dust and on the other in the image of God, he writes, 'There is a dialectical contrast in human life: human beings are both dust of the earth and image of God, both limited by their environment and free over against it.'[105] On the one hand, human beings have the capacity to transcend themselves and their environment, and on the other we are conditioned by our biological and psychological make-up and by the world around us. Living within this tension, Fiddes continues, generates anxiety, which is resolved either authentically by trust in God or inauthentically by finding security in worldly things. Following Tillich, he claims that the fall into a state of estrangement from God is not 'a logical necessity of creation' but rather an 'original fact', that is, something that all human beings in practice do, rather than something to which they once became predisposed as the result of a prehistoric crime.[106] It is this version of the narrative that Christian theology can construct from the event of revelation which Fiddes brings into dialogue with literary texts, since it represents, in his view, both a better reading of the Bible itself and can be more closely related than the 'U-shaped story' to 'the way that novelists and poets perceive the human situation today'.[107]

In some cases, Fiddes develops Edwards' arguments well. His reflection that our experience of the fallen world is in part an experience of the meaninglessness which troubles Ecclesiastes is a valuable addition to Edwards' theory of the pleasure of fiction in such a world. He is right to add that the novelty of the world of a story satisfies in a world which can appear characterized by meaningless repetition, in which there is 'nothing new under the sun' (Eccl. 1:9). He overstates the case, however, when he claims that, in constituting a new world in which the reader dwells whilst reading, literary works 'transcend themselves towards Mystery', and point towards inexpressible realities of ultimate concern to their readers. In the first place, his argument at this point is flawed by a lack of distinction between the imaginative work of the reader in constituting the new world projected by the text and that of the author in creating the text which allows the reader to do so. Hence, it is not clear, when Fiddes speaks of the imagination reaching out towards mystery, whether he means that the reader, in choosing to dwell in the world of the text, is or can be said to be reaching beyond the world of his ordinary experience to something of ultimate concern to him, or whether this is to be said of the author, in choosing to bring such a world into being. Whatever he intends, however, it is not true that literary texts necessarily lead the reader beyond his everyday experience to things of 'ultimate concern' to him. Fiddes argues that if this were not the case, the pleasure of reading fiction would be 'mere escapism' or 'mere fantasy', but in fact, even from the theological perspective I have developed from reflecting on Edwards' work, these may well constitute part of the pleasure of reading in a fallen world for certain readers of certain texts. Perhaps Fiddes already assumes as much in his use of the term 'literature', but it is only certain fictional and poetic texts that lead their readers to raise the question of their ultimate concern. Indeed it is precisely the nature of the concerns raised by a text that contributes to a reader's or a community of readers' judgement of its value. The extent to which an individual or a community accepts the values and the concerns projected by a text as ultimate determines the judgement such readers will make as to the value or merit of that text.

A similar judgement must be made with respect to Fiddes' claim that creative writing can be understood as a response to general revelation, namely that whilst there is some truth in it, the case is overstated. I agree with Fiddes' theology of grace, according to which we seek God because he first seeks us, but I disagree that literary works as such represent a seeking after God in the form of 'mystery', or that which is inexpressible in human experience. Some literary works – Larkin's 'High Windows', for example – are explicitly concerned with the mystery at the edges of human existence, but others – Plath's 'Daddy', say – are not. Hence, it seems to me true only at the most general level that creative writing represents a response, more or less conscious, to divine revelation. The creative writer's imagination works in response to his or her experience of human life in the world, in which, as Rom. 1:19–20 makes clear, its creator can be known. Insofar as God is knowable and present in the world, therefore, the creative writer, insofar as he or she responds imaginatively to the world, can be said to respond indirectly to the God who has chosen to reveal himself through it. Fiddes suggest a more directly informative theological perspective upon literary texts when he argues that, insofar as both literature and Christian theology are concerned with human experience, the concerns and values of a given text can be brought into dialogue with the reflections of Christian theology upon those concerns and values. As I have said, Fiddes takes too high a view of literary texts as a response to revelation and hence of their comparability to theology, which also constitutes such a response. Nevertheless, given that the worlds projected by literary texts and the world projected by the Biblical texts are, for the Christian, different in kind, since he or she believes the latter to be real, then the kind of dialogue Fiddes proposes constitutes a productive method of Christian literary criticism. It should be a part of Christian critical practice, where appropriate, to discuss the concerns and values projected by a text in the light of Christian faith and theology. Fiddes is right to add that this discussion should be a dialogue, in which theological interpretation of the Biblical revelation is held open to reform and revision in the light of the concerns of the text. As for Fiddes' discussion of the structure of the 'Christian story', whilst his discussion of the dialectic of freedom and limitation represents a cogent reading of the Bible, it does not seem to me necessary or productive in conducting a Christian critical practice to think of any one Biblical interpretation as the theological structure in whose terms all literary texts should be analysed. Fiddes' existential account of the basic structure of Christian theology is useful in bringing modern and contemporary texts into dialogue with Christianity, but, in my view, the Christian critic should be prepared to use whatever Biblical interpretation seems most appropriate – provided, of course, that it can be shown to be a convincing interpretation – for analysing the text or texts in question.

6.4   Religion in literature: Detweiler and Ledbetter

Since his earliest publications in the 1960s, the criticism of Robert Detweiler has focused on the religious dimensions, explicit and implicit, of narrative fiction, and in recent years he has come to emphasize these dimensions of postmodern fiction in particular. In 'Theological Trends of

Postmodern Fiction' (1976), he argues that there are certain characteristics of such fiction that have 'emerged with enough frequency and clarity to make [them] a familiar focus for discussion among theologically aware persons', that is, which lend themselves to theological interpretation.[108] He identifies four such characteristics – the need to let language speak itself, the disappearance of the subject, the evocation of presence and the shaping of alternative worlds. With respect to the first of these, Detweiler gives several examples from contemporary fiction in which the author strives 'to escape or transcend the imperialistic attitude ... toward knowledge and language', that is, to portray language not as an instrument controlled by his characters (the 'imperialistic' attitude) but rather as a network that surrounds them and 'speaks itself' through them. This trend can be interpreted theologically, Detweiler argues, insofar as it represents 'a continuation of the incarnation in the kerygmatic event'.[109] He means that in the Incarnation, the Word becomes flesh, but, in the proclamation of this gospel, Christ's incarnate flesh becomes word again. Both in the gospels and in the preaching of the gospel, Detweiler argues, the Word of God can be said to speak itself. The tendency of postmodern fiction to portray language as a trans-subjective network that speaks through rather than being spoken by the subject, therefore, represents a concern that such fiction shares with Christian theology. This can also be said, he argues, of the decentred and destabilized subject with which much postmodern fiction and theory is concerned. In the work of Robbe-Grillet, for example, 'points of view and centres of consciousness change rapidly because the self simply is not fundamental or important'.[110] This primary concern of postmodern fiction, Detweiler claims, 'reminds us of the Pauline death of the self, of putting off the old man, of being absorbed into something greater'.[111] In losing oneself in Christ, for St Paul, one becomes a member of his body, the church, and joins the community of believers. In a similar way, Detweiler argues, in postmodern theory and fiction, the disappearance of the self as a centre of consciousness gives way to collective and interactive models of identity. In contemporary fiction, he writes, 'the self is not to be found in the personality of the author or narrator or reader but rather ... in the interrelationship of the three a new collective identity is created'.[112] Hence he writes, '*koinonia*, the group consciousness of the church, may be a model for the artist searching for a way to express the *we* following the enervation of the self'.[113] The deconstruction of the subject as a stable centre of consciousness in postmodern fiction, that is, and the rise of dynamic and collective models of subjectivity in its place, is, for Detweiler, a concern not only of postmodern fiction but also of Christian theology. From a theological point of view, the characteristics he discerns in contemporary narratives represent fictional explorations of concepts dealt with in theology as the 'utterance of the word' and the 'redemption of the subject'.[114] Literary analysis of these narratives, he concludes, can therefore be seen to 'interact naturally and necessarily' with theological analysis. Ultimately, for Detweiler, this is because, in both narrative fiction and theology, 'the imagination, working in two kinds of discourse, shapes the faithful fictions in which and by which we live'.[115]

Detweiler develops this argument further in *Breaking the Fall* (1989), where he prefaces a series of 'religious readings' of contemporary fiction with two theoretical chapters. In the first, he again outlines some of the typical characteristics of postmodern narrative, in this case the central place of role-play in the concept of selfhood, the risk to such selfhood constituted by reading, and the use of language as play rather than as representation. These are of course well established generic characterizations, but in the course of them Detweiler makes some points especially worth mention. He takes a historical view of the development of the novel from the communally recited stories of pre-literate cultures, which 'served in their regular and ritualized retelling to confirm a people in their identity and challenged them to be worthy of their heritage'.[116] In our literate, secular and technologized culture, by contrast, the novel constitutes a story displaced from this communal context, written by a single author, produced and distributed in identical form, read in solitude and whenever the reader wishes, rather than on a special occasion. Detweiler writes, 'The novel, alienated from the communal roots of narrative, disseminated technologically and interpreted technically, becomes an ideal vehicle for the exploring self seeking to comprehend its separation, difference and individuality.'[117] In terms of the phenomenology of reading, this means that 'reading fiction can serve as a probe by offering the self other versions of what it might be'.[118] The novel, that is, represents narrative fiction particularly ordered towards the individual – and Detweiler adds that the postmodern narrative is especially ordered towards the multiplicity of the individual. The reader is therefore invited to see himself, to construct or reconstruct his sense of self, in terms determined by his experience of individual characters in the novel. Reading fiction, Detweiler writes, 'involves an excursion from the self to examine other selves and at the same time an evaluation of the self in terms of similarities and alternate possibilities of behaviour exhibited by those other selves'.[119] Indeed, this process works with respect not only to the reader's understanding of himself but also of his entire environment. This is the phenomenological function of metaphor, for Detweiler, which, in conjoining dissimilar images, forces the mind to conceive of a new and complex image that 'acts as a probe for establishing a deeper and more encompassing view of reality'.[120] Metaphor invites the reader to reconceive reality, and to read metaphorical language is to experiment with 'new patterns of knowledge that offer us greater choices of what we might believe, how we might respond'.[121] Like Ricoeur, Detweiler argues that this process occurs at the level of discourse in fiction. He writes, 'Metaphor or the literary text in this sense substitutes for reality by creating a new version of it, and for this reason writing and reading fictions pose a risk: they can lead us to change our minds and therefore our behaviour.'[122]

In his second chapter, Detweiler sets out a methodology for what he calls 'religious reading' of postmodern fiction so conceived. The first premise of such reading is that, as he has already suggested, 'writing and reading fiction are activities...through which we seek to replace whatever satisfactions were provided by intact storytelling communities'.[123] The novel is a narrative form written and read largely in private, arising with the increasing privatization of society in the eighteenth century. In Detweiler's view, it 'both celebrates this new condition and tries to compensate for it', that is, it offers both a form of entertainment for private leisure time and an imaginary portrayal of precisely the kind of communal life in which the reader as such does not participate.[124] A religious reading of such a genre, Detweiler claims, would be one which 'counters the privatising nature of writing and reading with participatory interpretations', that is, which transforms private response into communal response.[125] In practice, Detweiler thinks of this as a practice of 'contemplative fellowship' with the text rather than an analytical interpretation of it. He envisages a 'ludic interactive response' to texts, which will 'recuperate our conversations and remind us of the pleasures of trustful exchange based on principles of friendship rather than power'.[126] This kind of reading is religious in its 'openness to others', its 'willingness to accommodate and adapt' and its 'readiness to entertain the new...while honouring the old'.[127] In the second place, Detweiler argues, a religious reading would be one intended to 'aid the community's participation in the construction of myths and rituals against chaos'.[128] Here he makes use of Clifford Geertz's view of religion as cultural system which provides a community with a myth and a series of rituals which create a tolerable view of existence in the face of the rational doubt that it may ultimately be chaotic and uninterpretable. In this sense, a religious reading would be one in which 'a reader understands herself as part of a community engaged in simultaneously recognising, criticising and shaping the myths and rituals it lives by'.[129] It will be specifically religious, Detweiler claims, insofar as it emphasizes the festival dimensions of a text, which will include a kind of 'communal listening' to the text, which in turn constitutes a response to what Ricoeur calls its 'surplus of meaning', that is, to the interpreter's sense that the text means more than his interpretation can bring out. Pointing out that one interpretation of this surplus is Bakhtin's concept of the carnival, the holiday that for a limited period inverts the normal order and turns it into transgressive play, Detweiler argues that festival represents both an attempt to control excess and a means of increasing it. A religious reading, therefore, will 'uncover the elements of excess in the texts it addresses, and see them in their double role', both as 'witnesses to the great ineffability of existence' on the one hand, and as 'a reminder that the practice of religion, for all of its sublime moments, always remains close to humanity's most primitive impulses' on the other.[130] Detweiler describes three kinds of text that he believes are particularly susceptible to religious readings of the kind he has described, texts of pain, of love and of worship, and offers several readings of contemporary narratives which constitute various combinations of these three. These narratives, he claims, using a phrase of Lyotard's, represent their reading community's mode of alluding to the 'conceivable which cannot be presented'. His method of reading them is intended to be the first step in a communal gesture of celebrating this conceivable but unpresentable reality, in relation to which our community shapes its identity.

Detweiler's most theoretical statement, the concept of religious reading, is based on an anthropological rather than on a theological understanding of religion, and its principles do not therefore necessarily follow from the kind of theological reflection upon literature that I am proposing here. Detweiler's view of religion as a kind of communally enacted openness to mystery, especially as that is mediated through myth and ritual, is both wider and more indefinite than the Christian understanding of God's self-revelation and the human response to this revelation in Christian faith and practice, and is open to criticism from the perspective of this understanding. As Wesley Kort puts it in a review essay, Detweiler's argument implies 'a kind of bass continuo of confidence that when we give up on control, not chaos but some deeper or higher order of things will be disclosed', which, from the perspective of Christian anthropology, is ultimately misplaced.[131] Again, Kort asks Detweiler, 'Is there no demonic in your circle of the religious?', by which he means that the latter's concept of religion does not seem to include a basis for ethical judgements or for a response to evil. The concept of religious reading as a communal openness to the text and play with its innumerable potential senses, therefore, is not necessarily one that derives from the perspective of Christian theology. Detweiler's second definition of this concept is more useful from this perspective, in which he suggests that religious reading will consciously contribute to the reading community's construction of myths and rituals against chaos. His most important contribution here is to point out that it follows from the logic of Geertz's argument that the social function of religion is to construct such myths and rituals, that everyone needs and has a framework of beliefs about the nature of reality, and not only those who assent to beliefs of a specifically theological nature. What Detweiler proposes for 'religious' reading, therefore, is in fact true of all literary and cultural interpretation whatever, that it is a process in which the interpreter, both as an individual and as a member of a community, shapes and re-shapes the myths – that is, the fundamental concepts and narrative structures – by which he and his community understand themselves and the world. Detweiler's point about the phenomenology of reading fiction, therefore, is also well made. His historical perspective upon narrative as the development of a function that was originally and therefore remains essentially a communal and even ritualistic activity seems to me to depend upon the idea of a lost organic community whose actual existence would be very difficult to locate. Nevertheless, he is right to claim that reading narrative, and other literary forms, in the modern period is a process of putting the self into play, in which the reader experiments at the imaginary level with new senses of his own identity and of the world around him, which can, as Detweiler says, lead him to change his mind and therefore his behaviour.

Although Detweiler's concept of religious reading is expressed as a proposal for a more communal way to practise interpretation, in fact he tends to focus on the themes of community, festival, excess and so on at the level of the content of the texts he discusses. As he puts it at the beginning of his next book, *Uncivil Rites* (1996), in *Breaking the Fall* he had interpreted novels and stories as 'texts about persons seeking meaning for their lives through some sort of community', and that these communities cohered, if at all, 'through articulating and living out narratives of belief and commitment that their members inherited or created'.[132] His theoretical proposals for a communal and ritualistic method of reading in practice become an attention to the themes of community and ritual in the texts he addresses, an attention that he continues and develops in *Uncivil Rites*. In fact, this is part of the value of Detweiler's criticism. Whilst his proposals for a communal and celebratory practice of reading seem, as Kort suggests, unrealistic and utopian, his attention to and discussion of religious themes, both explicit and implicit, in the texts he analyses, is in fact a model of Christian critical practice. It seems to me that this kind of criticism, which discusses the religious and theological significance of certain themes or motifs in a text, constitutes a way in which Christian literary and cultural criticism could and should, where appropriate, proceed. One of the most convincing examples of this in Detweiler's own criticism is his theological analysis of the depiction of the dissolution of the self in postmodern fiction in terms of the dissolution of the old self envisaged by St Paul.

The religious functions of narrative fiction have also been emphasized in the criticism of Mark Ledbetter, who develops a theory of fiction initially influenced by the narrative ethics of Alisdair MacIntyre and Stanley Hauerwas. His first book, *Virtuous Intentions* (1989), is a study of what he calls the 'religious dimension of narrative', whose central claim is that 'narrative serves a religious function, namely, the discovery of virtue'.[133] Ledbetter understands religion in Mircea Eliade's terms, as 'the paradigmatic solution for every existential crisis', and so claims that narrative fiction has a religious aspect insofar as it both portrays an existential crisis in the lives of its characters and suggests a solution – in the form of a virtue – to which the characters can repeatedly turn to give meaning to their existence.[134] He writes, 'The completion of the crisis-solution dialectic is narrative's religious function.'[135] The motivation for writing and reading fiction, Ledbetter argues, is a 'desire for an ordered and coherent world-view', of the kind that mere experience of the world does not necessarily provide. This is a desire for something 'other' than the crises portrayed in the narrative, and this other, in Ledbetter's view, is typically 'a single virtue that dominates all other virtues'.[136] The solution portrayed by narrative fiction to the existential crises it represents, that is, is 'meaning for human existence that shows itself as a virtue for living the good life'.[137] Ledbetter isolates four basic elements of narrative structure – tone, atmosphere, plot and character – and argues that each 'points to, discovers and interprets a religious world-view'.[138] Tone, the ethos projected by the narrative voice, establishes the nature and qualities of the world which the reader enters on reading the narrative, and which are characteristics of the narrator's beliefs about that world. During reading, the reader tests these beliefs against those he himself holds as he comes to the text. Plot, Ledbetter argues, imposes order and meaning on the narrative world, and establishes a structure of 'repeatable time', opposed to the potentially chaotic flux in which readers live. He writes, 'A plot is ritual and repetitive and allows for a moment of return to a time that is stable and meaningful and that sets one free from the chaos and meaninglessness of the present.'[139] Most important, in terms of its religious function, in Ledbetter's view is the narrative element of character, because 'existential crises always confront characters and provide a situation in which virtue-establishing decisions are made'.[140] Characters, that is, are constantly confronted with moral and existential choices, and it is through this process of choices, Ledbetter argues, that 'a character comes to the point in the text where acquiescence is made to a particular virtue' which the character comes to accept as the essence of a meaningful human life. Ledbetter sees this moment of acceptance as an act of belief in the authority of a particular virtue as the way to live the good life. He analyses three novels in these terms, arguing that *philia* or family love, faith in God, and courage respectively are the dominant virtues that the characters of each come to discover and practise as a solution, at points of crisis in their lives, to the question of how to live well in a world characterized by such crises. In each case, Ledbetter cites the work of a theologian in whose thought this dominant virtue is conceived of in explicitly theological terms.

The importance of narrative so conceived, for Ledbetter, is that it is 'life-like', that is, that human beings understand themselves and their lives in terms of narrative. We tell stories, he writes, 'to reveal something about ourselves and to discover what gives identity, purpose and meaning to our existence'.[141] Narrative fictions, he claims, are constructed from the material of 'lived' narratives, that is, the stories we tell about our own lives in order to understand them. Both lived and fictional narratives, he argues, are motivated by a desire for a unity and a coherence to life that are not immediately given, and in both, characters who are constantly faced with moral and existential choices come to discover and live by virtues which give meaning and value to their lives. Ledbetter writes, 'Lived narrative, like fiction, reveals a particular virtue by which life is ordered and finds meaning.'[142] He follows Hauerwas in arguing that the value of fictional narratives in human life is that they constitute an 'excellent paradigm for self-discovery and exploring the virtuous life'.[143] Since we understand our own lives in narrative terms, we can learn about them from other, fictional narratives. Ledbetter writes, 'Observing characters in novels, we can encounter and learn from lived narrative's reflection in narrative fiction.'[144] The dominant virtue around which a fictional narrative can be seen to be ordered can suggest itself as a means of living the good life to its readers as it does to its characters. Ledbetter writes, 'Because we too are narrative beings, narrative fiction can equip us with tools of virtue with which to build our moral and religious lives.'[145] To put it more simply, 'Good literature is a way of looking at the world; it also suggests a way of living in the world.'[146]

In his next and latest book, *Victims and the Postmodern Narrative* (1996), Ledbetter continues to emphasize the ethical dimensions of narrative fiction, this time from the perspective of a postmodern ethics of the other. In this book, he argues that the ethical function of narrative fiction lies in its potential to 'reverse the course of rampant victimisation' in a world structured socially by the dominance and oppression of a large proportion of its inhabitants. He writes, 'Narrative has the power to liberate the victims of our society and to alert those of us who victimize, whether intentionally or otherwise, to how and why we violate the existence of those politically weaker than ourselves.'[147] It has this power, according to Ledbetter, as a result of its various modes of inscription of the stories of silenced and oppressed social groups who are given no voice in the narrative of history. Hence he writes, 'An ethic of writing is to discover and make heard silenced voices; an ethic of reading is to hear those voices.'[148] The first thing he means by this is that literary critics traditionally tend to think of narratives as unified and coherent wholes, interpreting apparent disruptions or gaps in the text in terms of their expectation of its unity and coherence. He also means that the narratives which have come to comprise the canon of Western literature are those which on the whole lend themselves to such interpretation. He calls this apparently 'right' reading of a text, to which institutional literary criticism is ordered, its 'master plot', and argues that every such plot, in privileging certain stories, specifically certain people's stories, excludes those of others, who can be called narrative's 'victims'.[149] The silenced voices of fictional narratives, that is, are often also the silenced voices of historical narratives. In response to this situation, Ledbetter proposes an ethical mode of reading, which sees the gaps and interruptions in a text as signs of the absence of certain stories which the narrative does not tell. He writes, 'Reading and writing which reveal absence are aware of the victim's peripheral existence in relation to the master plot's centred existence and in turn look for ways to tell narrative's story from the peripheral perspective.'[150] In practice, Ledbetter argues, this can be done through an attention to the representation of the human body in a given narrative. He associates the healthy body, neither diseased nor wounded, with the dominant social groups whose stories most narratives tell, and thinks metaphorically of such unified narratives themselves as healthy bodies. An ethic of reading, therefore, will attend to those places in a text that Ledbetter describes as 'narrative scarring', that is, the gaps and disruptions in a text where its silenced voices can be made heard.[151] He describes the narrative scar as follows: 'an apocalyptic moment in the text, an intruding otherness that is chaotic and crises-orientated and demands a new awareness on the part of the writer and reader and, in particular, the characters in the text'.[152] The scar raises the possibility, which an ethically minded critic must bring out, of another ethic altogether in the text than that implied by its dominant plot or traditional interpretation. Such scars can be recognized, Ledbetter claims, as moments of violence, physical or mental, perpetrated on the bodies of the characters in the narrative. Their ethical significance is determined by 'how the victim puts the violence to use to achieve an end other than the end intended by the violators'.[153] In the rest of the book, Ledbetter puts this kind of criticism into practice, attending to the moments of bodily violence in the texts he discusses and to the ethical significance of the response to this violence on the part of those whose stories the text apparently effaces. The value of such criticism, he argues, is that, in opening himself to the possibility of other stories in a text than those most immediately given or traditionally interpreted in it, the critic comes to open his own stories, that is, the narratives in whose terms he makes sense of his own life, to criticism and reinterpretation. Ledbetter writes, 'As a suspicious reader, certainly I will question a text's narrative claims which run counter to my personal narrative; yet more important . . . I will develop ways to be critical of narrative claims which reflect my own personal story.'[154] The most profound ethical effect a narrative can have, he argues, is that of altering or developing the narrative structure of the reader's own life.

As with Detweiler, Ledbetter's definition of religion is not one that derives specifically from Christian theology, although it is not inconsistent with the latter, and so his definitions of the religious functions of narrative do not necessarily follow from the theological perspective I am adopting here. Broadly speaking, Ledbetter's literary theory seems to me to be true in certain cases but not generally. With respect to his claim that novels can be interpreted in terms of a dominant virtue which is presented as a way to live the good life, that is, a fully human life, this is indeed true of certain novels – and Ledbetter's analyses of the three he discusses are on the whole convincing – but impossible to raise to the level of a truth about novels in general. Many novels simply do not present a resolution to crises in the form of a virtue – what would the dominant virtue of *The Bell Jar* be, for example, in which Esther ends the novel with the same existential questions and psychological traits as she began? The novel does not so much teach us a way to live well as suggest the impossibility of living well for an intelligent woman in America in the 1950s. Ledbetter's theory of reading, however, seems to me to be more generally true. He is right to argue that narratives project an ethos, which he calls 'tone', that is, that they project a world determined by the narrator's beliefs about its nature and qualities. In reading, the reader tests his own beliefs about the world against those expressed or implied in the text, and in certain cases will change them as a result. Again, it seems to me to be true that human beings understand themselves, in part at least, by thinking of their lives in narrative terms. Readers can therefore develop the narrative or narratives in whose terms they understand their own lives according to their understanding of fictional narratives. In short, as Ledbetter argues, in reading fiction, a reader can develop his understanding of himself and the world, and even, in certain cases, of how to live in the world. He develops this point well in the second book. His concept of a mode of criticism that attends to the silenced voices in a text, to the power-relations between those social groups represented in the text and those who are not represented or misrepresented, certainly constitutes a way of reading that is responsible to the other or to the socially marginalized. From a Christian perspective, this would constitute an ethical mode of criticism. It could not be said to exhaust the possibilities of an ethical approach to the text, since it is possible to make judgements concerning that which is given by the text as well as that which is absent from it, and indeed certain texts are explicitly concerned with social groups which have been marginalized by the dominant historical narratives of a given culture. Nevertheless, Ledbetter's mode of critical attention to the relationship between the stories of those groups marginalized by the dominant historical narratives of a given culture and its fictional narratives, constitutes a valuable method of literary criticism from the perspective of Christian ethics. He is right to argue that this kind of attention can lead a reader to attend to and even incorporate into his own self-understanding the stories marginalized by the dominant narratives in whose terms he understands his life. As Ledbetter claims, the profoundest ethical function of literary texts is that they can lead their readers to change and develop their understanding of the world and of how to live in it.

7
Conclusion

I am now in a position to set out the principles of a Christian literary theory which can be formulated in the contemporary culture which seems to reject the legitimacy of such a theory. Recent work in hermeneutics, I have argued, shows that the concepts of Christian literary theory and criticism are legitimate, insofar as these discourses are practised under the same conditions as every other mode of literary theory and criticism. Following Gadamer, I have argued that the situation in tradition by which interpretation of literary texts from the perspective of Christian faith and theology is characterized is shared by all acts of interpretation whatever. To think of literature from the perspective of Christian faith and theology is to do so in terms of a structure of pre-understandings that derives from the acceptance of the claims of a given tradition. This is not an exceptional mode of literary interpretation, since all such interpretation is so determined. There is no act of interpretation which is not determined in advance by the pre-understandings which derive from an interpreter's situation in traditions. This is not a conservative claim, in the sense that it does not recognize that traditions can be sources of ideology. On the contrary, I have argued, an individual accepts the claims of a given tradition on the basis of a rational judgement, and it is through precisely this process of judgement that he can also reject those claims which he judges to be ideological, or in any other way false. It is in this process of reinterpreting the claims of the past in the light of the concerns of the present that all tradition as such consists. I have further argued, following Fish's theory of interpretive communities, that the determination of Christian literary interpretation by the beliefs and values of the community of which the interpreter is a member is a characteristic of all acts of interpretation. Whilst Fish is wrong to claim that the meaning of a text is determined entirely by the interpretive strategies we use, he is right to claim that these strategies follow from an interpreter's membership of a complex set of interpretive communities, or social groups whose defining characteristics determine the ways in which their members interpret texts. To interpret the Bible as a text in whose truth-claim one can believe on the basis of the interpretive strategies shared by the church, therefore, is not an exceptional way of interpreting a text but rather an example of the way in which texts are always interpreted. To interpret literary texts from within the Christian community as well as the community of literary criticism is again precisely an example of the way in which such texts are always interpreted. Insofar as they share in the conditions of all literary theory and criticism whatever, therefore, I have argued that Christian literary theory and criticism are legitimate modes of these discourses.

I have gone on to argue that Christian theology is a discourse which can legitimately be used in literary theory and criticism after the specific critiques of such discourse posed by certain contemporary literary theories. In particular, I have shown that it can still be used after the critique of theological language posed by deconstruction. In the first place, Christian theology as such cannot be reduced to onto-theology, which is the object of deconstruction. In the second place, deconstruction itself works within the double bind of theology, using language, as the only medium available in which to do so, to indicate the wholly other than to which language applies. In particular, I have shown, deconstruction works within the problematic of negative theology, denoting the other by the dual strategy of negating the positive statements of a given tradition, and going on to negate all positive statement as such. Furthermore, as Derrida makes increasingly clear, deconstruction shares with theology a faith in the other which it denotes in this necessarily compromised way. Deconstruction does not prohibit or render meaningless the use of theological language in literary theory or criticism, therefore, since it remains within the circle of precisely such language itself. Rather, it makes clear a point which Christian theologians have always in principle recognized, that theology must remain continually critical of its own language. Theological statements cannot to be taken to be finally or certainly true, therefore, but rather as provisional articulations of the church's faith in that which lies beyond the world to which language can refer. Such statements are believed to be true, although their truth cannot be demonstrated. It is in this sense alone that theological language can be used in literary and cultural interpretation after deconstruction.

I have also shown that Christian theology can be used in literary interpretation after the critique of religion posed by Marxism, which remains an influential critique for politically committed forms of literary and cultural criticism. As an argument for atheism, the Marxist critique of religion is based upon a logical fallacy, inasmuch as the socio-economic determinants of religious beliefs do not constitute evidence for the truth or falsity of these beliefs. Whilst religious beliefs may be influenced by the social and economic conditions in which they are held, it does not follow from this, as Marxism claims, that they refer to no other reality than these conditions. The atheism of the Marxist world-view is ultimately an unproven hypothesis. Christian theology, therefore, remains in itself a legitimate discourse to use in literary interpretation after Marxism. Furthermore, whilst Marxism is right to claim that Christian theology has been used as an ideology, which serves to degrade human life, it is wrong to generalize from this historical fact to the essence of the Christian faith. Not only has Christian theology also been used to protest against social injustice, as Engels was aware, but the Christian faith is essentially a call to a fully human life, both individually and socially, as recent theology has emphasized. It remains ethically possible to use Christian theology in literary interpretation after the Marxist critique, therefore. Nevertheless, Marxism reminds such theology that it has historically functioned both to justify and to protest against social injustice and that it can still function in either way. It is only on the basis of a self-reflection in the light of this reminder that Christian theology can justifiably be used in literary and cultural interpretation after Marxism.

I have also argued that Christian theology can be used in literary interpretation after the critique of such theology posed by psychoanalysis. Freud's theory that the Christian faith is a theological expression of guilt which derives from the collective memory of an ancient parricide is, as he himself recognizes, a speculation that cannot be proved. Anthropology and the history of religion have rejected the premises upon which it is based, which render it unlikely to be true. Furthermore, as Freud also recognizes, his claim that religious beliefs are wish-fulfilments does not constitute evidence for their truth or falsity. Whilst religious beliefs may be expressions of infantile attitudes, it does not follow from this that there is no reality to which they correspond. It remains legitimate, therefore, to use Christian theology in literary and cultural interpretation after psychoanalysis. This claim is supported by those forms of psychoanalysis which acknowledge the possibility of the truth and the value of Christian beliefs. Nevertheless, Freud's claim that such beliefs can be a means of flight from reality and moral responsibility is true. Psychoanalysis reminds Christian theology that the faith upon which it reflects can function as an imaginary escape from the reality of human suffering, although it is in fact a call courageously to face and to improve this reality. It is only in the light of such a self-reflection that Christian theology can be used in literary theory and criticism after psychoanalysis.

Having established in this way that Christian theology can be used to understand and interpret literary and cultural works, I have argued that this can be done in the following ways. In the first place, literary texts are human works, and should be understood as such. Since the human person, according to Christian anthropology, is a unity of body and spirit, the literary works men and women produce are determined by both these aspects of their being. Insofar as the author is a bodily creature, I have argued, the insights of Marxist literary theory concerning the determination of literary and cultural works by the material conditions of their production are valid. Literary texts are determined by the social and economic conditions in which they are written, and can be fully understood only in the light of these conditions. I have argued that Christian literary criticism should analyse the social and economic relations which can be shown to be of relevance to a given text, and judge them in the light of Biblical social ethics. Insofar as an author is a spiritual creature, however, who finds fulfilment ultimately only in the relationship of love with God and with others for which he was created, the literary and cultural works he produces can express the desire for this kind of completely fulfilled human life by which his existence is characterized. Marxist literary theory speaks of the utopian desires expressed in literary works for the kind of fully human society that does not exist at present. From a Christian perspective, such works can express a desire for the kingdom of God, the kind of life lived in love with God and with others which constitutes the fulfilment of human desire. As spiritual creatures, men and women are faced with the question of the meaning of their existence, and their literary and cultural productions can constitute explorations of precisely that question.

I have argued that literary texts project a world, analogous to the real world of given objects, in which the reader dwells, at the level of his or her lived experience, whilst he or she reads. Part of the pleasure which derives from reading fictional works is that the worlds which they project, in which the reader dwells whilst reading, are in certain ways better and more satisfying than the world of the reader's everyday experience. This can be true at the level of the content of the world of the text, as in the happy endings of comic plots, but it is also true of the world of a fictional or poetic text as such. Simply by beginning, a literary text opens up a new world, free as such from the practical concerns, the suffering and the consequences of human evil by which the real world of the reader's experience is characterized. By ending, the text fixes that world and gives it a certain significance, which the world of the reader's experience does not necessarily possess. The world of a story, for example, has a logical progression towards an end, from whose perspective the lives of the characters represented in the story have a certain meaning. This is precisely the kind of certain meaning which its readers, who live, in Frank Kermode's phrase, in the middle of time, desire but are not guaranteed in their own lives. The world of the story, therefore, offers a temporary and imaginary fulfilment of this desire. The world of a text, through its fixation in writing, has a permanence that contrasts with the transitory quality of the reader's own experience, and, especially in poetic texts, a series of pleasing qualities which derive from its aesthetic formation. All these ways in which the world of a fictional or poetic text represents a better or more satisfying version of the world of the reader's experience can be understood, as Michael Edwards argues, as a response to the fallen nature of that world. Writing and reading fictional and poetic texts, that is, is in part an expression of the desire of human beings who live in a world characterized by original sin and its effects to live in a new and better world, transformed by its redemption from these effects. This is not necessarily a conscious aspect of the pleasure of reading a work of imaginative literature. Nevertheless, from the perspective of Christian theology, the fact that we write and read texts which project new and in certain respects more desirable worlds out of the material of our experience in this world, can be understood as an example of the way in which, according to Rom. 8:22–23, the creation awaits and strains towards its redemption. Certain literary texts articulate this desire at the level of their plot or content, as Edwards has shown in the case of tragedy. One way in which literary and cultural criticism can be practised from the standpoint of Christian faith, therefore, is analysis, where it can be shown to be appropriate, of the ways in which a given text responds to the fallen world of the author's experience and expresses a desire for the redemption of this world.

The world of a literary text can be opposed to the real world of the reader's everyday experience insofar as it is imaginary. Nevertheless, the experience of dwelling in the world of a text is also a part of the reader's experience in the real world, and I have argued that there is a dialectical relationship between the two. We understand literary texts on the basis of our experience as a whole, but, insofar as the text constitutes a new experience, it leads us to understand our experience as a whole in a new way. As Ricoeur argues, we understand ourselves in part through the worlds opened up to us by texts and utterances. The world of a literary text, therefore, can increase this understanding. To dwell in the world projected by a literary text can constitute an experience on whose basis a reader understands the world in which he or she dwells as such in a new way. I have argued that reading a fictional or poetic text constitutes, in varying degrees, the negative stage in a dialectic of self-understanding. On the one hand, insofar as the world of the text constitutes a new experience for the reader, it shows that his understanding of the world is incomplete. At the same time, this understanding is raised to a higher level as the reader incorporates the new experience of the text into a greater understanding of his experience as a whole. This is the basis of the ethical value of literature. A literary text projects a world determined by certain beliefs and values, which the reader interprets with reference to the structure of beliefs and values he holds as he begins to read, and *vice versa*. In interpreting the text, that is, a reader tests precisely the structure of norms in whose terms he interprets against those projected by the text. This process can lead him to develop and even altogether to change the beliefs about himself and the world which he held as he began to read. The extent of this negativity, that is, the extent to which a given text leads a reader to develop his self-understanding in this way, is an index of the value of the text to the reader.

It is in this sense that the Bible can be understood as a literary text among others. The Bible differs from literary texts insofar as it makes a truth-claim, in which the interpretive community of the church believes. Nevertheless, it shares with literary texts the property of projecting a world, determined by a specific structure of beliefs and values, in which the reader dwells, at the level of his lived experience, whilst reading. As with literary texts, in the process of interpreting the Biblical text, the reader understands these beliefs and values with reference to those which he or she brings to the text, and the latter with reference to those projected by the text. In this way, the reader can change his understanding of the world of his experience, and of how to live in it, as a result of his experience of the world of the text. The Bible differs from literary texts in demanding precisely this kind of change, on the basis of its claim to refer not only to a possible world of the reader's experience but to that which constitutes the ground of the world of his experience as such. It claims to project a world in whose terms the reader develops his self-understanding in the most authentic possible way. To understand the Bible as literature, through analysis of the ways in which its meanings are constructed through the devices of poetry and narrative, is to understand precisely how this claim is made.

The nature and qualities of the world projected by a fictional or poetic text will be an important object of analysis for Christian critical practice. I have argued that, since all interpretation is determined by the set of interpretive communities to which an individual belongs, to practice literary criticism from within both the Christian and the literary communities is an example of the way in which interpretation is always practised, and therefore legitimate. Christian literary critics are as such members of at least these two communities, and in practice of many more. This means that Christian literary criticism will be determined both by the standards of the community of academic literary criticism and by those of the church. In certain respects, therefore, Christian critical practice will use the critical methods shared by the community of literary criticism as such. I would argue that Christian critics can and should use all of these methods, except insofar as they contradict any article of the critic's Christian faith. I have argued that the methods of psychoanalytic criticism do not imply any such inconsistency, since human desire can be understood in terms of the theology of original sin and of the psychoanalytic theory of libido without contradiction. Where a psychoanalytic account of desire seems most appropriate in the interpretation of a literary text, therefore, a Christian critic could and should use it. In other respects, on the other hand, Christian critical practice will use methods which derive specifically from the critic's membership of the Christian community. The first of these, in my view, should be a kind of existential criticism, according to which the critic analyses the characteristics of the world projected by a given literary text in terms of Christian theology. The critic can compare the world of the text to the world as it understood from the perspective of Christian faith. The world of a given text is determined by a specific structure of principles and values, and it should be a method of Christian critical practice to analyse these principles and values in the light of a Christian theological reflection upon them. Furthermore, every text has a structure of concerns, some of which it projects as ultimate, that is, as that to which human life is most authentically ordered. Christian criticism should analyse these concerns in the light of Christian theology. Finally, I have argued that Christian criticism should conduct this theological reflection upon the world of a text in a dialogical manner. The theological reflections upon the Biblical revelation in whose terms the critic analyses the world of the text, that is, may be subject to critique and even reformulation in the light of the concerns and values projected by the text. Christian literary criticism should be a two-way process, in which the concerns of the text are interpreted in the light of a theology which remains open to critique in the light of these concerns.

Notes

1 Introduction

1 R. Barthes, *Image Music Text*, tr. S. Heath (London: Fontana, 1977), p. 147.
2 K. Mills, *Justifying Language: Paul and Contemporary Literary Theory* (Basingstoke and London: Macmillan, 1995), p. 2.
3 H. Küng, *Does God Exist? An Answer For Today*, tr. E. Quinn (London: Collins, 1980), p. 439.
4 Ibid., p. 461.
5 Ibid., p. 470.
6 C. Belsey, *Critical Practice* (London and New York: Routledge, 1980), p. 4.
7 G. Lindbeck, *The Nature of Doctrine: Religion and Theology in a Postliberal Age* (Philadelphia: The Westminster Press, 1984), p. 74.
8 *Dei Verbum* no. 2, in *The Documents of Vatican II*, tr. and ed. W. Abbott and J. Gallagher (New York: Association Press, 1966), p. 112.
9 K. Rahner, *Theological Investigations Vol. 1: God, Christ, Mary and Grace*, tr. C. Ernst (London: Darton, Longman and Todd, 1961), p. 47.
10 K. Rahner, *Foundations of Christian Faith: An Introduction to the Idea of Christianity*, tr. W. Dych (London: Darton, Longman and Todd, 1976), p. 377.
11 *Unitatis Redintegratio* no. 11, in *The Documents of Vatican II*, p. 354.
12 T. Eagleton, *Literary Theory: An Introduction* (Oxford: Blackwell, 1983), pp. 1–2.

2 On Deconstruction

1 J. Derrida, *Positions*, tr. A. Bass (London: Athlone, 1981), p. 40.
2 I. Kant, *Critique of Pure Reason*, A631/B659.
3 M. Heidegger, *Identity and Difference*, tr. J. Stambaugh (New York: Harper and Row, 1957), p. 54.
4 Ibid., p. 70.
5 Ibid., p. 60.
6 J. Derrida, *Of Grammatology*, tr. G. Spivak (Baltimore and London: Johns Hopkins University Press, 1976), p. 13.
7 Ibid., p. 14.
8 C. Raschke et al., *Deconstruction and Theology* (New York: Crossroad, 1982), p. 3.
9 Ibid., p. 4, 27.
10 M. Taylor, *Erring: A Postmodern A/theology* (Chicago and London: University of Chicago Press, 1984), p. 6.
11 Ibid., p. 5.
12 Ibid., p. 10.
13 Ibid., p. 13.
14 Ibid., p. 11.
15 Ibid., pp. 103–104.
16 Ibid., p. 104.

17 Ibid., p. 118.
18 J. Caputo, 'Mysticism and Transgression: Derrida and Meister Eckhart', *Derrida and Deconstruction*, ed. H. Silverman (New York and London: Routledge, 1989), p. 29.
19 J. Milbank, *Theology and Social Theory: Beyond Secular Reason* (Oxford: Blackwell, 1990), p. 295.
20 M. Taylor, *Erring*, p. 142.
21 Ibid., p. 98.
22 J. Milbank, *The Word Made Strange: Theology, Language, Culture* (Oxford: Blackwell, 1997), p. 41. In *After Writing: On the Liturgical Consummation of Philosophy* (Oxford: Blackwell, 1997), pp. 3–46, Catherine Pickstock argues that Plato cannot be held to privilege presence over difference in the way that Derrida asserts.
23 J. Milbank, *The Word Made Strange*, p. 85.
24 Ibid., p. 70.
25 Ibid.
26 Ibid., p. 74.
27 Ibid., p. 77.
28 Ibid., p. 78.
29 G. Ward, *Barth, Derrida and the Language of Theology* (Cambridge: Cambridge University Press, 1995), p. 255.
30 Ibid., p. 247.
31 K. Barth, *Church Dogmatics Vol. II: The Doctrine of God, 1st half-volume*, tr. T. Parker et al. (Edinburgh: T. & T. Clark, 1957), p. 57.
32 Ibid., p. 4.
33 K. Barth, *Church Dogmatics Vol. I: The Doctrine of the Word of God, Part 1*, tr. G. Bromiley (Edinburgh: T. & T. Clark, 1975), p. 91.
34 Ibid., p. 158.
35 Ibid., p. 159.
36 J. Derrida, *Of Grammatology*, p. 75.
37 K. Barth, *Church Dogmatics* I, 1, p. 194.
38 K. Barth, *Church Dogmatics* II, 1, p. 188.
39 G. Ward, *Theology and Contemporary Critical Theory* (Basingstoke and London: Macmillan, 1996), p. 24.
40 K. Hart, *The Trespass of the Sign: Deconstruction, Theology and Philosophy* (Cambridge: Cambridge University Press, 1989), p. 21.
41 Ibid., p. 29.
42 T. Wright, 'Behind the Curtain: Derrida and the Religious Imagination', *Through a Glass Darkly: Essays in the Religious Imagination*, ed. J. Hawley (New York: Fordham University Press, 1996), p. 279.
43 J. Derrida, *Of Grammatology*, p. 71, 98.
44 B. Ingraffia, *Postmodern Theory and Biblical Theology: Vanquishing God's Shadow* (Cambridge: Cambridge University Press, 1995), p. 221.
45 J. Dicenso, 'Deconstruction and the Philosophy of Religion: World Affirmation and Critique', *Philosophy of Religion* 31 (1992) 29.
46 B. Ingraffia, *Postmodern Theory and Biblical Theology*, p. 224.
47 Ibid., p. 222.
48 Ibid., p. 75.
49 P. Ricoeur, 'Biblical Hermeneutics', *Semeia* 4 (1975) 130.

50 T. Wright, 'Through a *Glas* Darkly: Derrida, Literature and the Specter of Christianity', *Christianity and Literature* 44 (1994) 74.
51 K. Barth, *Church Dogmatics* I, 1, p. 165.
52 G. Ward, 'Why is Derrida Important for Theology?', *Theology* 95 (1992) 265.
53 Ibid.
54 J. Derrida, *Writing and Difference*, tr. A. Bass (London: Routledge, 1978), p. 288.
55 J. Derrida, *Of Grammatology*, p. 14.
56 J. Derrida, *Writing and Difference*, p. 284.
57 K. Barth, *Church Dogmatics* I, 1, p. 164.
58 St Thomas Aquinas, *Summa Theologiae*, Ia 13, 2.
59 Ibid.
60 Ibid. Ia 13, 3.
61 Ibid. Ia 13, 2 ad 2.
62 K. Barth, *Church Dogmatics* II, 1, p. 187.
63 Ibid.
64 Ibid., p. 212.
65 Ibid., p. 214.
66 Ibid., p. 202.
67 J. Derrida, *Margins of Philosophy*, tr. A. Bass (New York and London: Harvester Wheatsheaf), p. 6.
68 J. Derrida, 'The Original Discussion of *"Différance"*', in *Derrida and Différance*, ed. D. Wood (Warwick: Parousia, 1985), p. 130.
69 Ibid., p. 132.
70 J. Derrida, 'How to Avoid Speaking: Denials', in *Derrida and Negative Theology*, ed. H. Coward and T. Foshay (New York: State University of New York Press, 1992), p. 77.
71 J. Derrida, 'The Original Discussion of *"Différance"*', p. 132.
72 J. Derrida, *Margins of Philosophy*, p. 6.
73 J. Derrida, 'How to Avoid Speaking', p. 77.
74 Ibid., p. 78.
75 Ibid.
76 M. Eckhart, 'Quasi stella matutina', in *Meister Eckhart: Teacher and Preacher*, tr. and ed. B. McGinn, F. Tobin and E. Borgstadt (New York: Paulist Press, 1986), p. 256.
77 J. Derrida, *Writing and Difference*, p. 337.
78 See D. Carabine, *The Unknown God. Negative Theology in the Platonic Tradition: Plato to Eriugena* (Louvain: Eerdmans, 1995), p. 282; R. Mortley, *From Word to Silence Vol. II: The Way of Negation, Christian and Greek* (Bonn: Hanstein, 1986), pp. 221–223.
79 R. Lees, *The Negative Language of the Dionysian School of Mystical Theology: An Approach to the Cloud of Unknowing* (Salzburg: Institut für Anglistik und Amerikanistik, 1983), p. 139.
80 D. Carabine, *The Unknown God*, p. 283.
81 Pseudo-Dionysius, *The Divine Names*, I.7 596C. All citations from Pseudo-Dionysius are taken from *Pseudo-Dionysius: The Complete Works*, tr. Colm Luibheid (London: SPCK, 1987).
82 Pseudo-Dionysius, *The Divine Names*, V.4 817C; I.3 589B.
83 See M. Heidegger, *Identity and Difference*, tr. J. Stambaugh (New York: Harper and Row, 1957), pp. 58, 70–71.

84 Pseudo-Dionysius, *The Divine Names*, II.11 949B; II.3 640B; IV.3 697A.
85 Ibid., I.4 589D.
86 Ibid., II.7 645A.
87 Ibid., II.11 649B.
88 See ibid., IV.13 712A.
89 Ibid., V.1 816B.
90 Ibid., V.2 816C.
91 Ibid., V.1 816B.
92 Ibid., V.6 820C.
93 Pseudo-Dionysius, *Letters*, IX.1 1105D.
94 Pseudo-Dionysius, *The Mystical Theology*, I.2 1000B.
95 J. Jones, 'Introduction', in *Pseudo-Dionysius Areopagite: The Divine Names and Mystical Theology* (Milwaukee: Marquette University Press, 1980), p. 20.
96 Pseudo-Dionysius, *The Mystical Theology*, I.2 1000B.
97 D. Turner, *The Darkness of God: Negativity in Christian Mysticism* (Cambridge: Cambridge University Press, 1995), p. 35.
98 Pseudo-Dionysius, *The Mystical Theology*, V 1048B.
99 Pseudo-Dionysius, *The Divine Names*, II.4 640D.
100 J. Jones, 'Introduction', p. 102.
101 M. Taylor, *nOts* (Chicago and London: Chicago University Press, 1993) pp. 48–49.
102 S. Wolosky, 'An "Other" Negative Theology: On Derrida's "How to Avoid Speaking: Denials"', *Poetics Today*, 19 (1998) 267.
103 J. Caputo, *The Prayers and Tears of Jacques Derrida: Religion Without Religion* (Bloomington: Indiana University Press, 1997), p. xxiv.
104 Ibid., p. 2, 7.
105 Ibid., p. 8.
106 Ibid.
107 J. Derrida, 'How to Avoid Speaking', p. 98.
108 J. Derrida, *Margins*, p. 6; 'How to Avoid Speaking', p. 82.
109 J. Derrida, 'How to Avoid Speaking', p. 82.
110 J. Derrida, 'Letter to John P. Leavey, Jr.', *Semeia*, 23 (1982) 61.
111 J. Derrida, *Writing and Difference*, p. 271.
112 J. Derrida, 'How to Avoid Speaking', p. 79.
113 J. Derrida, 'Circumfession', in J. Derrida and G. Bennington, *Jacques Derrida*, tr. G. Bennington (Chicago and London: University of Chicago Press, 1993), p. 3; *Specters of Marx*, tr. P. Kamuf (London and New York: Routledge, 1994), p. 35.
114 J. Derrida, *On the Name*, ed. T. Dutoit (Stanford: Stanford University Press, 1995), p. 43.
115 Ibid.
116 Ibid., p. 48.
117 Ibid., p. 54.
118 Ibid.
119 Ibid., p. 67.
120 J. Derrida, 'How to Avoid Speaking', p. 110.
121 J. Derrida, *The Gift of Death*, tr. D. Wills (Chicago and London: University of Chicago Press, 1995), p. 68.
122 J. Derrida, *Specters of Marx*, p. 28.
123 J. Derrida, 'How to Avoid Speaking', p. 109.

124 J. Caputo, 'Mysticism and Transgression', p. 30.
125 J. Derrida, 'Circumfession', p. 75.
126 J. Derrida, *Specters of Marx*, p. 28.
127 J. Derrida, 'Of an Apocalyptic Tone Newly Adopted in Philosophy', in *Derrida and Negative Theology*, ed. H. Coward and T. Foshay (New York: State University of New York Press, 1992), pp. 65–66.
128 J. Derrida, *Specters of Marx*, p. 59.
129 Ibid.
130 Ibid.
131 Ibid., p. 168.
132 Ibid.
133 J. Derrida, 'Faith and Knowledge: The Two Sources of "Religion" within the Limits of Reason Alone', *Religion*, ed. J. Derrida and G. Vattimo, tr. S. Weber et al. (Cambridge: Polity Press, 1998), pp. 52–53; 24–25.
134 Ibid., p. 17; *Specters of Marx*, p. 28.
135 J. Derrida, 'Faith and Knowledge', p. 19.
136 J. Derrida, 'Circumfession', pp. 154–155.
137 J. Derrida, 'Faith and Knowledge', p. 19.
138 Ibid., p. 18.
139 Ibid., p. 28.
140 Ibid., p. 44.
141 Ibid., p. 45.
142 Ibid.
143 J. Derrida, *The Gift of Death* p. 49; J. Caputo, *Deconstruction in a Nutshell: A Conversation With Jacques Derrida* (New York: Fordham University Press, 1997), p. 23.
144 Ibid., p. 24.
145 J. Caputo, *The Prayers and Tears of Jacques Derrida*, p. 139.
146 Ibid., p. 141.
147 Ibid.
148 J. Derrida, *On the Name*, p. 49.
149 J. Caputo, *The Prayers and Tears of Jacques Derrida*, p. 142.
150 J. Derrida, 'Faith and Knowledge', p. 17.
151 J. Caputo, *Deconstruction in a Nutshell*, p. 23.
152 J. Derrida, *Specters of Marx*, p. 168.
153 J. Derrida, 'Faith and Knowledge', p. 18; see pp. 26–30
154 Ibid., p. 19.
155 Ibid., p. 18.

3 On Marxism

1 K. Marx, 'Towards a Critique of Hegel's *Philosophy of Right*: Introduction', in *Karl Marx: Selected Writings*, ed. D. McLellan (Oxford: Oxford University Press, 1977), p. 63.
2 A. MacIntyre, *Marxism and Christianity* (London: Duckworth, 1968), p. 6.
3 K. Marx and F. Engels, *Collected Works* Vol. 1 (London: Lawrence and Wishart, 1975 ff.), p. 647.
4 Ibid., p. 639.

5 K. Marx, 'Forward to Thesis: *The Difference Between the Natural Philosophy of Democritus and the Natural Philosophy of Epicurus*', in K. Marx and F. Engels, *On Religion* (New York: Schocken, 1964), p. 15.

6 See H. Küng, *Does God Exist? An Answer for Today*, tr. E. Quinn (London: Collins, 1980), pp. 219–220.

7 F. Engels, 'Ludwig Feuerbach and the End of Classical German Philosophy', in *Marx and Engels: Basic Writings on Politics and Philosophy*, ed. L. Feuer (New York: Doubleday, 1989), p. 205.

8 L. Feuerbach, *The Essence of Christianity*, tr. G. Eliot (New York: Harper, 1957), p. 12.

9 Ibid., p. 4.

10 Ibid., p. 3.

11 Ibid., p. 14.

12 Ibid., p. 31.

13 Ibid., p. 26.

14 Ibid., pp. xxxvii–xxxviii.

15 Ibid., p. 270.

16 K. Marx, 'Towards a Critique of Hegel's *Philosophy of Right*', p. 63.

17 K. Marx and F. Engels, 'The Holy Family', in *Collected Works* Vol. 4, p. 135.

18 K. Marx, 'Towards a Critique of Hegel's *Philosophy of Right*', p. 63.

19 Ibid.

20 Ibid., p. 64.

21 Ibid.

22 Ibid.

23 Ibid., p. 69.

24 K. Marx, 'Theses on Feuerbach', in *Karl Marx: Selected Writings*, ed. D. McLellan (Oxford: Oxford University Press, 1977), p. 157.

25 K. Marx and F. Engels, 'The German Ideology', in *Collected Works* Vol. 5, p. 36.

26 Ibid.

27 K. Marx, *Capital: A Critique of Political Economy* Vol. 1, tr. B. Fowkes (London: Penguin, 1976), p. 494.

28 Ibid., p. 176.

29 Ibid., p. 172.

30 Ibid., p. 165.

31 Ibid., p. 173.

32 See D. McLellan, *Marxism and Religion: A Description and Assessment of the Marxist Critique of Christianity* (London: Macmillan, 1987), pp. 33–36.

33 K. Marx and F. Engels, *Collected Works* Vol. 2, p. 471.

34 F. Engels, 'Anti-Dühring', in *On Religion* p. 147.

35 Ibid.

36 Ibid.

37 Ibid., p. 148.

38 Ibid.

39 Ibid.

40 Ibid., p. 149.

41 F. Engels, 'Bruno Bauer and Early Christianity', in *On Religion* p. 195.

42 Ibid., p. 198.

43 Ibid., p. 196; 'The Book of Revelation', in ibid., p. 207; 'On the History of Early Christianity', in *Marx and Engels: Basic Writings on Politics and Philosophy* p. 175.

44 Ibid., p. 200.
45 Ibid., p. 202.
46 Ibid.
47 F. Engels, 'On the History of Early Christianity', p. 183.
48 F. Engels, 'The Book of Revelation', p. 206.
49 F. Engels, 'On the History of Early Christianity', p. 180.
50 Ibid., p. 169.
51 Ibid., p. 168.
52 Ibid., pp. 180–181.
53 Ibid., p. 169.
54 F. Engels, 'Ludwig Feuerbach and the End of Classical German Philosophy', in *Basic Writings on Politics and Philosophy* p. 237.
55 Ibid., p. 238.
56 F. Engels, 'The Peasant War in Germany', in *On Religion* p. 99.
57 F. Engels, 'Ludwig Feuerbach and the End of Classical German Philosophy', p. 239; 'The Peasant War in Germany', p. 100.
58 Ibid., p. 112.
59 Ibid.
60 F. Engels, 'Ludwig Feuerbach and the End of Classical German Philosophy', p. 240.
61 V. Lenin, 'Classes and Parties in Their Attitude to Religion and the Church', in *Collected Works* (Moscow: Foreign Languages Publishing House, and London: Lawrence and Wishart, 1960–1969), Vol. 15, p. 416.
62 D. McLellan, op. cit., p. 91.
63 V. Lenin, 'Socialism and Religion', in *Collected Works* Vol. 10 p. 83.
64 Ibid.
65 Ibid., p. 84.
66 V. Lenin, 'The Attitude of the Workers' Party to Religion', in *Collected Works* Vol. 15 p. 403.
67 Ibid., p. 402.
68 V. Lenin, 'Socialism and Religion', p. 85.
69 Ibid., p. 86.
70 Ibid., p. 87; 'The Attitude of the Workers' Party to Religion', p. 407.
71 Ibid., p. 406.
72 Ibid.
73 'V.I. Lenin to A.M. Gorky, November 1913', in *Lenin and Gorky: Letters, Reminiscences, Articles* (Moscow: Progress, 1973), p. 120; 'The Attitude of the Workers' Party to Religion', p. 409.
74 Ibid., p. 121.
75 V. Lenin, *Collected Works* Vol. 29, p. 134.
76 T. Damer, *Attacking Faulty Reasoning: A Practical Guide to Fallacy-Free Arguments*, 3rd edn, (Belmont, CA: Wadsworth, 1995), p. 12.
77 J. Mackie, 'Fallacies', in *The Encyclopaedia of Philosophy* Vol. 3, ed. P. Edwards (New York and London: Macmillan and the Free Press, 1967), p. 177.
78 H. Küng, op. cit., p. 204.
79 L. Feuerbach, *The Essence of Christianity*, p. 121.
80 H. Küng, op. cit., p. 210.
81 K. Marx, 'Towards a Critique of Hegel's *Philosophy of Right*', p. 69.

82 F. Engels, 'Ludwig Feuerbach and the End of Classical German Philosophy', p. 219.

83 H. Küng, op. cit., p. 245.

84 N. Lash, *A Matter of Hope: A Theologian's Reflections on the Thought of Karl Marx* (London: Darton, Longman and Todd, 1981), p. 159.

85 Ibid., pp. 160–161.

86 R. Bigler, *The Politics of German Protestantism: The Rise of the Protestant Church Elite in Prussia, 1815–1848* (Berkeley and London: University of California Press, 1972), p. 7.

87 W. Shanahan, *German Protestants Face the Social Question Vol. I: The Conservative Phase 1815–1871* (Notre Dame: University of Indiana Press, 1954), p. 194.

88 A. McGovern, *Marxism: An American Christian Perspective* (Maryknoll, NY: Orbis), p. 91.

89 See W. Doyle, *The Oxford History of the French Revolution* (Oxford: Oxford University Press, 1989), pp. 136–146, 396–398.

90 H. Daniel-Rops, *The Church in an Age of Revolution 1789–1870*, tr. J. Warrington (London: J.M. Dent, 1965), p. 153.

91 Pius IX, *Syllabus of Errors* (1864), n. 76. The text can be found at http://listserv.american.edu/catholic/church/papal/pius.ix/p9syll.html.

92 Ibid., n.18.

93 Quoted in A. McGovern, op. cit., p. 92.

94 K. Marx, 'The Communism of the Paper *Rheinischer Beobachter*', in *On Religion* p. 83.

95 J. Bonino, *Christians and Marxists: The Mutual Challenge to Revolution* (Grand Rapids, MI: Eerdmans), p. 59.

96 R. Garaudy, *The Alternative Future: A Vision of Christian Marxism*, tr. L. Mayhew (Harmondsworth: Penguin, 1976), p. 88.

97 R. Garaudy, *From Anathema to Dialogue: The Challenge of Marxist-Christian Co-operation*, tr. L. O'Neill (London: Collins, 1967), p. 87; *The Alternative Future* p. 85.

98 Ibid., p. 87.

99 A. McGovern, op. cit., p. 250.

100 Vatican Council II, 'Pastoral Constitution on the Church in the Modern World' nn. 41, 57, in *Vatican Council II: The Conciliar and Post-Conciliar Documents*, ed. A. Flannery (Dublin: Dominican Publications, 1992).

101 Ibid., n. 26.

102 Ibid., n. 12.

103 G. Girardi, *Marxism and Christianity*, tr. K. Traynor (Dublin: Gill and Son, 1968), p. 74.

104 Ibid., p. 77.

105 Ibid., p. 82.

106 See N. Lash, op. cit., p. 142; H. Küng, op. cit., pp. 254–255.

107 Ibid., p. 254.

108 A. McGovern, op. cit., p. 255.

109 H. Küng, op. cit., p. 252.

110 R. Garaudy, *From Anathema to Dialogue*, p. 87.

111 Second General Conference of Latin American Bishops, 'Justice' § 1, in *The Church in the Present-Day Transformation of Latin America in the Light of the*

Council Vol. II: Conclusions, ed. L. Colonnese (Bogotá: General Secretariat of CELAM, 1970).

112 Ibid., n. 3.
113 Ibid., nn. 16, 20.
114 J. Miranda, *Marx and the Bible: A Critique of the Philosophy of Oppression*, tr. J. Eagleson (Maryknoll, NY: Orbis, 1974), p. xix.
115 E. Lévinas, *Totality and Infinity: An Essay On Exteriority*, tr. A. Lingis (Pittsburgh: Duquesne University Press, 1969), p. 46.
116 J. Miranda, op. cit., p. xx.
117 Ibid., p. xvii.
118 Ibid., p. 44
119 Ibid.
120 Ibid., p. 45.
121 Ibid.
122 Ibid., p. 48.
123 Ibid.
124 Ibid., p. 56.
125 Ibid., p. 58.
126 Ibid.
127 Ibid., p. 163.
128 Ibid., p. 170.
129 Ibid., p. 181.
130 Ibid.
131 Ibid., p. 184.
132 Ibid., p. 187.
133 Ibid.
134 Ibid., p. 250.
135 P. Berryman, 'Latin American Liberation Theology', in *Theology in the Americas*, ed. S. Torres and J. Eagleson (Maryknoll, NY: Orbis, 1976), p. 72.
136 C. Cranfield, *A Critical and Exegetical Commentary on the Epistle to the Romans* Vol. 1 (Edinburgh: T. & T. Clark, 1975), p. 129; J. Fitzmyer, *Romans: A New Translation with Introduction and Commentary* (London: Chapman, 1993), p. 289.
137 C. Cranfield, op. cit., p. 194.
138 J. Dunn, *The Theology of Paul the Apostle* (Edinburgh: T. & T. Clark, 1998), pp. 119–123.
139 Ibid., p. 112.
140 J. Fitzmyer, op. cit., p. 474.
141 W. McKane, *A Critical and Exegetical Commentary on Jeremiah* Vol. I (Edinburgh: T. & T. Clark, 1986), p. 213.
142 J. Mays, *Hosea: A Commentary* (London: SCM, 1969), p. 63.
143 J. Miranda, op. cit., p. xvii.
144 Congregation for the Doctrine of the Faith, 'Instruction on Certain Aspects of the "Theology of Liberation"' (1984), intro. http://www.vatican.va/roman_curia/congregations/cfaith/documents/rc_con_cfaith_doc_19840806_theology-liberation_en.html.
145 L. Boff and C. Boff, *Introducing Liberation Theology*, tr. P. Burns (Tunbridge Wells: Burns & Oates, 1987), p. 28.
146 Ibid.

147 G. Gutiérrez, *A Theology of Liberation: History, Politics, Salvation*, tr. C. Inda and J. Eagleson (London: SCM, 1988), p. 86.
148 Ibid., p. 88.
149 Ibid.
150 Ibid., p. 89.
151 Ibid.
152 Ibid., p. 91.
153 Ibid., p. 97.
154 Ibid., p. 96.
155 Ibid., p. 97.
156 Ibid.
157 Ibid., p. 24.
158 Ibid., p. 102.
159 Ibid., p. 103.
160 Ibid., p. 24.
161 Ibid.
162 L. Boff, *Jesus Christ Liberator: A Critical Christology for Our Time*, tr. P. Hughes (London: SPCK, 1980), p. 52.
163 Ibid.
164 Ibid., p. 53.
165 Ibid., p. 55.
166 Ibid., p. 63.
167 Ibid., p. 72.
168 J. Sobrino, *Christology at the Crossroads: A Latin American Approach*, tr. J. Drury (London: SCM, 1978), p. 53.
169 Ibid.
170 L. Boff, op. cit., pp. 50–51.
171 See R. Charles, *Christian Social Witness and Teaching: The Catholic Tradition from Genesis to* Centesimus Annus, Vol. II (Leominster: Gracewing, 1998), pp. 10–12.
172 Leo XIII, *Encyclical Letter On the Condition of the Working Classes:* Rerum Novarum, tr. N.C.W.C. (Boston: St Paul, 1942), n. 6.
173 Ibid.
174 Ibid., n. 31.
175 Ibid., nn. 53, 59.
176 Ibid., 22.
177 Paul VI, *Octagesimo Adveniens* n. 26. The text can be found in *Proclaiming Justice and Peace: Documents from John XXIII to John Paul II*, ed. M. Walsh and B. Davies, 2nd edn (London: CAFOD/Collins, 1991).
178 John Paul II, *Sollicitudo Rei Socialis* n. 21. The text can be found in *The Logic of Solidarity: Commentaries on Pope John Paul II's Encyclical on Social Concern with the Complete Text of the Encyclical* ed. G. Baum and R. Ellsberg (Maryknoll, NY: Orbis, 1989), pp. 1–62.
179 John Paul II, *Encyclical* Redemptor Hominis (London: Catholic Truth Society, 1979), n. 14.
180 John Paul II, *Encyclical Letter On Human Work*: Laborem Exercens, tr. Vatican (Boston: St Paul, 1981), n. 1.
181 Ibid., n. 6.
182 Ibid., n. 7.

183 Ibid., n. 8.
184 John Paul II, *Encyclical Letter* Centesimus Annus: *On the Hundredth Anniversary of* Rerum Novarum, tr. Vatican (Boston: St Paul, 1991), n. 33.
185 Ibid., n. 35.
186 John Paul II, *Laborem Exercens* n. 13.
187 Ibid.
188 John Paul II, *Centesimus Annus* n. 13.
189 Ibid., n. 44.
190 Ibid., n. 13.
191 Ibid.
192 Ibid., n. 24
193 Ibid.
194 Ibid., n. 41.
195 Ibid.
196 Ibid.
197 Vatican Council II, 'Pastoral Constitution on the Church in the Modern World', n. 13.
198 John Paul II, *Centesimus Annus* n. 25.
199 Ibid.
200 R. Niebuhr, *Moral Man and Immoral Society: A Study in Ethics and Politics* (New York: Charles Scribner's Sons, 1932), p. 164.
201 Ibid., p. 196.
202 Ibid., p. 197.
203 P. Tillich, 'Religious Socialism' in *Political Expectation*, ed. J.L. Adams (Macon, GA: Mercer University Press, 1971), p. 46.
204 P. Tillich, 'Christianity and Marxism', in ibid., p. 91.
205 P. Tillich, 'Religious Socialism', p. 52.
206 P. Tillich, 'Christianity and Marxism' p. 89–90; Wolfhart Pannenberg, *Systematic Theology* Vol. 2, tr. G. Bromiley (Edinburgh: T. & T. Clark, 1991), p. 176.
207 St Augustine, *Confessions* I, 1, 1.
208 R. Niebuhr, *The Nature and Destiny of Man: A Christian Interpretation* Vol. I (London: Nisbet, 1941), p. 50.
209 *Catechism of the Catholic Church* (London: Geoffrey Chapman, 1994), n. 27.

4 On Psychoanalysis

1 See S. Freud, 'The Question of a Weltanschauung', in *The Penguin Freud Library*, ed. A. Richards and A. Dickson (London: Penguin, 1973–1986), vol. 2, pp. 193–219. This edition will hereafter be cited as *PFL*.
2 S. Freud, 'Totem and Taboo', in *PFL*, vol. 13, p. 79.
3 Ibid., p. 82.
4 Ibid., p. 83.
5 Ibid., p. 85.
6 Ibid., p. 86.
7 Ibid., p. 192.
8 Ibid., pp. 192–193.
9 Ibid., pp. 203–208.

10 Ibid., p. 206.
11 Ibid., p. 209.
12 Ibid., p. 216.
13 Ibid., pp. 356–370.
14 Ibid., p. 384.
15 S. Freud, 'The Future of an Illusion', in *The Standard Edition of the Complete Psyhcological Works of Sigmund* Freud, tr. and ed. J. Strachey et al. (London: The Hogarth Press and The Institute of Psycho-Analysis, 1953–1974), Vol. XXI, p. 30. This edition will hereafter be cited as *SE*.
16 Ibid., p. 18.
17 Ibid.
18 Ibid., p. 43.
19 Ibid., p. 41.
20 S. Freud, 'Totem and Taboo', p. 190.
21 Ibid., p. 192.
22 Ibid.
23 Ibid., p. 204.
24 Ibid., p. 211.
25 Ibid., p. 217.
26 Ibid., p. 220.
27 A. Kroeber, *The Nature of Culture* (Chicago and London: University of Chicago Press, 1952), p. 302.
28 Ibid.
29 C. Lévi-Strauss, *The Elementary Structures of Kinship*, tr. J. Bell, J. von Sturmer and R. Needham (Boston: Beacon Press, 1969), p. 491.
30 Ibid. Lévi-Strauss also objects to Freud's equation of ontogenesis and phylogenesis. He writes, 'The most primitive culture is still an adult culture, and as such is incompatible with infantile manifestations even in the most highly developed civilisation.' (Ibid., p. 92)
31 S. Freud, 'Totem and Taboo', p. 193.
32 A. Kroeber, *The Nature of Culture*, p. 302.
33 A. Kroeber, *Anthropology* (London: Harrap, 1923), pp. 300–316.
34 A. Radcliffe-Brown, *Structure and Function in Primitive Society: Essays and Addresses* (New York and London: The Free Press, 1952), p. 122.
35 Ibid. In *Freud and the Problem of God* (New Haven: Yale University Press, 1979), p. 67, Hans Küng writes that the claim that any form of religion was everywhere original is 'a dogmatic postulate, not a historically proved fact'.
36 A. Radcliffe-Brown, op. cit., p. 122.
37 Ibid., pp. 157–161.
38 S. Freud, 'Totem and Taboo', p. 159.
39 S. Freud, 'The Future of an Illusion', p. 33.
40 Ibid.
41 Ibid., p. 43. See Freud's letter to Oskar Pfister of 9 February 1909, in which he writes, 'In itself psychoanalysis is neither religious nor irreligious but an impartial tool'. *Psychoanalysis and Faith: The Letters of Sigmund Freud and Oskar Pfister*, ed. H. Meng and E. Freud (London: Hogarth, 1962), p. 17.
42 H. Küng, *Freud and the Problem of God*, p. 76.
43 Ibid., p. 78.

44 S. Freud, 'The Future of an Illusion', p. 37.
45 C. Jung, 'Psychoanalysis and the Cure of Souls', in *Psychology and Religion: West and East. Collected Works of C.G. Jung, Vol. 11*, tr. R. Hull (London: Routledge and Kegan Paul, 1958), p. 349.
46 C. Jung, *Psychology and Religion* (New Haven: Yale University Press, 1938), p. 4.
47 Ibid., p. 6.
48 Ibid., p. 47.
49 Ibid., p. 149.
50 Ibid., p. 46.
51 Ibid., p. 57.
52 Ibid., p. 63.
53 Ibid., p. 71.
54 Ibid., pp. 71–72.
55 Ibid., p. 73.
56 Ibid., p. 99.
57 Ibid., p. 112.
58 C. Jung, 'Psychotherapists or the Clergy', in *Psychology and Religion: West and East*, p. 334.
59 C. Jung, 'Transformation Symbolism in the Mass', in *Psychology and Religion: West and East*, p. 296.
60 See *Letters of C.G. Jung*, ed. G. Adler and A. Jaffé, vol. 2 (London: Routledge, 1976), p. 575.
61 E. Fromm, *Psychoanalysis and Religion* (London: Victor Gollancz, 1951), p. 29.
62 Ibid., p. 36.
63 Ibid., p. 42.
64 Ibid., p. 43.
65 Ibid., p. 44.
66 Ibid., p. 70.
67 Ibid., p. 81.
68 Ibid., p. 82.
69 Ibid., p. 83.
70 Ibid., p. 85.
71 Ibid., p. 92.
72 Ibid., p. 98.
73 R. Webster, *Why Freud Was Wrong: Sin, Science and Psychoanalysis* (London: Harper Collins, 1995), p. 7.
74 Ibid., p. 314.
75 Ibid., p. 330.
76 S. Kirschner, *The Religious and Romantic Origins of Psychoanalysis: Individuation and Integration in Post-Freudian Theory* (Cambridge: Cambridge University Press, 1996), p. 77.
77 R. Webster, op. cit., p. 311.
78 See R. Walsh, *Neoplatonism* (London: Duckworth, 1972), pp. 37–93.
79 M. Abrams, *Natural Supernaturalism: Tradition and Revolution in Romantic Literature* (New York and London: Norton, 1971), pp. 146–154.
80 S. Kirschner, op. cit., p. 180.
81 Ibid., p. 183.
82 Ibid.
83 S. Freud, 'The Dissolution of the Oedipus Complex', in *SE*, vol. XIX, p. 173.

84 S. Kirschner, op. cit., p. 185.
85 S. Freud, *Introductory Lectures on Psychoanalysis. PFL*, vol. 1, p. 380.
86 S. Kirschner, op. cit., pp. 190–191.
87 Ibid., p. 7.
88 P. Vitz and J. Gartner, 'Christianity and Psychoanalysis, Part I: Jesus as the Anti-Oedipus', *Journal of Psychology and Theology* 12 (1984) 5.
89 Ibid. 8.
90 Ibid.
91 Ibid. 13. Freud also attributes love for the father to the infant. Vitz and Gartner acknowledge this but argue that in practice Freud is more concerned with the infant's aggression towards him.
92 Ibid.
93 St Thomas Aquinas, *Summa Theologiae*, Ia–IIae 82, 1.
94 Ibid.
95 Ibid., Ia–IIae 82, 3.
96 Council of Trent, *Decree on Original Sin* (1546), no. 5, http://history. hanover.edu/texts/trent/ct05
97 St Augustine, *De Civitate Dei*, XIV, 14.
98 Ibid., XIV, 15.

5 Hermeneutics

1 H.-G. Gadamer, *Truth and Method*, rev. ed., tr. J. Weinsheimer and D. Marshall (London: Sheed and Ward, 1989), p. 4.
2 M. Heidegger, *Being and Time*, tr. J. Macquarrie and E. Robinson (Oxford and Cambridge, MA: Blackwell, 1962), pp. 182–188.
3 Ibid., pp. 191–192.
4 Ibid., p. 194.
5 Ibid., p. 195.
6 H.-G. Gadamer, op. cit., p. 267.
7 Ibid., p. 270.
8 Ibid., p. 271.
9 Ibid., p. 270.
10 Ibid., p. 276.
11 Ibid.
12 Ibid., pp. 276–277.
13 Ibid., p. 277.
14 Ibid., p. 279.
15 Ibid.
16 Ibid., p. 280.
17 Ibid.
18 Ibid., p. 281.
19 Ibid.
20 Ibid., p. 282.
21 Ibid.
22 Ibid., p. 284.
23 Ibid., p. 290.
24 Ibid., p. 301.

25 Ibid., p. 302.
26 Ibid., p. 304.
27 Ibid., p. 306.
28 Ibid.
29 J. Habermas, *On the Logic of the Social Sciences*, tr. S. Nicholsen and J. Stark (Cambridge, MA: MIT Press, 1988), p. 86.
30 Ibid., p. 167
31 Ibid.
32 See J. Habermas, *Knowledge and Human Interests*, 2nd edn, tr. J. Shapiro (Cambridge: Polity Press, 1987), p. 310.
33 J. Habermas, *On the Logic of the Social Sciences*, p. 168.
34 Ibid.
35 Ibid.
36 Ibid., p. 169.
37 Ibid.
38 Ibid.
39 Ibid., p. 170.
40 Ibid.
41 Ibid.
42 Ibid.
43 Ibid., p. 172.
44 Ibid., p. 88.
45 Ibid., p. 172.
46 Ibid.
47 Ibid., p. 174.
48 Ibid., p. 187.
49 H.-G. Gadamer, 'Rhetoric, Hermeneutics and the Critique of Ideology: Metacritical Comments on *Truth and Method*', in *The Hermeneutics Reader: Texts of the German Tradition from the Enlightenment to the Present*, ed. K. Mueller-Vollmer (Oxford: Blackwell, 1985), p. 286.
50 Ibid.
51 Ibid., p. 283.
52 Ibid.
53 Ibid., p. 284.
54 Ibid., p. 286.
55 Ibid., p. 282.
56 J. Habermas, 'The Hermeneutic Claim to Universality', tr. J. Bleicher, in *The Hermeneutic Tradition: From Ast to Ricoeur*, ed. G. Ormiston and A. Schrift (Albany: State University of New York Press, 1990), p. 252.
57 Ibid., p. 256.
58 Ibid.
59 Ibid., p. 264.
60 Ibid., p. 267.
61 Ibid., p. 269.
62 H.-G. Gadamer, 'Reply to My Critics', tr. G. Leiner, in *The Hermeneutic Tradition*, p. 277, 282.
63 Gadamer, 'Rhetoric, Hermeneutics and the Critique of Ideology', p. 291.
64 Gadamer, 'Reply to My Critics', p. 288.
65 Ibid., p. 289.

66 Gadamer, *Truth and Method,* p. 277.
67 P. Ricoeur, 'Hermeneutics and The Critique of Ideology', in *Hermeneutics and the Human Sciences: Essays on Language, Action and Interpretation,* tr. and ed. J. Thompson (Cambridge: Cambridge University Press, 1981), p. 99.
68 Gadamer, 'Reply to My Critics', p. 288.
69 See F. de Saussure, *Course in General Linguistics,* tr. R. Harris (London: Duckworth, 1983), pp. 8–11.
70 P. Ricoeur, *Interpretation Theory: Discourse and the Surplus of Meaning* (Fort Worth: Texas Christian University Press, 1976), p. 6.
71 R. Barthes, 'Introduction to the Structural Analysis of Narratives', in *Barthes: Selected Writings,* ed. S. Sontag (London: Fontana, 1982), p. 295.
72 P. Ricoeur, 'Biblical Hermeneutics', *Semeia* 4 (1975) 51.
73 P. Ricoeur, *The Rule of Metaphor: Multi-Disciplinary Studies in the Creation of Meaning in Language,* tr. R. Czerny et al. (London: Routledge, 1978), p. 69.
74 Ibid., pp. 66–69.
75 P. Ricoeur, *Interpretation Theory,* p. 12.
76 Ibid., p. 9.
77 Ibid.
78 P. Ricoeur, *The Rule of Metaphor,* p. 70.
79 P. Ricoeur, *Interpretation Theory,* p. 20.
80 Ibid., p. 25.
81 P. Ricoeur, 'The Hermeneutical Function of Distanciation', in *Hermeneutics and the Human Sciences,* p. 139.
82 P. Ricoeur, *Interpretation Theory,* p. 30.
83 Ibid., p. 31.
84 Ibid., p. 34.
85 P. Ricoeur, 'What is a Text? Explanation and Understanding', in *Hermeneutics and the Human Sciences,* p. 148.
86 P. Ricoeur, *Interpretation Theory,* p. 36.
87 Ibid.
88 Ibid., p. 35.
89 P. Ricoeur, 'Toward a Hermeneutic of the Idea of Revelation', in *Essays on Biblical Interpretation,* ed. L. Mudge (London: SPCK, 1981), p. 100.
90 P. Ricoeur, *Interpretation Theory,* p. 37.
91 P. Ricoeur, 'The Hermeneutical Function of Distanciation', p. 142.
92 Ibid.
93 Ibid.
94 P. Ricoeur, 'What is a Text?', p. 152.
95 P. Ricoeur, *Interpretation Theory,* p. 36.
96 Ibid., p. 87.
97 Ibid., p. 94.
98 P. Ricoeur, 'The Hermeneutical Function of Distanciation', p. 143.
99 Ibid.
100 P. Ricoeur, *Interpretation Theory,* p. 94.
101 P. Ricoeur, 'Appropriation', in *Hermeneutics and the Human Sciences,* p. 193.
102 P. Ricoeur, 'Philosophical Hermeneutics and Biblical Hermeneutics', in *From Text to Action: Essays in Hermeneutics II,* tr. K. Blarney and J. Thompson (London: Athlone, 1991), p. 90.
103 Ibid., p. 92.

104 P. Ricoeur, 'Toward A Hermeneutic of the Idea of Revelation', p. 80.
105 P. Ricoeur, 'Philosophical Hermeneutics and Biblical Hermeneutics', p. 92.
106 P. Ricoeur, 'Toward A Hermeneutic of the Idea of Revelation', p. 76.
107 Ibid., p. 93.
108 P. Ricoeur, 'Philosophical Hermeneutics and Biblical Hermeneutics', p. 96.
109 P. Ricoeur, 'Toward A Hermeneutic of the Idea of Revelation', p. 104.
110 Ibid.
111 Ibid., 'Philosophical Hermeneutics and Biblical Hermeneutics', p. 97.
112 P. Ricoeur, 'Biblical Hermeneutics', p. 107.
113 Ibid., p. 108.
114 Ibid., p. 111. See Mk. 1:15, Lk. 17:21.
115 Ibid., p. 110.
116 Ibid., p. 115.
117 Ibid., p. 119.
118 Ibid., p. 120.
119 Ibid., p. 123.
120 Ibid.
121 Ibid., p. 125.
122 P. Ricoeur, 'Philosophical Hermeneutics and Biblical Hermeneutics', p. 99.
123 Ibid.
124 S. Fish, *Is There a Text in This Class? The Authority of Interpretive Communities* (Cambridge, MA and London: Harvard University Press, 1980), p. 28.
125 Ibid., p. 27.
126 Ibid., p. 149.
127 Ibid., p. 158.
128 Ibid., p. 167.
129 Ibid., p. 163.
130 Ibid., p. 165.
131 Ibid.
132 Ibid., p. 167.
133 Ibid., p. 171.
134 S. Fish, *Doing What Comes Naturally: Change, Rhetoric and the Practice of Theory in Literary and Legal Studies* (Oxford: Clarendon Press, 1989), p. 30.
135 Ibid., p. 31.
136 Ibid.
137 S. Fish, *Is There a Text in This Class?*, p. 349.
138 Ibid., p. 306.
139 Ibid.
140 Ibid., p. 311.
141 Ibid., p. 316.
142 Ibid., p. 318.
143 Ibid., p. 319.
144 Ibid.
145 Ibid., p. 320.
146 Ibid.
147 Ibid.
148 Ibid., p. 321.
149 Ibid., p. 335.
150 Ibid., p. 332.

6 Christian Literary Theory

1 K. Mills, *Justifying Language: Paul and Contemporary Literary Theory* (Basingstoke and London: Macmillan, 1995), p. 2.
2 Ibid., p. 25.
3 Ibid., p. 37.
4 Ibid., p. 29.
5 Ibid., p. 25.
6 Ibid., p. 47.
7 Ibid., p. 45.
8 Ibid., p. 76.
9 Ibid., p. 82.
10 Ibid., p. 86.
11 Ibid.
12 Ibid., p. 106.
13 Ibid., p. 141.
14 Ibid.
15 Ibid.
16 Ibid., p. 148.
17 Ibid., p. 154.
18 Ibid., p. 158.
19 Ibid., p. 172.
20 Ibid., p. 10.
21 B. Ingraffia, *Postmodern theory and Biblical Theology: Vanquishing God's Shadow* (Cambridge: Cambridge University Press, 1995), p. 241.
22 Ibid., p. 4.
23 Ibid., p. 6.
24 Ibid., p. 13.
25 Ibid., p. 64.
26 Ibid., p. 65.
27 Ibid., p. 67.
28 Ibid., p. 73.
29 Ibid., p. 75.
30 T. Sheehan, 'Heidegger's "Introduction to the Phenomenology of Religion", 1920–1921', in *A Companion to Martin Heidegger's 'Being and Time'*, ed. J. Kockelmans (Washington: University Press of America, 1986), p. 56.
31 B. Ingraffia, op. cit., p. 116.
32 Ibid., p. 122.
33 Ibid., p. 136.
34 Ibid., p. 137.
35 Ibid., p. 162.
36 Ibid., p. 184.
37 Ibid., p. 222.
38 Ibid., p. 240.
39 V. Cunningham, *In the Reading Gaol: Postmodernity, Texts, History* (Oxford and Cambridge, MA: Blackwell, 1994), p. 363.
40 Ibid., p. 396.
41 Ibid., p. 402, 403.
42 Ibid., pp. 383–386.

43 D. Jasper, *Coleridge as Poet and Religious Thinker: Inspiration and Revelation* (London and Basingstoke: Macmillan, 1985), p. 3.
44 Ibid., p. 9.
45 Ibid., p. 40.
46 D. Jasper, *The New Testament and the Literary Imagination* (Basingstoke and London: Macmillan, 1987), p. 98.
47 Ibid., p. 14, 16.
48 Ibid., p. 36.
49 Ibid., p. 52.
50 Ibid., p. 98.
51 D. Jasper, *The Study of Literature and Religion: An Introduction*, 2nd edn (Basingstoke and London: Macmillan, 1992), p. 5.
52 Ibid., p. 100.
53 Ibid., p. 121.
54 Ibid., p. 124.
55 Ibid., p. 131.
56 T. Wright, *Theology and Literature* (Oxford and New York: Blackwell, 1988), p. 2.
57 Ibid., p. 4.
58 Ibid., p. 10.
59 Ibid., p. 42.
60 Ibid., p. 67.
61 Ibid., p. 82.
62 Ibid.
63 Ibid., p. 106.
64 Ibid., p. 110.
65 Ibid., p. 110.
66 Ibid., p. 121.
67 Ibid., p. 129.
68 Ibid., p. 139.
69 Ibid., p. 149.
70 Ibid., p. 152.
71 Ibid.
72 Ibid., p. 128.
73 M. Edwards, *Towards a Christian Poetics* (London and Basingstoke: Macmillan, 1984), p. 1.
74 Ibid.
75 Ibid., p. 4.
76 Ibid., p. 8.
77 Ibid., p. 10.
78 Ibid., p. 11.
79 Ibid., p. 12.
80 Ibid.
81 Ibid., p. 73.
82 Ibid.
83 Ibid., p. 74.
84 Ibid.
85 Ibid., p. 75, 90.
86 Ibid., p. 16.

87 G. Chaucer, 'The Prologue of the Monk's Tale' ll. 1973–1976, *The Riverside Chaucer*, ed. L. Benson (Oxford: Oxford University Press, 1987), p. 241.
88 Ibid., p. 25.
89 Ibid., p. 48.
90 Ibid., p. 53.
91 Ibid., p. 47.
92 Ibid.
93 Ibid., p. 7.
94 P. Fiddes, *Freedom and Limit: A Dialogue Between Literature and Christian Doctrine* (Basingstoke and London: Macmillan, 1991), p. 5.
95 Ibid., p. 7.
96 Ibid., p. 8.
97 Ibid., p. 11.
98 Ibid., p. 12.
99 Ibid.
100 Ibid., p. 30.
101 Ibid.
102 Ibid., p. 31.
103 Ibid., p. 32.
104 Ibid., p. 34.
105 Ibid., p. 52.
106 Ibid., pp. 59–62.
107 Ibid., p. 62.
108 R. Detweiler, 'Theological Trends of Postmodern Fiction', *Journal of the American Academy of Religion* 44 (1976) 225.
109 Ibid., p. 226.
110 Ibid., p. 230.
111 Ibid.
112 Ibid.
113 Ibid., p. 231.
114 Ibid., p. 235.
115 Ibid., pp. 236–237.
116 R. Detweiler, *Breaking the Fall: Religious Readings of Contemporary Fiction* (Basingstoke and London: Macmillan, 1989), p. 9.
117 Ibid., p. 11.
118 Ibid.
119 Ibid.
120 Ibid., p. 21.
121 Ibid., p. 22.
122 Ibid., p. 25.
123 Ibid., p. 30.
124 Ibid., p. 31.
125 Ibid., p. 33.
126 Ibid., p. 34.
127 Ibid., p. 35.
128 Ibid., p. 36.
129 Ibid., p. 38.
130 Ibid., pp. 40–41.

131 W. Kort, 'Doing "Religion and Literature" in a Postmodernist Mode', *Christianity and Literature* 39 (1990) 195.

132 R. Detweiler, *Uncivil Rites: American Fiction, Religion and the Public Sphere* (Urbana: University of Illinois Press, 1996), p. 2.

133 M. Ledbetter, *Virtuous Intentions: The Religious Dimension of Narrative* (Atlanta: Scholars Press, 1989), p. 1.

134 See M. Eliade, *The Sacred and the Profane*, tr. W. Trask (New York: Harcourt Brace, 1959), p. 210.

135 Ibid., p. 6.

136 Ibid., p. 7.

137 Ibid., p. 8.

138 Ibid., p. 11.

139 Ibid., p. 14.

140 Ibid., p. 15.

141 Ibid., p. 71.

142 Ibid.

143 Ibid., p. 78.

144 Ibid.

145 Ibid.

146 Ibid.

147 M. Ledbetter, *Victims and the Postmodern Narrative, or, Doing Violence to the Body: An Ethic of Reading and Writing* (Basingstoke and London: Macmillan, 1996), p. x.

148 Ibid., p. 1.

149 Ibid., p. 2, 3.

150 Ibid., p. 6.

151 Ibid., p. 16.

152 Ibid., p. 18.

153 Ibid., p. 19.

154 Ibid., p. 143.

Bibliography

Aquinas, T. *Summa Theologiae*, Blackfriars edition and translation, 60 vols (London and New York: Eyre and Spottiswoode, 1964–1976).

Barth, K. *Church Dogmatics Vol. II: The Doctrine of God, 1st half-volume*, tr. T. Parker et al. (Edinburgh: T. & T. Clark, 1957).

Church Dogmatics Vol. I: The Doctrine of the Word of God, Part 1, tr. G. Bromiley (Edinburgh: T. & T. Clark, 1975).

Baum, G. and Ellsberg, R., eds. *The Logic of Solidarity: Commentaries on Pope John Paul II's Encyclical on Social Concern with the Complete Text of the Encyclical* (Maryknoll, NY: Orbis, 1989).

Belsey, C. *Critical Practice* (London and New York: Routledge, 1980).

Bigler, R. *The Politics of German Protestantism: The Rise of the Protestant Church Elite in Prussia, 1815–1848* (Berkeley and London: University of California Press, 1972).

Berryman, P. 'Latin American Liberation Theology'. *Theology in the Americas*, ed. S. Torres and J. Eagleson (Maryknoll, NY: Orbis, 1976), pp. 20–83.

Boff, L. *Jesus Christ Liberator: A Critical Christology for Our Time*, tr. P. Hughes (London: SPCK, 1980).

Boff, L. and Boff, C. *Introducing Liberation Theology*, tr. P. Burns (Tunbridge Wells: Burns & Oates, 1987).

Bonino, J. *Christians and Marxists: The Mutual Challenge to Revolution* (Grand Rapids, MI: Eerdmans, 1976).

Caputo, J. 'Mysticism and Transgression: Derrida and Meister Eckhart'. *Derrida and Deconstruction*, ed. H. Silverman (New York and London: Routledge, 1989), pp. 24–39.

Deconstruction in a Nutshell: A Conversation With Jacques Derrida (New York: Fordham University Press, 1997).

The Prayers and Tears of Jacques Derrida: Religion Without Religion (Bloomington: Indiana University Press, 1997).

Carabine, D. *The Unknown God. Negative Theology in the Platonic Tradition: Plato to Eriugena* (Louvain: Eerdmans, 1995).

Catechism of the Catholic Church (London: Geoffrey Chapman, 1994).

Charles, R. *Christian Social Witness and Teaching: The Catholic Tradition from Genesis to Centesimus Annus*, vol. II (Leominster: Gracewing, 1998).

Congregation for the Doctrine of the Faith. 'Instruction on Certain Aspects of the "Theology of Liberation"' (1984). http://www.vatican.va/roman_curia/congregations/cfaith/documents/rc_con_cfaith_doc_19840806_theology-liberation_en.html.

Coward, H. and Foshay, T., eds. *Derrida and Negative Theology* (New York: State University of New York Press, 1992).

Cranfield, C. *A Critical and Exegetical Commentary on the Epistle to the Romans Vol. 1* (Edinburgh: T. & T. Clark, 1975).

Cunningham, V. *In the Reading Gaol: Postmodernity, Texts, History* (Oxford and Cambridge, MA: Blackwell, 1994).

Damer, T. *Attacking Faulty Reasoning: A Practical Guide to Fallacy-Free Arguments*, 3rd edn (Belmont, CA: Wadsworth, 1995).

Daniel-Rops, H. *The Church in an Age of Revolution 1789–1870*, tr. J. Warrington (London: J.M. Dent, 1965).

Derrida, J. *Of Grammatology*, tr. G. Spivak (Baltimore and London: Johns Hopkins University Press, 1976).

Writing and Difference, tr. A. Bass (London: Routledge, 1978).

Positions, tr. A. Bass (London: Athlone, 1981).

Margins of Philosophy, tr. A. Bass (New York and London: Harvester Wheatsheaf, 1982).

'Letter to John P. Leavey, Jr.'. *Semeia*, 23 (1982) 61–62.

'The Original Discussion of *"Différance"'*. *Derrida and Différance*, ed. D. Wood (Warwick: Parousia, 1985), pp. 130–132.

'How to Avoid Speaking: Denials'. *Derrida and Negative Theology*, ed. H. Coward and T. Foshay (New York: State University of New York Press, 1992), pp. 73–142.

'Of an Apocalyptic Tone Newly Adopted in Philosophy'. *Derrida and Negative Theology*, ed. H. Coward and T. Foshay (New York: State University of New York Press, 1992), pp. 25–71.

Specters of Marx, tr. P. Kamuf (London and New York: Routledge, 1994).

On the Name, ed. T. Dutoit (Stanford: Stanford University Press, 1995).

The Gift of Death, tr. D. Wills (Chicago and London: University of Chicago Press, 1995).

'Faith and Knowledge: The Two Sources of "Religion" within the Limits of Reason Alone'. *Religion*, ed. J. Derrida and G. Vattimo, tr. S. Weber et al. (Cambridge: Polity Press, 1998).

Derrida, J. and Bennington, G. *Jacques Derrida*, tr. G. Bennington (Chicago and London: University of Chicago Press, 1993).

Detweiler, R. 'Theological Trends of Postmodern Fiction', *Journal of the American Academy of Religion* 44 (1976) 233–37.

Breaking the Fall: Religious Readings of Contemporary Fiction (Basingstoke and London: Macmillan, 1989).

Uncivil Rites: American Fiction, Religion and the Public Sphere (Urbana: University of Illinois Press, 1996).

Dicenso, J. 'Deconstruction and the Philosophy of Religion: World Affirmation and Critique'. *Philosophy of Religion* 31 (1992) 29–43.

Dunn, J. *The Theology of Paul the Apostle* (Edinburgh: T. & T. Clark, 1998).

Eagleton, T. *Literary Theory: An Introduction* (Oxford: Blackwell, 1983).

Eckhart, M. *Meister Eckhart: Teacher and Preacher*, tr. and ed. B. McGinn, F. Tobin and E. Borgstadt (New York: Paulist Press, 1986).

Edwards, M. *Towards a Christian Poetics* (London and Basingstoke: Macmillan, 1984).

Feuerbach, L. *The Essence of Christianity*, tr. G. Eliot (New York: Harper, 1957).

Fiddes, P. *Freedom and Limit: A Dialogue Between Literature and Christian Doctrine* (Basingstoke and London: Macmillan, 1991).

Fish, S. *Is There a Text in This Class? The Authority of Interpretive Communities* (Cambridge, MA and London: Harvard University Press, 1980).

Doing What Comes Naturally: Change, Rhetoric and the Practice of Theory in Literary and Legal Studies (Oxford: Clarendon Press, 1989).

Fitzmyer, J. *Romans: A New Translation with Introduction and Commentary* (London: Chapman, 1993).

Freud, S. *Introductory Lectures on Psychoanalysis*, tr. J. Strachey (London: Penguin, 1973).

New Introductory Lectures on Psychoanalysis, tr. J. Strachey (London: Penguin, 1973).

The Origins of Religion: Totem and Taboo, Moses and Monotheism and Other Works, tr. J. Strachey (London: Penguin, 1985).

'The Future of an Illusion', *The Standard Edition of the Complete Psychological Works of Sigmund Freud*, tr. and ed. J. Strachey et al. (London: The Hogarth Press and The Institute of Psycho-Analysis, 1953–1974), vol. XXI, pp. 3–56.

Fromm, E. *Psychoanalysis and Religion* (London: Victor Gollancz, 1951).

Gadamer, H.-G. *Truth and Method*, rev. ed., tr. J. Weinsheimer and D. Marshall (London: Sheed and Ward, 1989).

'Rhetoric, Hermeneutics and the Critique of Ideology: Metacritical Comments on *Truth and Method*'. *The Hermeneutics Reader: Texts of the German Tradition from the Enlightenment to the Present*, ed. K. Mueller-Vollmer (Oxford: Blackwell, 1985), pp. 274–292.

Reply to My Critics', tr. G. Leiner, in *The Hermeneutic Tradition From Ast to Ricoeur*, ed. G. Ormiston and A. Schrift (Albany: State University of New York Press, 1990), pp. 273–297.

Garaudy, R. *The Alternative Future: A Vision of Christian Marxism*, tr. L. Mayhew (Harmondsworth: Penguin, 1976).

From Anathema to Dialogue: The Challenge of Marxist-Christian Co-operation, tr. L. O'Neill (London: Collins, 1967).

Girardi, G. *Marxism and Christianity*, tr. K. Traynor (Dublin: Gill and Son, 1968).

Gutiérrez, G. *A Theology of Liberation: History, Politics, Salvation*, tr. C. Inda and J. Eagleson (London: SCM, 1988).

Habermas, J. *On the Logic of the Social Sciences*, tr. S. Nicholsen and J. Stark (Cambridge, MA: MIT Press, 1988).

Knowledge and Human Interests, 2nd edn, tr. J. Shapiro (Cambridge: Polity Press, 1987).

'The Hermeneutic Claim to Universality', tr. J. Bleicher. *The Hermeneutic Tradition*: pp. 245–272.

Hart, K. *The Trespass of the Sign: Deconstruction, Theology and Philosophy* (Cambridge: Cambridge University Press, 1989).

Heidegger, M. *Identity and Difference*, tr. J. Stambaugh (New York: Harper and Row, 1957).

Being and Time, tr. J. Macquarrie and E. Robinson (Oxford and Cambridge, MA: Blackwell, 1962).

Ingraffia, B. *Postmodern Theory and Biblical Theology: Vanquishing God's Shadow* (Cambridge: Cambridge University Press, 1995).

Jasper, D. *Coleridge as Poet and Religious Thinker: Inspiration and Revelation* (London and Basingstoke: Macmillan, 1985).

The New Testament and the Literary Imagination (Basingstoke and London: Macmillan, 1987).

The Study of Literature and Religion: An Introduction, 2nd edn (Basingstoke and London: Macmillan, 1992).

Readings in the Canon: Written for Our Learning (Basingstoke: Macmillan, 1994).

John Paul II, Pope. *Encyclical* Redemptor Hominis (London: Catholic Truth Society, 1979).

Encyclical Letter On Human Work: Laborem Exercens, tr. Vatican (Boston: St Paul, 1981).

Encyclical Letter Centesimus Annus: *On the Hundredth Anniversary of* Rerum Novarum, tr. Vatican (Boston: St Paul, 1991).

Jones, J. 'Introduction'. *Pseudo-Dionysius Areopagite: The Divine Names and Mystical Theology* (Milwaukee: Marquette University Press, 1980).

Jung, C. *Psychology and Religion: West and East. Collected Works of C.G. Jung, Vol. 11*, tr. R. Hull (London: Routledge and Kegan Paul, 1958).

Psychology and Religion (New Haven: Yale University Press, 1938).

Kirschner, S. *The Religious and Romantic Origins of Psychoanalysis: Individuation and Integration in Post-Freudian Theory* (Cambridge: Cambridge University Press, 1996).

Kort, W. 'Doing "Religion and Literature" in a Postmodernist Mode', *Christianity and Literature* 39 (1990) 193–198.

Kroeber, A. *The Nature of Culture* (Chicago and London: University of Chicago Press, 1952).

Anthropology (London: Harrap, 1923).

Küng, H. *Does God Exist? An Answer for Today*, tr. E. Quinn (London: Collins, 1980).

Freud and the Problem of God (New Haven: Yale University Press, 1979).

Lash, N. *A Matter of Hope: A Theologian's Reflections on the Thought of Karl Marx* (London: Darton, Longman and Todd, 1981).

Ledbetter, M. *Virtuous Intentions: The Religious Dimension of Narrative* (Atlanta: Scholars Press, 1989).

Victims and the Postmodern Narrative, or, Doing Violence to the Body: An Ethic of Reading and Writing (Basingstoke and London: Macmillan, 1996).

Leo XIII, Pope. *Encyclical Letter On the Condition of the Working Classes*: Rerum Novarum, tr. N.C.W.C. (Boston: St Paul, 1942).

Lévi-Strauss, C. *The Elementary Structures of Kinship*, tr. J. Bell, J. von Sturmer and R. Needham (Boston: Beacon Press, 1969).

Lees, R. *The Negative Language of the Dionysian School of Mystical Theology: An Approach to the Cloud of Unknowing* (Salzburg: Institut für Anglistik und Amerikanistik, 1983).

Lenin, V.I. 'Classes and Parties in Their Attitude to Religion and the Church'. *Collected Works* (Moscow: Foreign Languages Publishing House, and London: Lawrence and Wishart, 1960–1969), vol. 15, pp. 410–420.

'Socialism and Religion'. *Collected Works*, vol. 10, pp. 83–87.

'The Attitude of the Workers' Party to Religion'. *Collected Works*, vol. 15, pp. 402–413.

Lenin, V.I. and Gorky, M. *Lenin and Gorky: Letters, Reminiscences, Articles* (Moscow: Progress, 1973).

Lindbeck, G. *The Nature of Doctrine: Religion and Theology in a Postliberal Age* (Philadelphia: The Westminster Press, 1984).

MacIntyre, A. *Marxism and Christianity* (London: Duckworth, 1968).

Marx, K. *Capital: A Critique of Political Economy* Vol. 1, tr. B. Fowkes (London: Penguin, 1976).

Karl Marx: Selected Writings, ed. D. McLellan (Oxford: Oxford University Press, 1977).

Marx, K. and Engels, F. *On Religion* (New York: Schocken, 1964).

Marx and Engels: Basic Writings on Politics and Philosophy, ed. L. Feuer (New York: Doubleday, 1989).

'The German Ideology'. *Collected Works Vol. 5: Marx and Engels; 1845–47* (London: Lawrence and Wishart, 1976).

Mays, J. *Hosea: A Commentary* (London: SCM, 1969).

McGovern, A. *Marxism: An American Christian Perspective* (Maryknoll, NY: Orbis, 1980).

Liberation Theology and its Critics: Towards an Assessment (Maryknoll, NY: Orbis, 1989).

McKane, W. *A Critical and Exegetical Commentary on Jeremiah*, vol. I (Edinburgh: T. & T. Clark, 1986).

McLellan, D. *Marxism and Religion: A Description and Assessment of the Marxist Critique of Christianity* (London: Macmillan, 1987).

Meng, H. and Freud, E. *Psychoanalysis and Faith: The Letters of Sigmund Freud and Oskar Pfister* (London: Hogarth, 1962).

Milbank, J. *Theology and Social Theory: Beyond Secular Reason* (Oxford: Blackwell, 1990).

The Word Made Strange: Theology, Language, Culture (Oxford: Blackwell, 1997).

Mills, K. *Justifying Language: Paul and Contemporary Literary Theory* (Basingstoke and London: Macmillan, 1995).

Miranda, J. *Marx and the Bible: A Critique of the Philosophy of Oppression*, tr. J. Eagleson (Maryknoll, NY: Orbis, 1974).

Mortley, R. *From Word to Silence Vol. II: The Way of Negation, Christian and Greek* (Bonn: Hanstein, 1986).

Mays, J. *Hosea: A Commentary* (London: SCM, 1969).

Niebuhr, R. *Moral Man and Immoral Society: A Study in Ethics and Politics* (New York: Charles Scribner's Sons, 1932).

The Nature and Destiny of Man: A Christian Interpretation Vol. I (London: Nisbet, 1941).

Pannenberg, W. *Systematic Theology*, vol. 2, tr. G. Bromiley (Edinburgh: T. & T. Clark, 1991).

Pope Pius IX, *Syllabus of Errors* (1864). http://listserv.american.edu/catholic/church/papal/pius.ix/p9syll.html.

Pseudo-Dionysius. *Pseudo-Dionysius: The Complete Works*, tr. C. Luibheid (London: SPCK, 1987).

Radcliffe-Brown, A. *Structure and Function in Primitive Society: Essays and Addresses* (New York and London: The Free Press, 1952).

Rahner, K. *Theological Investigations Vol. 1: God, Christ, Mary and Grace*, tr. C. Ernst (London: Darton, Longman and Todd, 1961).

Foundations of Christian Faith: An Introduction to the Idea of Christianity, tr. W. Dych (London: Darton, Longman and Todd, 1976).

Raschke, C., et al. *Deconstruction and Theology* (New York: Crossroad, 1982).

Ricoeur, P. 'Biblical Hermeneutics', *Semeia* 4 (1975) 29–148.

Interpretation Theory: Discourse and the Surplus of Meaning (Fort Worth: Texas Christian University Press, 1976).

The Rule of Metaphor: Multi-Disciplinary Studies in the Creation of Meaning in Language, tr. R. Czerny et al. (London: Routledge, 1978).

Hermeneutics and the Human Sciences: Essays on Language, Action and Interpretation, tr. and ed. J. Thompson (Cambridge: Cambridge University Press, 1981).

Essays on Biblical Interpretation, ed. L. Mudge (London: SPCK, 1981).
From Text to Action: Essays in Hermeneutics II, tr. K. Blarney and J. Thompson (London: Athlone, 1991).
Figuring the Sacred: Religion, Narrative and Imagination (Minneapolis: Fortress, 1995).
Second General Conference of Latin American Bishops, *The Church in the Present-Day Transformation of Latin America in the Light of the Council Vol. II: Conclusions*, ed. L.M. Colonnese (Bogotá: General Secretariat of CELAM, 1970).
Shanahan, W. *German Protestants Face the Social Question Vol. I: The Conservative Phase 1815–1871* (Notre Dame: University of Indiana Press, 1954).
Sobrino, J. *Christology at the Crossroads: A Latin American Approach*, tr. J. Drury (London: SCM, 1978).
Taylor, M. *Erring: A Postmodern A/theology* (Chicago and London: University of Chicago Press, 1984).
nOts (Chicago and London: Chicago University Press, 1993).
Tillich, P. *Political Expectation*, ed. J. Adams (Macon, GA: Mercer University Press, 1971).
Turner, D. *The Darkness of God: Negativity in Christian Mysticism* (Cambridge: Cambridge University Press, 1995).
Vatican Council II: The Conciliar and Post-Conciliar Documents, ed. A. Flannery (Dublin: Dominican Publications, 1992).
Vitz, P. and Gartner, J. 'Christianity and Psychoanalysis, Part I: Jesus as the Anti-Oedipus'. *Journal of Psychology and Theology* 12 (1984) 4–14.
Walsh, M. and Davies, B. *Proclaiming Justice and Peace: Documents from John XXIII to John Paul II*, 2nd edn (London: CAFOD/Collins, 1991).
Ward, G. 'Why is Derrida Important for Theology?'. *Theology* 95 (1992) 263–270.
Barth, Derrida and the Language of Theology (Cambridge: Cambridge University Press, 1995).
Theology and Contemporary Critical Theory (Basingstoke and London: Macmillan, 1996).
Webster, R. *Why Freud Was Wrong: Sin, Science and Psychoanalysis* (London: Harper Collins, 1995).
Wolosky, S. 'An "Other" Negative Theology: On Derrida's "How to Avoid Speaking: Denials"' *Poetics Today*, 19 (1998) 261–280.
Wright, T. *Theology and Literature* (Oxford and New York: Blackwell, 1988).
'Through a *Glas* Darkly: Derrida, Literature and the Specter of Christianity', *Christianity and Literature* 44 (1994) 73–92.
'Behind the Curtain: Derrida and the Religious Imagination'. *Through a Glass Darkly: Essays in the Religious Imagination*, ed. J. Hawley (New York: Fordham University Press, 1996), pp. 276–295.

Index